St. George Marc

Family Favorites
COOKBOOK

*An International
Collection of Recipes*

Sponsored By Ladies Altar Society

December 2014

Disclaimer: All efforts were made to see that the recipes were as accurate as given and the right person was credited for submitting the recipe.

Order Additional Copies from:

St. George Maronite Catholic Church
ATTN: Ladies Altar Society
6070 Babcock Road
San Antonio, TX 78240

St. George Phone: 210-695-5937
Call for pricing + shipping and handling cost, if shipped.

ISBN: 978-1889391-43-4

Library of Congress Control Number: 2014953484

Dedication and Thanks

In memory of founding members of Ladies Altar Society who are the reason for our existence and preservation of our culture.

To all of the members of St. George Church and beyond that contributed recipes and made this book become a reality.

Father Charles Khachan for supporting the Ladies Altar Society and encouraging us to produce this cookbook.

To Ladies Altar Society members, past and present, for their continued support and countless hours of work in producing this cookbook for our parish.

Table of Contents

St. George Maronite Catholic Church History

The first Lebanese immigrants arrived in San Antonio in the 1880's. Until the mid-1920's, the Maronite immigrants worshipped in a Roman Latin Rite Church near their community in the downtown area.

On January 20, 1925, Father George Aziz of Lebanon stopped in San Antonio on his way to visit relatives in south Texas and Mexico. He was asked by the San Antonio Maronite community to stay and serve as their priest. Father Aziz consented and with the local Catholic Bishop's permission, the original congregation of St. George Maronite Catholic Church was established.

Within months, the Maronite Lebanese community and parishioners collected enough money to buy land located at the southeast corner of Pecos and West Main Street, which included a small frame building. This was used as the first church and the upstairs served as the priest's residence. This was the first and only Maronite Church to exist in the southwestern United States for a period of fifty three (53) years.

By the early 1930's, the original congregation of just over fifty members had grown large enough to merit the need for a larger church building. In 1932, the construction of a new church was begun on the same property and was completed in 1934. During this time, Father Aziz was replaced by Father Elias Najem.

In 1948, Father John Trad arrived at a very critical time in the church history. The church building would have to be relocated to make way for a newly proposed IH35 Highway. New land was acquired at 501 North Frio Street and Morales. Because of limited funds; materials from the old church were used to build the new church, brick by brick. Even then, the construction required additional cost. The deficit was paid in part due to the diligent efforts of Father Trad, who sought help from Maronites in other Texas cities, Oklahoma and Mexico. The Ladies of the parish were also of great assistance to Father Trad who was barely able to meet his monthly needs during this critical period.

In 1962, the Ladies Altar Society began hosting weekly Lebanese dinners as fundraisers and in 1963, *"Magic is the Night"* annual fundraiser gala kicked-off. In 1968, the church experienced another crisis. The church on Frio had been condemned by an urban renewal project and would have to be moved.

On March 15, 1974, land on Babcock Road was purchased, twelve miles north of Metropolitan San Antonio. Father Wlademar Akekee, the priest at the time, celebrated the first liturgy at the Babcock property in the temporary chapel.

In 1976, a banquet hall and rectory were completed and in 1980, the present St. George Maronite Catholic Church was dedicated. In 1987, a second banquet hall was completed. In 1990, the Congregation of Maronite Lebanese Missionaries took over the staffing of St. George. Father Abdallah E. Zaidan was assigned to our parish. In 2000, The Maronite Community Center was constructed, which included a gymnasium, classrooms, meeting rooms, storage, a kitchen and a dining area.

Today, we continue to be a parish growing in size and activities. The ladies of the church continue to regularly sponsor scheduled Lebanese luncheons, bake sales and assist with the *Magic is the Night* cooking. St. George Maronite Church has hosted NAM and Southern Federation Conventions. Various church organizations sponsor BINGO sessions to help support the expenses of the church. The church continues to participate in the San

Antonio Folklife Festival and also sponsors an annual Lebanese Festival on the grounds of the church. Many other family activities, religious services, sessions and education, fellowships, picnics, sport events and tournaments, etc. are conducted and sponsored by St. George Maronite Catholic Church.

The motivation of those early pioneer families is still present in the many descendants. Under the direction and assistance of our pastor, Father Charles Khachan, M.L.M., we strive to educate and teach people of all backgrounds the richness of the Maronite Catholic Liturgy and Traditions. In the 21st Century we strive to be even more committed to meeting the challenges of defining and preserving our faith and our tradition for our children and our children's children.

Lebanese Glossary, Tools, and Ingredients

As in any country, ingredients and spices can vary widely depending upon which region or part of the country where you are from. Ingredients availability often plays a role in their usage in foods in their region or part of the country.

Allspice is dried unripened fruit of the pimento tree. It is named allspice because the discoverers thought it combined the flavors of cinnamon, nutmeg and cloves. Use allspice in flavoring meat and vegetable dishes.

Anise are seeds of the anise plant (a member of the parsley family) tastes like liquorice or fennel. Use anise as a spice in baked goods and alcoholic beverages.

Burghul (also known as bulghur or bulgur) is crushed wheat which has been parboiled and dried, used in Middle Eastern cooking. It comes in several grades, #1 (small), #2 (medium), #3 (coarse) to use in various dishes according to the preferences of the cook.

Chickpeas (garbanzo beans) are used extensively for hummus as well as other dishes. Chickpeas are available in cans or dry.

Clarified butter is butter fat produced by cooking the butter of the milk solids that float and need to be skimmed off and/or also sink to the bottom so the fat can be poured off. Clarified butter has a higher smoke point and a longer shelf life without refrigeration.

Cumin is a spice with a nutty, peppery flavor that is a member of the parsley family native of Egypt. Cumin has health benefits because it contains iron and benefits digestion.

Farina is made from cereal grains (usually semolina). Use farina in place of flour in cookies and other sweets.

Filo dough (phyllo dough) is a very thin dough that is often used for making desserts such as baklava.

Flower waters, such as rose water and orange blossom (flower) water, are used in desserts and puddings.

Garlic is widely known for its pungent flavor and used in flavoring meats and salads. It has been used for medicinal purposes dating back 4000 years. Most health benefits are derived from using garlic raw.

Hummus (also spelled homos, hummous, humus, hommos) is a dip made from garbanzo beans (chickpeas), Tahini, and garlic.

Laban is yogurt made from whole or skim milk. If placed in cheesecloth with salt and allowed to drain overnight it becomes lebne.

Kibbee is a dish of finely ground lamb mixed with wheat (bulgur), onions, spices, and pine nuts and baked, or sometimes eaten raw. In the U.S., beef is used often in place of lamb.

Maamoul (also spelled Mamoul or Mamool) is a cookie filled with nuts or dates. Special molds are used so a design is created for the cookie. Use this mold for kibbee, other meats or just use your imagination.

Mint, especially spearmint, is used for flavoring meats, salads, vegetables, etc.

Mortar and pestle is a tool used to grind spices or nuts to the consistency you desire.

Olives are indispensable items to have on hand that garnish many Lebanese dishes. The fruitier, heavier, and darker, the better-and-closer to the type used in the Middle East.

Olive oil is essential for Lebanese cooking.

Orange blossom water is a by-product when distilling orange blossoms for their essential oil. Used in flavoring syrup for pastries and sweet baked cakes and cookies.

Parsley is the world's most popular herb known for its delicious flavor and healing properties. It is rich in Vitamin C, A, folic acid, beta-carotene and zinc. Use parsley in salads and meat dishes.

Pine nuts are elongated oval shaped nuts that derive from certain species of pine trees found in Middle East. Pine nuts are expensive because each nut is encased in a thin hard shell that has to be removed by hand. Use pine nuts in stuffings, various meats and desserts such as sfoof.

Rose water is a by-product from distilling rose petals for their essential oils. Use rose water to flavor pastries and syrup.

Sesame seed is one of the oldest seed crops known, begun over 4000 years ago. The seeds are used to flavor pastries and used to make Tahini.

Tahini is ground sesame seed paste that is used in hummus and many other dishes. Tahini is thick like peanut butter.

Vegetable reamer is a small hollow cylindrical shaped tool used to core squash or other vegetables.

Wooden spoons with long handles are great for cooking because they do not get hot or scratch your pans.

Stainless steel whisks are indispensable for blending sauces or mixing dry ingredients into liquids.

Zaatar is Arabic for thyme. Zaatar is a mixture of thyme, ground sumac, and toasted sesame seeds and very aromatic. Zaatar is commonly mixed with olive oil and pasted onto pita bread, then toasted in oven and eaten. Zaatar is also used for dips and as an appetizer. Find zaatar spice in middle eastern stores.

Lebanese and Middle Eastern Cuisine

Entrées

Lebanese Meat Pastry Rolls
Michele Chebib

Pastry

5 cups plain flour
1 cup vegetable oil
½ pkg. yeast
1 tsp. salt
½ stick margarine
2 tsp. sugar
Water as needed

Filling

4 medium onions, chopped
6 Tbsp. oil or butter
4 tsp. salt
½ tsp. pepper
½–1 tsp. allspice or cinnamon
1 cup pine nuts (optional)
2 lb. ground meat
4 Tbsp. vinegar
4 Tbsp. lemon juice

Pastry: Dissolve yeast in ½ cup of water, and then add sugar. Meanwhile sift flour and salt together, then add oil, butter, and yeast; mix. Add enough water to make soft dough. Knead until smooth. Add more water, if needed. Cover and let rise 30–45 minutes before rolling out.

Filling: Heat oil and lightly brown pine nuts, remove pine nuts and set aside. Brown onions, then add meat and allspice. When meat is almost cooked, add pine nuts, then vinegar and lemon juice. To complete the rolls, divide the pastry dough into 4 parts. Take one of the parts and roll into a thin sheet on a floured board. Cut into strips about 3" x 4." Put about 2 teaspoons of filling in the middle of each strip and roll up firmly. Place on parchment paper or well-greased baking tray. Brush top with melted butter or ghee and bake in 350°F. for 15 minutes.

Variations:

1) Add 2 tablespoons of tomato paste, ½ cup well-drained, chopped tomatoes, and 2 tablespoons of parsley to filling.
2) Use 3 cups of cooked chicken, 2 tablespoon of chopped parsley or green onions, salt, pepper, and 2 unbeaten eggs in place of the meat filling.
3) Substitute a mixture with 3 cups grated cheddar cheese, 2 tablespoons chopped parsley, and pinch of cayenne pepper for meat filling.

Baked Fish

1 large red snapper
Salt
2 large onions
Tahini
Oil
2 lemons (optional)
2 cloves garlic
1 large brown sack

Oil a large brown sack place large red snapper inside and close the sack. Bake at 350°F. until done.

Remove from sack and place in a long pan. Slice onions into long pieces and sauté in oil. Pour over the fish. Mash garlic into a paste with salt and blend completely. Add 1 cup Tahini and gradually add water stirring until mixture is comparable to a medium thick gravy. Add lemon juice gradually, mix well and pour over fish and onions. Return to oven (upper part) for about 2 or 3 minutes.

Chicken and Onion Stew
(Bassaliyeh)
Yield: Serves 6

1 large fryer about 4 lb., cut up
2 tsp. salt
½ tsp. pepper
2 Tbsp. lemon juice
½ cup rendered butter
½ tsp. cinnamon
5 cups water
6 large onions, sliced

Rub chicken with salt and spices and partially fry in butter in skillet. Remove chicken to heavy saucepan add water to cover. Sauté onions in skillet with remaining butter until golden and translucent, add to chicken and broth with lemon juice. Continue cooking on low until chicken is done or broth is slightly thickened. Serve with cooked rice.

Chicken Rice Soup
(Shouraba il roz)
Yield: Serves 6–8

1 whole chicken, cut into sections
Salt and pepper (to taste)
2 cups celery, chopped
¼ tsp. cinnamon
¼ tsp. allspice
½ cup rice

Cover chicken pieces with water and simmer until tender. If foam appears on top of water skim and discard. After chicken has cooked for about 45 minutes add celery, spices and seasonings. When celery is soft add rice and cook another 20 minutes. Serve with chicken on the bone or debone and return meat to soup prior to serving.

Note: Use cinnamon stick in place of ground cinnamon.

Cabbage Rolls
(Yabrah)
Margaret Andry Karam

1½ lb. ground beef
1 cup rice, washed
2 cups water
1 large cabbage
2 cloves garlic
1 tsp. allspice or to taste
3 tsp. dried mint
1 tsp. salt
¼ tsp. pepper
¼–½ cup lemon juice

Wash rice and pour into large bowl. Then add meat and the above ingredients and mix together. Set aside. Fill large pan with water and bring to boil. Core cabbage and place in boiling water and pull leaves off as they wilt. Place each leaf on board and take out core in center, making 2 parts to each leaf. Place 1 tablespoon meat mixture in center of each part. Roll like a cigar. Place a few bones or cabbage ends in the bottom of kettle. Place cabbage rolls in kettle, cover the rolls with it. Add garlic, mint, and cover. Cook on high heat until a rapid boil then reduce heat to low for half-hour.

Dough (for Meat Fingers or Spinach Pies)
Margaret Karam
Yield: About 36 meat sticks

4 cups flour
1 cup butter (OR ½ cup oleo and ½ cup canola oil)
1 cup hot water
1 tsp. salt
Small pinch of yeast

Mix all together using a mixer. Roll into balls and then flatten. Fill with meat and bake at 375°F. until they are brown.

Note: For spinach pies, add ½ package of yeast.

Cabbage Rolls
Minnie Mery

1 large or 2 small heads cabbage
1 cup rice (parboiled or Uncle Ben's)
1 lb. ground round or hamburger (90-10%)
2 tsp. salt
1 tsp. allspice
¼ tsp. cinnamon
⅛ tsp. black pepper
4 large cloves of garlic
1 Tbsp. dry mint or 2 Tbsp. fresh mint
¼ to ½ cup lemon juice

Remove core using a triangular cut around core. Then put cabbage in a big pot and bring to a boil to loosen leaves; separate with a fork. As leaves become limp, remove and place in pan to cool. Cut out heavy center stems from leaves. If leaf is large, cut in two lengthwise.

Wash and rinse rice until clear. Mix rice with pound of ground round or hamburger being careful not to break rice. Add salt, allspice, cinnamon, nutmeg, and pepper. Mix well. Place about a tablespoon of meat mixture on each leaf along rib lengthwise, and roll up like a cigar. Arrange in compact rows over a layer of cabbage ribs placing closed side down. Cover rolls with water and lemon about ½" higher than top. Sprinkle tablespoon of salt over the top. Place 3 to 4 cloves of garlic on top of cabbage. Sprinkle dry mint on top of cabbage. Cover with leftover leaves and invert a plate and place over cabbage so cabbage rolls remains firm and submerged in the pan. Cook over low heat 45 minutes to an hour.

Eggplant Stew
Yield: 6–8

1 pound ground round, cubed
5 medium eggplants, diced
1 large onion, diced
3 + 1 Tbsp. oil
16 oz. can tomatoes
1 tsp. salt
½ tsp. black pepper
¼ tsp. allspice

Brown meat in 3 tablespoons of oil, add onion and continue cooking until onion is translucent. Add 8 ounces of water and continue cooking meat and onion for 30 minutes. Then add eggplant, tomatoes, salt, pepper, and allspice. Bring to a boil and simmer for 30 minutes.

Burghul with Tomatoes
(Burghul a Banadoora)

Lina Noujeim

2 cups coarse burghul
2 cups onions, chopped
2 Tbsp. oil
2 lb. tomatoes crushed (can be substituted with tomato sauce or tomato paste)
Salt, allspice and black pepper to taste

Heat oil and lightly brown the onions; add tomatoes, salt and spices and let boil for 5 minutes.

Wash burghul and add to sauce. Burghul should be covered with the sauce. If not, add water.

Boil and reduce heat until done.

Egyptian Bean and Vegetable Soup
(Ful Nabed)
Sue Guergues

½ cup chopped onions
2 cloves garlic, pressed
¼ cup olive oil
1 tsp. cumin
2 bay leaves
1 long carrot, chopped
1 cup tomatoes
3½ cups vegetable stock
2 cups canned or cooked fava beans
¼ cup fresh parsley, chopped
1 Tbsp. fresh lemon juice
Salt and pepper to taste
½ tsp. paprika
¼ tsp. cayenne pepper (optional)
5 cups water

In a large soup pot, sauté the onions and garlic in olive oil. Add cumin, paprika, cayenne, bay leaves, carrots, and water; cook on medium for 5 minutes. Stir in chopped tomatoes and vegetable stock, and simmer until carrots are tender, usually about 15 minutes. Finally add fava beans, parsley, and lemon juice. Add salt and pepper to taste.

Note: This is a popular Egyptian soup that is simple and nutritious. Serve with pita bread and garnish with fresh mint leaves.

Falafel
Michele Chebib

1 lb. of chickpeas soaked overnight (you can do ½ lb. of fava beans and ½ lb. of chickpeas)
2 cloves of garlic crushed
1 large brown onion chopped finely
4 large spring onions chopped finely
½ hot red or green pepper chopped finely (optional)
1 level Tbsp. baking soda
3 Tbsp. plain flour
1 cup finely chopped parsley
1 teaspoon of ground coriander
1–1½ tsp. cumin (optional)
1½ Tbsp. salt
½ tsp. black pepper
Oil for frying

Drain the beans and rinse well in cold water. If the beans are not skinless, skin them. Pound or grind the beans (if grinding, put them through the fine blade of the mincer twice). Mix in the crushed garlic, chopped onions, spring onions and hot pepper, then add the remaining ingredients. Pound or blend the mixture to a smooth paste and let rest for at least one hour. Take walnut sized lumps of the mixture and mold into round flat shapes 1½" in diameter. Allow to rest for further 15 minutes, then deep fry them in oil until golden brown. Serve hot with Garlic Paste accompanied by a tomato and cucumber salad and tahini sauce.

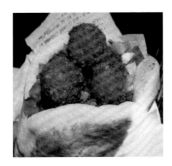

Fried Meat Triangles

Filling:

1 lb. lean ground beef
1 tsp. salt
¼ cup oil
1 small onion, finely chopped
Pepper
½ tsp. Spice Mix

Pastry:

2 cups flour
1 tsp. salt
¼ cup butter
1 egg
Cold water
Oil for deep frying

Spice Mix:

5 cardamom pods
2 pieces cinnamon bark
½ tsp. whole cloves
2 Tbsp. cumin seeds
1 tsp. black cumin seeds
½ nutmeg, grated fine

Heat oil in pan and gently fry onion until transparent. Add meat, increase heat and fry until lightly browned. If too dry, add a little water to moisten, and add pepper, spice mix, and salt. Remove from heat.

Sift flour and salt into bowl, add butter and rub into flour lightly with fingertips until well distributed. Beat egg lightly in cup, measure and add enough cold water to make ½ cup liquid.

Pour liquid into flour mixture and mix to soft dough. Cover and leave to rest for 15 minutes. Then roll out dough in approximately 6" diameter circles and fill with meat mixture. Fold and seal dough. Deep fry until golden brown. Drain on paper towel.

Grape Leaves

Cook: 20 minutes on top of stove Time: 2–3 hours depending on quantity

Use fresh, frozen or bottled grape leaves; (if fresh, make sure the bottom of leaves are a nice green, and smooth. If it is white and rough, do not use this leaf!) If using bottled grape leaves, be sure and rinse each leaf thoroughly as they are packed with salty brine.

Rinse with warm water to loosen. Put leaves in strainer to drain. Transfer leaves from strainer to cookie sheet (with sides), use cookie sheet to cut the stems from the grape leaves. Do not cut into the leaf; just trim the stem close to the leaf. Roll the leaves, as it keeps the excess water from getting all over table.

Filling:

Mix the following together.
1½–2 lb. lean ground beef
1 cup Uncle Ben's Converted Rice
1 tsp. salt per lb. meat
½ tsp. pepper
½–1 tsp. allspice
Cinnamon (to taste)
Lemon juice from 3–4 lemons
Oil

You will need more of the spices than you would expect, but you will have to taste until suitable. Put about a teaspoonful of meat mixture on inside bottom edge of grape leaf. Roll up, bringing in sides and rolling up.

Cooking: Use lamb or beef bones, broken grape leaves or tomato slices on bottom of the pan, which helps keep leaves from burning in bottom of pan. Place grape leaves separately into pot with folded edge down. Stagger rolls in rows, one going one direction, the next going opposite way. Pack tightly. Place an inverted ovenproof/microwavable plate on top of grape leaves, to keep the leaves from bobbling up while cooking.

Cover to top with water. May want to add salt. Add juice of 3–4 lemons, add lemon juice with the water, and a little oil. Cook for about 20–30 minutes or until rice is done, on medium heat.

How to Fold Grape Leaves

Meatless Grape Leaves

Candy Monsour

1 cup lentils
1 large jar of *Orlando* brand grape leaves
1½ cup dry cracked wheat
1 bunch green onions or 1 large onion chopped fine
2 tsp. cumin
2 tsp. mint
Salt and pepper to taste
⅓ to ½ cup oil
1 Tbsp. lemon juice
2 cups water
1 Tbsp. butter

Soak 1 cup lentils for ½ day until soft. Drain. Then add other ingredients, mix well, and use about 1 heaping tablespoon onto a grape leave and roll. Put 1 tablespoon butter in bottom of pan and melt. Then place leftover grape leaves on bottom of pan.

Lay rolled grape leaves in pan fairly tight. Add 2 cups water with 1 Tbsp. lemon juice. Grape leaves will not be covered. Bring to a boil, then simmer 45 minutes.

Lebanese Green Beans and Rice

2 cans green beans
1 1b. round steak or lean beef, cubed
½ cup olive oil
1 large onion, diced
8 oz. can tomato sauce
2 buttons garlic (optional)
½–1 tsp. salt (to taste)
¼–½ tsp. pepper (to taste)
½ tsp. allspice (to taste)

Sauté onion and garlic in oil until lightly browned. Add meat, salt, pepper, and allspice. After browning put meat in a 3 quart sauce pan. Add 3 cups water (the water from green beans can be used). Cook over medium heat until the meat is tender. Add tomato sauce and simmer 20–30 minutes. Pour green beans into the mixture and simmer another 10 minutes. Serve over rice.

Meat & Rice
Hashweh
Louise Malouff
Time: 30 minutes

1–2 lb. beef, cubed
1 cup Uncle Ben's converted rice (1 cup uncooked = 2 cups
   cooked rice)
1–2 tsp. salt
¼ –½ tsp. pepper
Cinnamon, to taste (start with 1–2 tsp)
1 stick of butter

Brown beef in 1 stick of butter.

Rinse rice in colander, to remove starch. Add water, according to rice directions, let mixture come to a boil. Add rice into pan with meat, salt, pepper, and cinnamon to taste. Cook on low to medium heat until rice is done, about 20 minutes.

Meat Filling

(Hashweh)
Cheryl Smith
Yield: 2 lb.

2 lb. ground beef (85-15%)
2 medium white onions, chopped
2 tsp. salt
¼ tsp. black pepper
¾ tsp. allspice
½ cups pine nuts (optional)

Brown meat and onion in frying pan; sprinkle salt, pepper, and allspice evenly over meat. If possible, break the meat into small chunks while cooking until it is done. Drain any excess grease. Spread filling in a large cookie sheet. Allow to cool, then crumble into small pieces. Use for Kibbeh stuffing, meat pie filling, or for meat finger stuffing.

Note: Filling can be made in advance and frozen in plastic bag so you have some on hand when you want it for a recipe.

Hint: *If you are trying to dry parsley or lettuce in a hurry, try rolling the leaves in a microfiber cloth. The microfiber readily absorbs the water so it dries the leaves quickly.*

Grape Leaves
Marie Saleh

2 lb. ground beef (85%–15% or 80%-20%)
1 cup rice (Uncle Ben's or converted rice)
½ large yellow onions, minced finely
1 Tbsp. salt
1 tsp. (heaping) pepper
1 tsp. (heaping) allspice, ground
¾ cup crushed tomatoes
¼ cup oil
⅓ cup (4½ Tbsp.) butter, melted
¼ cup lemon juice
2 large jars Orlando brand California grape leaves

Mix thoroughly, and then use about 1 tablespoon of mixture to roll grape leaves. Cook. (See page 23).

Iraqi Biryani
Susan Rizzo
Prep time: 35 minutes Cook time: 45 minutes

¼ cup vegetable oil
1 medium carrot cut into medium cubes
1 medium onion sliced
½ cup frozen green peas thawed
2 Tbsp. raisins
¼ tsp. ground black pepper
Pinch of saffron filaments (or dash of turmeric for color)
½ cup almonds, peeled and toasted
2 Tbsp. ghee or butter
¾ cup vermicelli
2 cups rice washed
2 cubes chicken bouillon
1½ tsp. 7 spice
4-4½ cups water

In a medium saucepan, heat oil and sauté onion until it is tender then add green peas, raisins, black pepper, saffron leaves or turmeric, almonds, and carrot. Stir until well combined and set aside (add salt to your taste).

In a medium pot, melt the ghee, add the vermicelli and stir until vermicelli has changed to golden brown. Add rice, chicken bouillon cubes and spices (add salt, if needed). Stir for 15–30 seconds, then add the water and stir constantly until it boils. Cover and simmer over a low heat for 20 minutes or until rice is cooked.

Combine together and serve.

Kafta Meat Loaf

Michele Chebib

Oven 350°F. Time: 40 minutes Yield: 4–6 servings

2 lb. ground beef or lamb
1 cup parsley, finely chopped
1 tsp. allspice
1 cup onion, chopped
1 Tbsp. salt
½ tsp. black pepper
3 Tbsp. tomato paste
1 cup water

Mix all of the ingredients together except tomato paste and water in a large bowl incorporating well.

Spread the kafta mixture evenly over a large baking pan, 10" x 13" pan about an inch thick. Bake at 350°F. oven until lightly browned, about 10 minutes.

Mix the tomato paste with the water. Pour the tomato mixture over the meat in the pan; continue baking until half the tomato mixture is absorbed into the meat, about another 20 minutes.

Remove from the oven, place on a hot plate keeping at medium heat until most of the juice is absorbed into the meat (usually about 10 minutes.)

Cut into squares. Serve hot with potatoes and cooked vegetables.

Kafta
Father Ghassan Mattar

4 lb. ground meat
3 Tbsp. allspice
2 red onions, chopped finely
16 oz. can tomato paste or (2) 8 oz. cans
4 Tbsp. (¼ cup) salt
1 Tbsp. cinnamon
1 Tbsp. black pepper
2–3 bunches of parsley (depending on size), finely chopped

Line cooking sheet with parchment paper.

Finely chop parsley. Set aside. Chop 2 red onions, finely. Set aside.

Combine meat, allspice, onion, salt, cinnamon, black pepper, and some parsley. Mix, then add remaining parsley and tomato paste until well combined. Shape into desired shape, usually about size of a cigar, and place on baking sheet. Cover, and freeze at this point for about 12 hours.

When ready to cook, grill until done. Put in a large casserole dish until ready to serve.

Kibbeh

Marie Saleh

Oven 350°F. Time: 30 minutes Yield: 8" x 8" pan

2 lb. extra lean ground beef (Kibbeh meat)
½ tsp. black pepper
½ tsp. allspice
1 Tbsp. salt
¾–1 large onion, pulverized or to taste
2⅔ cups burghul
¼ cup fresh mint, pulverized with onion
Oil

Filling

1 lb. ground beef (85%-15%)
1 large onion, diced
½ tsp. allspice
1 tsp. salt
¼ tsp. black pepper
⅓ cup pine nuts (optional)

Cover burghul with water. Allow to soak for short time (15–30 minutes), then using strainer, drain. Add burghul to meat. Sprinkle and spread other ingredients over meat and burghul. Mixing and combining well by hand using a pushing and pulling action similar to kneading dough; dip hands in ice water, if needed. Put meat in mixer bowl and add about 10 to 12 regular ice cubes, and allow mixer to mix thoroughly.

Filling: Brown the meat, onions, and pine nuts. Sprinkle salt, pepper, and allspice over meat mixture. Drain away grease. Spread filling over large jelly roll pan to cool. After it cools, break the meat into small pieces so the filling is crumbly.

Put a quarter cup (¼") of oil and spread in a 8" X 8" pan. Divide the kibbeh in half. Spread the first half over the bottom of the pan. Smooth out the layer evenly, and if necessary, dip your hand in ice water to facilitate the smoothing. Then spread the filling evenly over the top of the first layer. Then spread the rest of the kibbeh by forming patties in your hand or spread the kibbeh onto a piece of saran warp evenly to cover the entire surface of the 2 layers. Smooth the edges and top using the ice water to help. Then score the kibbeh into equal squares or diamond shape. Run a knife around the edge of the pan to loosen the kibbeh away from the sides of the pan. Make a hole in the corners of the kibbeh with your little finger. Let the kibbeh rest about an hour in the refrigerator before baking.

To bake, preheat the oven to 350°F. Pour about one-third (⅓) cup of oil over the top and bake for about 30 minutes or until done.

Potato Kibbeh
(Kibbeh Batata)

2 lb. potatoes
2 cups fine burghul (soaked)
3 yellow onions, diced
3 Tbsp. oil
2 Tbsp. dried mint
Salt and pepper to taste
1 cup walnuts

Cook, peel and mash potatoes. Finely chop (or grate) ½ cup of onions, mix with dried mint, salt and pepper and add to the mashed potatoes. Chop the remaining onions and cook in oil until brown.

Add the soaked burghul to the potatoes and mix until well blended. Spread the mixture in a platter, top with the cooked onions and sprinkle with the walnuts.

Raw Kibbeh
(Kibbeh nayyeh)

Reggie Raba

3¾–4 lb. top sirloin beef (clean off fat and gristle for about 3 lb.
    clean, cubed beef)
2 cups #2 burghul wheat (soaked 30–45 minutes)
1 small white onion, chopped
½–¾ cup fresh mint
1–1½ Tbsp. salt
1–2 tsp. black pepper
1 Tbsp. allspice
Oil

Take cubed meat, a little onion, and 2–3 mint leaves at a time and grind in meat grinder until all are ground.

Drain wheat. Mix by hand into the ground meat mixture. Sprinkle the salt, pepper, and allspice over meat and mix well. Grind meat again. Taste, and add more salt and/or allspice, if needed.

Grind meat again. Serve with pita bread, oil, and green onions.

Kibbeh
Louise Malouff
Oven 350°F. Time: 30+5 minutes Yield: 8" x 8" pan

2 lb. ground lean meat (kibbeh)
1½ cups burghul (wash, and soak in water for at least 20 minutes, then drain all water)
1 medium white onion, grated
Salt (start with 2 tsp. salt or to taste)
Pepper (start with ½ tsp. or to taste)
Allspice (start with ½ tsp. or to taste)
Cinnamon (if desired)

Mix above ingredients together well.

Use butter, oleo, or oil to grease pan, put kibbeh into pan, smoothing top to make it even and look nice. If using butter or oleo, make about five holes, two on each side, and one in the middle on top of kibbeh and insert butter into the holes. If oil is used, brush top of entire layer of kibbeh with the oil.

Bake at 350 °F. for at least ½ hour, cooking until done. To brown the top put under broiler for the last 5 minutes.

Kibbeh can also be eaten raw or fried like a hamburger. If eaten raw, mound onto a plate, and garnish with green onions, can also place sliced white onion around kibbeh.

Note: If kibbeh shrinks ½" or more from sides of pan, an insufficient amount of burghul was utilized.

Kibbeh

Julie Malouff

Oven 350°F. Time: 30–45 minutes Yield: 8" x 8" pan

2 lb. very lean ground beef
2 cups burghul (1 cup / lb. meat)
Black pepper, coarse
Allspice
Nutmeg
Salt
Olive oil
Green onions
White onions

Put lean ground beef in large bowl. Soak burghul in another bowl of tepid water.

Grind white onions to puree. Use black pepper liberally; mix with meat. Add pureed onions, mix well into meat. Squeeze out water from burghul wheat; then add burghul to meat. On top, liberally sprinkle allspice. Lightly sprinkle nutmeg. Add salt to taste, and mix well. Dip hands in ice water while mixing. Put kibbeh on serving platter. Indent cross with hands in middle. Put sliced white onions or green onions on the side. Drizzle olive oil on each serving.

To bake, cover bottom of pan with olive oil. Place meat in pan and cut meat into diamond shapes. Put olive oil lightly on top. Bake at 350°F. for 30 to 45 minutes. Check at 20 minutes to pour off excess grease. Put in broiler to make crusty.

Note: Scramble leftover kibbeh with eggs or fry into a patty.

Kibbeh with Quinoa
Eleanor Khattar
Oven 350°F. Time: 30–45 minutes Yield: 9" x 9" pan

2 lb. kibbeh meat
½ tsp. black pepper
½ tsp. allspice
1 Tbsp. salt
¾–1 large onion, pulverized
2½ cups quinoa, cooked (1 cup uncooked)
¼ cup fresh mint, pulverized with onion
2 cups water

Filling

1 lb. ground beef (85%–15%)
1 large onion, diced
½ tsp. allspice
1 tsp. salt
¼–½ tsp. black pepper
⅓ cup pine nuts (if desired)

In a small saucepan, bring two cups of water to a boil over high heat. Meanwhile rinse the quinoa in a fine mesh strainer with cold water. Then add to boiling water, cover the pot, reduce the heat to low cooking the quinoa about 15 minutes or until it is tender and the liquid is absorbed. Place the quinoa in a large bowl to cool.

While quinoa is cooking, pulverize the onion and mint. Add to a large bowl. Then add salt, pepper, onions, and allspice; mix. After quinoa cools, add onion mixture to the quinoa. Add quinoa mixture to the meat. Mixing and combining well by hand using a pushing and pulling action similar to kneading dough; dip hands in ice water, if needed. Put meat in mixer bowl and add about 10 to 12 regular ice cubes, and allow mixer to mix thoroughly.

Filling: Brown the meat, onions, and pine nuts. Sprinkle salt, pepper, allspice, over meat mixture. Drain away grease. Spread hashwet over large jelly roll pan to cool. After it cools, break the meat into small pieces so the filling is crumbly. (2nd layer)

Oil 9" x 9" pans with ½ cup of oil. Spread a little less than half of the kibbeh meat over the pan evenly. Make a second layer with the filling distributed over the top of first layer evenly. Then spread the remaining meat over the top. (An easy way to spread the meat is to spread out on a piece of plastic wrap, then transfer onto the second layer.). Cut the kibbeh into pieces and score. Using your little finger to separate corners of the kibbeh. Pour a half cup of oil over the kibbeh and cook in a 350°F. oven for 30 minutes or until done.

Meat Pie

(Lahambajeen)

Oven: 400°F. Time: 20 minutes

Dough

5½ cups flour
2 cups oil
½ tsp. salt

Mix together and knead. Fill with meat and pine nuts.

Filling

2 lb. ground beef (90–10%)
1 large onion
2 tsp. salt
1 tsp. allspice
¾ tsp. cinnamon (if desired)
Pine nuts (optional)

Sauté onion in small amount of oil for a couple of minutes until translucent, then add meat and continue cooking until done. Add salt and spices. Reserve for filling.

To form the pies: Flatten a ball of dough into a disk. Roll out into a circle about 5–6" wide and 1/8" thick. Place about 2 tablespoons of filling onto the center of the dough. Fold the edges of the dough over the filling. Form 2 edges together, then bring up the third side. Pinch the seams to seal. Add a small hole in the center. Bake.

Koushari

Sue Guergues

1 cup brown lentils
3 cups water
1 cup macaroni noodles
1 cup short grain rice
2 Tbsp. olive oil
3+4 cups water
1 cup tomato purée
2 large onions
¼ cup olive oil
1 garlic clove finely chopped

Place lentils in a sieve and wash well, place in a large pot and add 3 cups water, bring to boil uncovered then simmer for ¾ hour covered. Drain and keep aside.

Clean same pot. Add 4 cups water bring to boil; add 2 teaspoons of salt and macaroni, stir constantly until it boils, and cook uncovered until tender. Drain and keep aside. Clean pot again and dry.

Wash rice and drain, heat oil in pot and fry rice over medium heat for 3 minutes, add 2 cups water and 1 teaspoon salt bring to boil cover and simmer over low heat 15 minutes until tender, remove cover and take off the heat for 5 minutes.

With fork toss lentils, macaroni and rice. Warm tomato puree. Thinly slice the onions, and fry in oil over medium heat until golden. Cook garlic for a minute. Add tomato and onions to rice, lentils and macaroni.

Note: This is classified as an 'oil' dish by Coptic Egyptians and is prepared during periods of fasting when animal products cannot be eaten.

Lebanese Chicken and Rice

2 large chicken fryers
2 lb. Uncle Ben's rice
¼ lb. butter
1½ lb. meat, coarsely ground
Salt (start with 1–1½ tsp.)
Pepper (start with ½ tsp.)
Allspice, to taste (start with ½ tsp.)
4 cups chicken broth
Water

Wash chicken fryers; sprinkle with seasoning inside and out; then put in a covered roaster and bake in 350°F. oven until done. Meanwhile, melt butter in a pan; add meat, salt, pepper, and allspice and brown. Soak rice in hot salted water for 30 to 60 minutes. Drain rice and add with pine nuts to butter and meat mixture, stirring until the rice is coated with butter. Add 4 cups broth and water. Cook over medium flame until rice is done and all the water is absorbed. Season to taste. Place rice around chicken and return to oven, heat thoroughly. Serve.

Lentils and Wheat (Mujadarah)
Soumaya Diab Doenges

2 cups lentils, brown
8 cups water
1 cup burghul (#1)
2 medium onions, sliced into half circles
¼ cup olive oil
Salt

Cook lentils in water over medium heat, uncovered. In about 15 minutes, taste to see if the lentils have softened.

Meanwhile, sauté onions in oil until soft and golden brown or smoky. After the lentils have softened, add sautéed onion, wheat, and salt. Cook for about 15 to 20 minutes until water is absorbed.

Lebanese Grape Leaves
Mary Ann Karam

1 jar grape leaves (Orlando brand)
3 lb. lean ground meat
3 cups long grain rice
½ to 1 tsp. allspice (more or less to taste)
½ to 1 tsp. cinnamon (more or less to taste)
Salt and pepper to taste
1 stick butter
3 beef soup bones (the flatter the better to fit into pan)
Juice of 8 lemons

Mix rice, meat and spices. Rinse grape leaves and cut hard stems off. Place meat mixture, the size of your forefinger in the middle of leaf and begin to roll. Start from bottom, folding leaf inwards on both sides. *Grape leaves should be the shape and size of a small cigar.* You can at this time place into freezer bag and put into freezer until needed. Or if ready to cook, place leftover leaves in bottom of large pot place bones on top of leaves. Arrange rolled grape leaves in layers in the pot alternating layers of rolls. Sprinkle with small amount of salt, melt 1 stick of butter and drizzle over leaves. Fill pot ½ full with water and lemon juice. Place plate upside down on top of leaves and bring to a boil then reduce heat and simmer about 1 hour to complete cooking. Remove plate and let grape leaves rest a few minutes prior to serving.

Serve with traditional Lebanese yogurt sauce accompanied with tossed salad and kibbeh for a full meal.

Lebanese Lamb and Rice

Yellow onion, chopped
2 Tbsp. butter
1 cup rice
2 cups water
⅛ cup pine nuts
½ tsp. cinnamon
½ tsp. allspice
Salt (about 1 tsp.)
1 lb. ground lamb

Brown lamb in a bit of butter and set aside. Sauté onion in remainder of butter, until tender. Add the rice, then sauté until rice is barely golden brown.

Add the water, pine nuts, cinnamon, allspice, cooked lamb and salt. Bring to boil, cover and reduce heat to low, cook 30 minutes or until rice is done.

Variation: Use boneless lamb that is cut up into bite size pieces.

Lentil Stuffed Grape Leaves
Time: Simmer about 1 hour

Soak lentils until soft 1 cup
About 1½ cups dry cracked wheat
Bunch of green onions or 1 big onion
Salt, pepper
2 tsp. cumin use more as desired
3 Tbsp. dry mint
⅓–½ cup oil
2 cups water
1 Tbsp. lemon juice

Add all ingredients to drained, soaked lentils. Roll mixture in grape leaf. Put 1 tablespoon butter in pot and melt. Add 2 cups water (not covered) and 1 tablespoon of lemon juice. Simmer about 1 hour.

Lebanese Stuffed Zucchini
(Koossa)

Susan Rizzo
Yield: 4 servings

12 medium zucchini, rinsed
½ lb. ground beef or lamb
2 cups rice soaked in warm water 30 minutes
2 Tbsp. pine nuts, skillet-toasted in 1 Tbsp. olive oil (if desired)
½ tsp. cumin
½ tsp. cinnamon
½ tsp. ground coriander
1 tsp. ground allspice
1 tsp. salt
½ tsp. black pepper
½ cup onion, finely chopped
3 Tbsp. tomato paste
8 cups water

Cook the meat in 1 tablespoon olive oil, stirring to break it up. Add the seasonings and cook another few minutes (about 10 minutes total). Drain the rice. Mix it with the meat and pine nuts and seasonings in a bowl. Cover and set aside.

Trim ends of each zucchini. Hollow out each zucchini with a peeler or sharp, thin, flexible knife, taking care not to pierce the bottoms. Stuff each zucchini half-way up with the meat mixture.

Fry the chopped onion with 1 to 2 tablespoons olive oil in a pan large enough to cook the zucchini in. When the onions are translucent, add the tomato paste and 8 cups water, bring to a boil. Check seasonings and salt to taste. Place the zucchini in the sauce. Cook for 30 minutes on medium heat. To test for doneness, pierce one zucchini with a toothpick or thin knife. When tender and the rice is cooked, remove them to a platter and keep warm.

Reduce the sauce by boiling it another 15 minutes or until thick. Spoon the reduced sauce over the zucchini and serve.

Macaroni with Garlic
(Toom)

Susu (Souraya Sarkis)

Flour
Water
Salt
1 clove fresh garlic, minced
3–4 Tbsp. olive oil
Salt to taste
2 Tbsp. lemon juice
Mint to taste

Mix 1 cup flour with water and salt to make dough. Mix with hand, roll with hands into a thin cigar shape. Cut into ½" pieces.

Boil water with salt, drop dough into boiling water, approximately 5–7 minutes until cooked through.

Marinade: In a separate bowl mix garlic, olive oil, salt, lemon juice and mint. Drain pasta and add to marinade.

Green Beans & Tomatoes with Meat
(Loobyeh)
Louise Malouff

1½–2 pounds beef, cubed
1 medium onion, chopped
Garlic
16 oz. pkg. frozen or 2 cans green beans (regular cut beans or French-style cut beans)
Italian Seasoning
Oregano
Salt
Pepper
1 to 3 cans (8 oz.) tomato sauce (and more if making more)

Brown meat with onions and garlic.

Add tomato sauce, spices, and green beans - simmer. Cook over low heat until done. Serve over Lebanese rice.

Note: Adjust to suit your own taste, so go easy at first – have enough sauce to cover meat and green beans. If you like a thicker paste, use tomato paste. If using paste, use 3 cans of water for each can of paste.

Meat Balls
(Kafta)
Stove top and Oven: 350°F.

1 lb. ground beef
1 small onion, diced
½ cup parsley, chopped fine
1 Tbsp. mint
2 garlic buttons, grated fine
1 egg
1 tsp. salt
½ tsp. pepper
½ tsp. allspice

Combine all of the ingredients in a mixing bowl. Shape into patties or balls, and brown with a small amount of oil. After browning, drain off oil, put in a casserole dish, and add 1 can tomato sauce and a can of water. Bake at 350°F. until it thickens in the oven. Serve.

Pre-Ground Raw Kibbeh
(Kibbeh nayyeh)
Reggie Raba

3 1b. very lean pre-ground beef
2 cups burghul, soaked
1½ Tbsp. salt
¾–1 Tbsp. black pepper
1–1½ Tbsp. allspice
White onion   } Equal portions of white onion and mint
Fresh spearmint ∫ pulverized = 1⅛ cups

Soak burghul in water for 20 to 45 minutes. Drain. Then add salt, pepper, and allspice to wheat; mix thoroughly. Add wheat mixture to ground beef to thoroughly mix with meat. Then run through meat grinder. Serve on dish with green onions, pita bread, and oil.

Meat Ball Soup

Meatball

1 lb. ground beef
1 small onion, finely ground
½ cup parsley, finely chopped
1 Tbsp. mint (optional)
1 tsp. salt or to taste
½ tsp. pepper or to taste
½ cup crackers, finely ground
½ green pepper (optional)
1 egg

Soup

Butter or oleo, enough to fry meat balls
1 small can tomato sauce
½ cup rice, rinsed
2 to 3 cups water

Mix first eight ingredients together. Form meat into balls the size of a marble then fry in butter. Place into large sauce pan, add tomato sauce, seasonings and 2 to 3 cups water, mix well. Simmer for about 30 minutes then add rice. Cook until rice is done, serve with crackers.

Meat Pies
Oven: 400°F. Time: 15–20 minutes Yield: 12–14 pies

Dough

3 cups flour
⅔ cup oil
1¼ tsp. salt
1 Tbsp. yeast (½ package)
¼ cup water and ¾ cup water

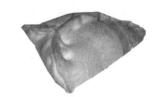

Meat Filling

1 lb. ground beef
1 white onion, diced
2 Tbsp. lemon juice
½ tsp. allspice
1 tsp. salt
½ tsp. black pepper

Filling: Start browning the beef in a frying pan; add onions. Continue cooking until onions are translucent and the beef is cooked. Add salt, pepper, allspice, and lemon juice. Set aside.

Dough: In a mixing bowl, dissolve the yeast in one-fourth (¼) cup water. Add salt, flour, and oil plus remaining water. Add more water if needed to make dough soft and pliable like bread dough. Let dough rise 30 minutes.

Roll out the dough to ¼" thickness. Using a biscuit cutter, cut the dough into rounds. Gather the remaining dough, roll and then cut into rounds; continue until all the dough is used.

Place a tablespoon of the meat mixture and fold in half (half moon) or into triangles by bring the dough up from 2 sides and then the remaining side to form a triangle and pinching the edges together. Bake in a 400°F. oven in a greased pan or parchment covered pan for 15–20 minutes until lightly browned.

Meat Balls with Peas and Tomato Sauce

1 lb. ground beef or lamb, mixed if desired
2 tsp. salt
¼–½ tsp. allspice (or to taste)
½ tsp. cinnamon (optional or to taste)
½ stick + 2 Tbsp. butter
1 medium onion, minced
½ tsp. pepper
¼ cup pine nuts
16 oz. can whole tomatoes
6 oz. can tomato puree
½–1 cup peas

Mix the ground meat with onions and spices. Shape into walnut size balls, make a hole in each meat ball with finger and fill with 4 or 5 pine nuts. Reshape meat back into a ball so all nuts are covered. Sauté meat balls in butter using a 2-quart saucepan. Add tomatoes and tomato puree. Cook until tomato sauce thickens and meat is tender, approximately 45 minutes. Add peas and cook for 20 more minutes. Add lemon juice during final minutes of cooking. Serve over hot cooked rice.

Meat Omelet
(Ijjeh)

1 large onion, chopped
½ tsp. salt
½ cup rendered butter
½ tsp. allspice
¼ lb. unsalted butter
½ tsp. pepper (to taste)
1 lb. coarsely ground beef or lean lamb
1 dozen eggs
1 Tbsp. cornstarch diluted with 2 Tbsp. milk
1 bunch parsley, chopped

Sauté onions in butter until soft. Add meat and continue cooking on low until meat is done and majority of moisture is gone. Add chopped parsley, salt and spices; set aside to cool. Beat eggs well until foamy. Add cornstarch mixture and combine with meat mixing well. Pour into a buttered baking dish and bake in a preheated oven at 375°F. until thickened and done. Cut into small squares and serve hot.

Mujadarah (Lentils and Rice)
Janie Ashmore

1 cup uncooked lentils (Rinse, look for rocks)
4 cups water
1 tsp. salt
¼ tsp. pepper
1 large onion, chopped
½ cup uncooked rice (rinse)

Rinse lentils, add water and bring this to boil then time for 20 minutes. Add rice and spices. Cook another 20 minutes on low to medium heat until rice is done and all water is gone.

On the side, chop onions and sauté them in another saucepan with little oil until slightly brown. After rice and lentils are done top with onions and serve.

Note: *Want a soup?* Add about 6–7 cups water. Add 2–3 tablespoons rice, and other vegetables like carrots and celery. Then add ½ cup of lentils for a delicious soup.

Meat Fingers
Gloria Benson

Oven: 350–400°F. Time: 10 minutes Yield: 50 fingers

Dough

6 cups flour
1¾ cups butter, melted
1¼ cups lukewarm water

Stuffing

2 lb. ground beef (85%-15%)
1 large onion
Pine nuts (optional)
Salt to taste (about 2 tsp. to start)
½ tsp. black pepper
allspice (start with ½ tsp. or to taste)

Add butter and water to flour, continue as you would a pie crust. Form dough into balls. Roll balls into thin crust. Spread with meat mixture and roll in shape of a finger. Bake fingers on a jelly roll pan at 350°F. to 400°F. for 10 minutes or until golden brown.

Meatless Grape Leaves
Marie Saleh

1 jar "Orlando" brand grape leaves
1 cup rice
1 cup chopped parsley
1 cup diced tomatoes
¼ to ½ cup minced onions
¼ tsp. pepper
1 tsp. salt
¼ tsp. allspice
⅓ cup oil
2 Tbsp. fresh lemon juice

Combine well in a large bowl. Use about 1 tablespoon of the mixture to roll into a grape leaf in usual fashion.

Pack into a deep pan in criss-cross fashion. Freeze at this point, or cover grape leaves with water. Bring to a boil and cook for about 20 minutes or until about two-thirds (⅔) of the water is absorbed. Combine 6 cups of water and 1 to 2 cups of lemon juice, then heat to boiling in microwave; add to grape leaves and cook for about 10 to 20 minutes more or until done.

Hint: Grape leaves are usually available in Mediterranean or international stores. The Orlando brand grape leaves are a good choice.
Variation: Add a dash cayenne pepper.

Meat Loaf with Potatoes and Carrots
Serves 8-10

Meatloaf

½ cup onions, diced
2 tsp. salt
⅛ tsp. pepper
½ tsp. allspice
⅛ tsp. cinnamon (if desired)
⅔ cup parsley, chopped finely
2 lbs. ground beef
1 egg, beaten
2 Tbsp. flour
⅓ cup water

Veggies

8 medium potatoes, peeled and cut into quarters
8 medium carrots, peeled and cut into quarters
2 medium onions, remove skin and cut into quarters
½ tsp. salt (or to taste)
¼ tsp. pepper
8 oz. can tomato sauce + 1 can water

Place onion in mixing bowl. Add salt, pepper, allspice, cinnamon, and parsley, and mix well. Add the egg, flour, and water, and mix together very well. Shape meat into a loaf and place into a baking pan. Bake at 350°F. for 15 minutes while preparing the vegetables.

Peel and quarter potatoes and carrots. Remove onion skins and root, and cut onions into quarters. Remove meatloaf from oven. Arrange vegetables around meatloaf in the baking dish. Sprinkle vegetables with salt and pepper. Reserve a tablespoon of sauce then mix remainder of tomato sauce with a can of water to half-way cover meatloaf and vegetables. Spread top of meat loaf with reserved tomato sauce. Return baking dish to a 350°F. for an hour, basting periodically with tomato sauce in pan.

Lentils & Rice
(Mujadarah)
Louise Malouff
Time: 40 minutes +

1 cup lentils
1 cup rice
3 cups water
Salt to taste (it takes a lot of salt; start with 1 tsp.)
½ cup olive oil

Prior to cooking go through Lentils making sure there are no foreign objects mixed in with them, wash and rinse thoroughly.

Cook over low heat (about 20 minutes). When lentils are soft, add 1 cup rice that has been rinsed thoroughly to remove starch. If lentils become too thick, add more water. Cook another 20 minutes or until rice is done.

Fry chopped or slivered onions in oil until browned. Save some onions for garnish on top of lentils. When rice and lentils are almost done, add onions. Garnish with browned onions.

Mom's 'Meat Sticks'
Louise Malouff
Oven: 450–475°F. Prep Time: 2 hours
Cook Time: 12–15 minutes

3 cups flour
1 tsp. salt
2 sticks melted butter or oleo (Fleischmann's)
½ cup lukewarm water

Add salt to flour and gradually add melted butter with fork working well into dough. Do NOT use spoon!!

Gradually add water, working into dough. Cover dough and let set about 45 minutes. In meantime, fix the filling.

Filling:

2 medium onions, chopped
1 lb. ground beef
Salt and pepper
Allspice
Pine nuts (toasted) (optional)
2–3 lemons

Sauté onions in oleo. Add beef, and brown. Add salt, pepper, and allspice to taste. Add pine nuts, if desired. Simmer until done. Add juice of 2–3 lemons. Set aside. Go back to dough after 45 minutes.

Roll into small balls (golf ball size). ***Keep dough covered at all times!!*** Use rolling pin to roll out individually. Fill with meat mixture using with as little juice as possible. Roll each individually into a long *cigar,* closing ends.

Can be frozen cooked or uncooked (I prefer to freeze uncooked) when freezing uncooked, layer them on cookie sheet until frozen, then combine in package. If frozen, thaw 1 hour, then bake.

Moussakas
Eggplant, Meat and Béchamel Casserole
Oven: 400°F. Time: 45 minutes, let stand for 15 minutes

5 lb. eggplant (aubergines)
½ cup olive oil
2 garlic cloves, sliced
1 large onion
1½ lb. lean meat (beef)
3 cups puréed fresh or canned tomatoes
Salt, pepper
½ tsp. sugar
2 egg whites, lightly beaten
½ cup chopped parsley
6 Tbsp. bread crumbs
3 cups Béchamel sauce *recipe below
½ cup heavy cream
3 eggs lightly beaten
1 cup grated Kefalotyri or Romano Cheese

Wash and trim eggplants, slice into ½" thick rounds. Sprinkle with salt leave them to drain in colander for 2 hours. Rinse, squeeze gently, and pat dry with paper towels. Fry in hot oil until lightly brown on both sides. Drain and set aside. Sauté garlic and onion add meat and stir for 10 minutes. Pour in tomatoes add sugar, season to taste. Simmer covered until liquid evaporates. Allow to cool, and mix in the lightly beaten egg whites and chopped parsley. Arrange half of eggplant slices in a layer on the bottom of 12" x 14" buttered ovenproof dish sprinkled with 2 tablespoons of bread crumbs and spread over half meat sauce. Sprinkle with grated cheese and bread crumbs. Repeat with remaining eggplant, spread rest of meat sauce and top with remaining grated cheese and bread crumbs.

*Note: At this stage you may cover well and freeze the dish. When ready to bake completely thaw first.

Prepare 3 cups thick béchamel sauce. Stir in the cream and eggs. Pour the sauce over the moussakas and bake at 400°F. for 45 minutes. Let stand for 15 minutes before cutting and serving.

Note: Can use half sliced potatoes or zucchini.

Béchamel Sauce

1 cup of milk
3 Tbsp flour
3 Tbsp butter
Salt, pepper
Pinch of nutmeg

Heat milk in small pan and using a heavy sauce pan melt butter. Stir in flour and sauté 2–3 minutes. Pour in the hot milk, stirring constantly with a wire whisk to blend mixture smoothly. Cook for about 15 minutes stirring with whisk to prevent sauce from sticking. Remove from heat add salt, pepper and nutmeg. Pour over moussakas and bake.

Stuffed Bell Peppers OR Squash (or Zucchini)

Janie Ashmore

1 lb. meat, chuck or ground
¾ cup rice
8 oz. can tomato sauce
2 tsp. salt
1 tsp. pepper
Dried mint
Little allspice

Mix all of the above in bowl. Stuff peppers or other vegetables. In large pan put another small can of tomato juice with enough water to come to half the peppers. Bring to boil, then lower flame; cover for 20–25 minutes or until rice is cooked.

Okra with Meat
(Bamieh)

Yield: Serves 6 to 8

2 lb. fresh baby okra
½ cup unsalted butter
2 large onions, chopped
2 lb. cubed beef or lamb, 2" squares
1 tsp. salt
2 cups water
½ tsp. pepper
1 tsp. coriander (optional)
2 cloves garlic, crushed
½ cup lemon juice
6 oz. can tomato paste

Wash okra and leave to dry. Trim off stems after drying and brush with half the butter. Broil in oven until light brown on all sides. Sauté onions in the remaining butter in large pan, add cubed meat, salt and pepper and continue cooking on low until meat is tender. Mash garlic and coriander add to meat. Add broiled okra, tomato paste, one cup of water and the lemon juice. Adjust salt and spices according to taste. Cook on low until okra is done and juice has thickened.

Note: You can leave out tomato paste and make stew cooked with lemon juice and water only. Serve over cooked rice.

Pumpkin Kibbeh

Soumaya Diab Doenges

Oven: 450°F. Time: 40 minutes

2.2 lb. (1 Kg.) pumpkin
5 Cups #1 (fine) burghul
1 dry onion for the mix
Bunch of parsley
1 tsp. mint
Green marjoram
1 tsp. allspice
1 tsp. cinnamon
1 tsp. 7 Spices
1½ Tbsp. flour

For the Stuffing:

1 small box of raisins
1 large bag of spinach

Peel and cut the pumpkin after removing the seeds. Boil the pumpkin until it is soft and done. Add the burghul to the hot pumpkin without soaking it in a kibbeh bowl. Chop and add the parsley, mint, marjoram, allspice, seven spices, and cinnamon; add flour, if needed. Spread the mix into a teflon pan. Spread the stuffing in the middle. Spread remaining stuffing on top. Cut into squares. Add little olive oil on top to cover the tray and bake for about 40 minutes at 450°F.

Raw Kibbeh
(Kibbeh nayeh)
Yield: 3½ cups

1 lb. very lean ground beef or lamb
1 cup burghul (#1 fine), washed and soaked
1½ cups ground onion, pulverized in food processor
⅛ tsp. ground cinnamon (optional)
½ tsp. ground allspice
2 Tbsp. salt
¼ to ½ tsp. black pepper to taste

Combine in a large bowl, burghul, onion, cinnamon, allspice, salt and pepper; mix well. Then add to meat and mix together. (A food processor or heavy duty mixer can be used to combine.) Serve in a plate, using a fork or dull knife to press a pattern into the meat OR place in a mound in a shallow dish and draw grooves across the mound in a star shape with a fork, passing through the center point with each stroke. Put a slight indentation in the center of the mound and trickle olive over the raw kibbeh. Serve with green onion and bits of pita bread.

Roast Leg of Lamb

(Faketh laham ghanam)

Yield: Serves 6 to 8

5 lb. leg of lamb
1 tsp. salt
2 cloves garlic (minced)
1 bay leaf (crushed)
¼ tsp. pepper
¼ tsp. marjoram
¼ tsp. sage
¼ tsp. ginger
¼ tsp. thyme
1 Tbsp. olive oil

Rinse and dry lamb then with small knife cut ¼" gashes along the top surface of lamb. Combine all spices except olive oil and mix well. Then rub spice mixture into meat so that all gashes are completely filled. Rub roast all over with olive oil. Sear in pre-heated oven 500°F. for 15 minutes, then reduce temperature to 350°F. and roast about ½ hour. When meat is about half cooked, add parboiled potatoes and onions if desired.

Eggplant Casserole
Sheik Al Mehshe

Oven: 350°F. Time: 30 to 35 minutes

2 large eggplants (dark)
1 lb. ground meat
1 large can tomato puree or paste diluted with water
2 cloves garlic, minced
¼ cup pine nuts, optional
Salt and pepper to taste
½ tsp. allspice
2 or 3 Tbsp. butter
Oil
1 onion, diced

Sauté onion in butter until tender and add ground meat, salt and pepper. Cook until done. Add half of garlic and pine nuts. Set aside to cool.

Peel and slice eggplants into 1" thick round slices (or long ways). Salt eggplant slices and lay on cookie sheet or tray to draw out water and bitter taste.

Here are 2 ways to cook the eggplant. You may fry them, then lay them on paper towels to draw out grease OR you may brush with oil on both sides and place on greased cookie sheet. Brown on both sides in an oven broiler.

Place eggplant in a baking dish or casserole, spread ½ of meat mixture over top, then layer eggplant again, then again the 2nd half of meat mixture. Top with last of eggplant.

Pour the (diluted to your preference) tomato sauce that has been mixed with the garlic, salt, pepper, and allspice over eggplant.

Serve over Lebanese Rice.

Shish Kebob
Louise Malouff
Prep Time: Marinate for 24 hours

Chuck Roast, cubed
Oil
Garlic
Salt and Pepper
Taylor Red Lake Country Wine (or your favorite)

Marinate for 24 hour in refrigerator. Turn occasionally while marinating. Place onto skewers alternating with onions (quartered), mushrooms, tomatoes, and green peppers (sliced big or chunked). Grill until done.

Spinach Pies
Oven: 450°F. Time: 20 minutes Yield: 3 dozen

Dough recipe (page 38)

3 large white onions, finely diced
½ cup oil
2 (16 oz.) pkg. frozen spinach, thawed with water squeezed out
1 cup lemon juice (or to taste)
1 tsp. salt (to taste)
½ tsp. black pepper (to taste)

Prepare dough according to recipe. Cover and set aside while preparing spinach. Saute onion in oil. Then add spinach and saute for 2–3 minutes. Add lemon juice, salt, and pepper and cook for another minutes. Set aside.

For each pie: Pinch a piece of dough about the size of a golf ball, then flatten to form a circle using a tortilla press to ⅛" thick. In center, place about a tablespoon of spinach mixture. Pull up 3 sides to form a triangle. Pinch the edges together taking care not to get juice on the edges or pie will not close. A little flour helps close them if you do get juice on the edges. Place on a parchment sheet and bake for 450°F. for 20 minutes or until golden brown.

Stuffed Squash

(Koossa)

Kathy Birkner

Cooking Time: 1 hour Yield: 12 squash

12 yellow squash
1 lb. ground beef
Juice 1 lemon
12 oz. can diced tomatoes
8 oz. can tomato sauce
1 cup rice
2 tsp. allspice (or to taste)
½ tsp. cinnamon (optional)
1 tsp. granulated garlic powder
2 tsp. salt
½ tsp. black pepper
1 Tbsp. dried mint, minced with hands
8 oz. can of water + more

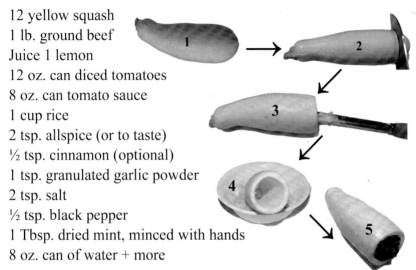

Cut bottoms off squash, and core, removing all of the pulp and seeds taking care not to break into the side of the squash using a squash corer. Save bottoms for squash tops recipe.

Rinse rice to remove starch. Combine meat, allspice, salt, pepper, garlic, and mint; mix well. Stuff each squash *loosely* allowing room for rice to expand during cooking. Arrange squash in a deep pan. Pour tomatoes, tomato sauce, and can of tomato sauce filled with water over squash. Put in enough water to cover squash along with lemon juice. Place an inverted plate over squash to hold them down in pan. Cook covered, slowly, for about 45–60 minutes or until done.

Note: If you do not have time to core the squash, dice squash, then combine with meat mixture. Add tomatoes, tomato sauce and water; stir to combine. Bring to a boil, then simmer about 30 minutes or until done.

Stuffed Squash

1 lb. ground meat
1 cup rice
2 tsp. salt
10–12 squash (yellow, green, or white)
½ tsp. ground black pepper
1 can tomato paste
½ tsp. allspice

Wash squash and scoop out as much of the insides as possible leaving a hollow shell. (A squash corer can be bought at some Arabic specialty stores.) Mix all the meat, rice, salt, pepper, and allspice. Add ½ can of tomato paste. Fill hollowed out squash with meat mixture and stack in pan. Use remaining tomatoes mixed with water and ½ tsp. salt to cover squash. Cook for 1 to 1 ½ hours or until tender when pierced with fork.

Beef & Potato Stew

(Yakhnet Batata)

Louise Malouff

1 lb. beef, cubed
½ onion, diced (if desired)
Butter or oleo, or salad oil
3 potatoes, cubed
Salt and pepper (to taste)
Italian seasoning (to taste)
Oregano (to taste)
Basil (to taste)
1–2 8 oz. cans tomato sauce

Brown meat and onions in either butter or oleo or salad oil. Add potatoes to meat. Add salt, pepper, Italian seasoning, oregano, and basil. Add tomato sauce (to thickness desired).

Cover and cook on medium low heat until done. Cook until potatoes are soft or desired consistency.

Lebanese and Middle Eastern Cuisine

Appetizers
Salads
Dressings
Veggies
Miscellaneous
Drinks

Baba Ghanouj

Cathy Van Delden

2 large black eggplants
5 large cloves garlic or 8 small cloves
4 large juicy lemons or frozen lemon juice
4 Tbsp. Tahini
Dried mint
Olive oil

Peel and puree garlic until a paste consistency.

Liberally puncture eggplants with a fork. Cook in microwave on high for at least 10 minutes on each side or until soft OR cook under a broiler until the eggplant skin is charbroiled all around

OR grill until the skin is charred all around

OR cook on top of the stove in an old frying pan until charred.

Insure the eggplant is soft and cooked inside. After the eggplant is cooked, put in a colander and run cold water over eggplant for 3 to 5 minutes.

Cut the top off and slice bottom off...cut the eggplant in half lengthwise, then cut the half in half. Remove the meat of the eggplant from the peel.

If a food processor is available, puree eggplant meat with garlic paste. If food processor is not available, use hands to mash the eggplant, then using a strong spoon, whip it until it reaches a puree state.

Then add the Tahini and thoroughly incorporate the mixture. Then add lemon juice and thoroughly incorporate. If desired, add more lemon juice and salt to taste.

Let set in refrigerator for at least 1 hour before serving.

To serve: Put in a deep plate, form a groove around the middle, pour olive oil over the top and sprinkle with dried mint.

Baba Ghanouj

Louise Malouff

Oven: 400°F. Cook time: 30–40 minutes

1 eggplant
¼ cup lemon juice
¼ cup Tahini
2 Tbsp. sesame seeds
2 cloves garlic, minced
Salt & pepper to taste
1½ Tbsp. olive oil

Lightly grease a baking sheet.

Place eggplant on baking sheet & make holes in the skin with a fork. Roast eggplant for 30–40 minutes turning occasionally or until soft. Remove from oven, place in a large bowl of cold water. Remove from water and peel skin off.

Place eggplant, lemon juice, Tahini, sesame seeds and garlic in food processor or electric blender and puree.

Season mixture with salt & pepper to taste. Transfer eggplant mixture to a medium size bowl. Slowly mix in olive oil. Refrigerate for 3 hours before serving.

Note: A roasted eggplant dip or spread. Delicious served with flat bread, pita bread or vegetables alongside hummus (garbanzo dip) or on its own.

Chickpea Salad
(Salata Hommus)

15 oz. can chickpeas
¼ cup olive oil
6 cloves garlic, mashed
2 Tbsp. lemon juice
1 Tbsp. mint, finely chopped

Drain and rinse chickpeas 2–3 times. Allow to drain well in colander.

Place chickpeas in serving bowl and add lemon juice. Mix gently, taking care not to mash the chickpeas. Add garlic and mint, mixing well. Drizzle with olive oil. Serve immediately.

Spinach Salad

1 large bunch of spinach, washed and chopped (bite size pieces)
1 clove garlic
1 tsp. salt
¼ cup lemon juice (1 lemon)
1 Tbsp. dry mint
¼ cup parsley, finely chopped
Dash black pepper
3-4 green onions, finely chopped
3 Tbsp. olive oil

Wash spinach; shake to move excess water. Chop into bite sized pieces. Set aside.

Crush garlic and salt together with a mortar and pestle, then place in a mixing bowl. Add remainder of ingredients along with the spinach. Toss together well. Serve immediately.

Eggplant with Sesame Oil

Yield: 4–6 as an appetizer

1 medium eggplant (dark skinned)
2 cloves garlic
Salt (to taste)
2 Tbsp. water
2 Tbsp. pine nuts
3 Tbsp. sesame oil
2 Tbsp. lemon juice
2 Tbsp. parsley (chopped)

Broil eggplant with skin on, turning it frequently. Remove skin under cold water and mash eggplant. Pound the garlic with salt, add sesame oil, lemon juice and water, mix with eggplant and stir well. Spread on platter and garnish with pine nuts and parsley. Serve with toasted pita triangles.

Chickpeas Salad

Soumaya Diab Doenges

1 1b. dried chickpeas (Garbanzo beans)
6-8 cups of water
Dried mint (to taste)
Garlic, minced (to taste)
Oil
Dash lemon juice
Tomatoes, diced

Rinse beans and put in a large pot. Add 6 to 8 cups of water. Let soak overnight (at least 6 to 8 hours). Drain and rinse. Then add 6 cups of water to the drained chickpeas and cover. Bring to a boil and simmer for about 45 minutes to an hour or until desired tenderness. Drain. Set aside.

Sauté garlic in oil in pan until tender; then combine with chickpeas, mint, lemon juice, and tomatoes. Serve.

Father's Famous Garlic Paste

Father Ghassan Mattar

Full Recipe

1 cup peeled garlic cloves with dry end removed
   (keep cold before using)
3 cups canola oil (also keep cold before using)
⅓ cup water and crushed ice
1 tsp. salt
2 Tbsp. lemon juice

Keep garlic cloves and oil in refrigerator at least 2–3 hours or overnight.

Place garlic and water and ice mixture in a food processor. Process to a fine dice. Stop, scrape sides, and continue processing to a puree (consistency of mashed potatoes). With processor running, add oil in a very fine stream. Add all of the oil in this manner. When all of the oil has been processed and with the processor still running, add salt and lemon juice. Process for another minute. Place in glass jar(s) and let set in refrigerator for at least one day before using. The paste will keep up to *three* months in the refrigerator.

This garlic paste is great with anything, but it is especially good with vegetables, chicken, beef, and lamb. You can even use it in a salad.

One-Third (⅓) Recipe

⅓ cup peeled garlic dry end removed (keep cold before using)
1 cups canola oil
⅛ cup water and crushed ice (i.e. 1 oz. = 2 Tbsp.) Or use very cold water
⅓ Tbsp. salt (= 1 tsp.)
⅔ Tbsp. lemon Juice(= 2 tsp.)

Fattoush

5 cups toasted pita bread, torn into 1 inch pieces
2 tomatoes, diced
1 cucumber, diced
¼ cup parsley, chopped
¼ cup green onions, chopped
¼ cup green pepper, diced
1 half head of romaine lettuce, torn into small pieces
3 cloves garlic, crushed
½ cup lemon juice
¾ cup olive oil
¼ cup fresh mint, chopped
Salt and pepper to taste

In a large bowl, combine lettuce, bread, cucumber, tomatoes, green peppers, onions, and parsley together. Toss gently.

Make dressing in a small bowl combining garlic, olive oil, lemon juice, and mint. Mix well. Pour dressing over salad and serve.

Variations: Add chickpeas for a heartier salad. The great thing about fattoush is that you can add and delete veggies from the recipe according to taste.

Garlic Dip

Yield: 1⅓ cups dip

½ cup sour cream
½ cup mayonnaise
2 to 3 garlic buds (try 3 buds first time, add more if desired)
1 tsp. salt
⅓ cup chili sauce
¼ tsp. freshly ground pepper

Blend together sour cream and mayonnaise. Mince garlic and add to sour cream mixture *OR* mince garlic and blend with salt, then add to sour cream mixture. Add remaining ingredients.

Cucumber–Laban Salad

Khyar bi laban

Yield: 6 servings

2 large cucumbers
2 cloves garlic or ½ tsp. garlic powder
¼–½ tsp. salt or to taste
1 quart yogurt
2 tsp. pulverized dried mint or 1 Tbsp. chopped fresh mint

Peel and quarter, then slice the cucumbers into halfs or quarters or use without peeling. Mash garlic with salt in a pestle and mortar, then add to cucumbers, garlic, and mint to yogurt.

Green Beans with Tomato Sauce

Gloria Monek Karina

2¾ lb. string green beans
1 cup olive oil
1 lb. 10 oz. tomatoes
1 Tbsp. tomato paste
2 medium onions, chopped
2 Tbsp. parsley, chopped
Salt (about 1 tsp.)
Pepper (about ¼ tsp.)

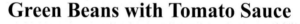

Trim the beans and snap in half. Wash in a pot of water. Sauté onions in hot oil until soft. Add strained tomatoes or paste diluted in 2 cups water to onions. Bring to a boil. Drain the beans in colander. Add the parsley, salt, pepper, and enough water to cover the beans. Cook over medium heat until only oil remains as a sauce.

Variation: Add ½ tsp. of allspice.

Lebanese Green Beans and Rice

2 cans green beans
1 1b. round steak or lean beef, cubed
½ cup olive oil
1 large onion, diced
8 oz. can tomato sauce
2 buttons garlic (optional)
½–1 tsp. salt (to taste)
¼–½ tsp. pepper (to taste)
½ tsp. allspice (to taste)

Sauté onion and garlic, if using in oil until lightly browned. Add meat, salt, pepper, and allspice. After browning put meat in a 3 quart sauce pan. Add 3 cups water (water from green beans can be used). Cook over medium heat until the meat is tender. Add tomato sauce and simmer 20–30 minutes. Pour green beans into the mixture and simmer another 10 minutes. Serve over rice.

Simply Hummus

Kathy Birkner

15 oz. can garbanzo beans (chickpeas), drain liquid and save
1 clove garlic
4 Tbsp. Tahini (sesame seed paste)
½ tsp. salt
4 Tbsp. lemon juice (1 lemon)

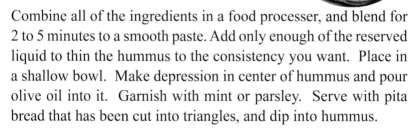

Combine all of the ingredients in a food processor, and blend for 2 to 5 minutes to a smooth paste. Add only enough of the reserved liquid to thin the hummus to the consistency you want. Place in a shallow bowl. Make depression in center of hummus and pour olive oil into it. Garnish with mint or parsley. Serve with pita bread that has been cut into triangles, and dip into hummus.

Variation: Use a lettuce leaf in place of pita bread as a scoop to reduce calories.

Hummus

Susan Rizzo

15 oz. can chickpeas, or garbanzo beans
¼ cup fresh lemon juice, about 1 large lemon
¼ cup Tahini
Half of a large garlic clove, minced or more to taste
2 Tbsp. olive oil, plus more for serving
½ to 1 tsp. kosher salt, depending on taste
1 tsp. dry garlic chutney powder, use more if you like it spicy
2 to 3 Tbsp. water
Dash of ground paprika for serving

In the bowl of a food processor or hand pulsar, combine Tahini and lemon juice. Process for 1 minute. Scrape sides and bottom of bowl then turn on and process for 30 seconds. The extra time helps "whip" or "cream" the Tahini, making smooth and creamy hummus possible.

Add olive oil, minced garlic, dry garlic chutney powder and the salt to whipped Tahini and lemon juice. Process for 30 seconds, scrape sides and bottom of bowl then process another 30 seconds.

Open can of chickpeas, drain liquid then rinse well with water. Add half of the chickpeas to the food processor then process for 1 minute. Scrape sides and bottom of bowl, add remaining chickpeas and process for 1 to 2 minutes or until thick and quite smooth.

If the hummus is too thick or still has tiny bits of chickpea, slowly add 2 to 3 tablespoons of water until the consistency is perfect. Scrape the hummus into a bowl then drizzle about 1 tablespoon of olive oil over the top and sprinkle with paprika. Serve with pita chips.

Store homemade hummus in an airtight container and refrigerate up to one week or freeze in airtight container.

How to Soak and Cook Dried Chickpeas

Kathy Birkner

Chickpeas are a staple in Middle Eastern cooking, and are used for hummus and falafel. While it is fast and simple to use canned chickpeas, dried chickpea are more economical and really easy to prepare. Extra chickpeas can be frozen for later use.

Before cooking dried chickpeas, you have to soak them. Place chickpeas in a large bowl and cover completely with cold water. Allow to soak overnight or around 12 hours.

After the chickpeas have soaked, drain, then transfer them to a large cooking pot. Cover with water twice the amount of chickpeas and bring to a boil; cover and simmer for an 45 minutes to an hour. Do a taste test at this point to make sure they are tender enough for your liking. Drain and cool for 15 minutes.

Once chickpeas are cooled, they are ready to use. Cooked chickpeas can keep for up to three days, if covered in the refrigerator, or freeze in an airtight container for about a month.

Laban (Yogurt)

Minnie Karam Mery

Yield: 1 qt.

1 qt. whole milk
1 Tbsp. plain yogurt starter

Pour milk into a saucepan. Put on stove over low heat, stir in one direction until it comes to a boil or when it raises, immediately take off the fire and let cool. When you can put your little finger in to milk and count to ten, it is the correct temperature to add the starter. Put a tablespoon of yogurt starter in a cup of the heated milk; stir together and then add to remaining milk. Cover. Wrap pot with old towel or a blanket, and set in a warm spot in the house; leave undisturbed for 24 hours. Then put in the refrigerator.

Lebanese Butter Beans

1 lb. dried lima beans
1 (No. 303) can tomatoes
1½ lb. round steak, cubed
½ cup tomato paste
1 large onion
Salt and pepper (to taste)
Cinnamon (to taste)
1 clove garlic, minced
1 cup water

Wash lima beans 3 or 4 times checking for bad beans or small rocks. Soak beans overnight in cold water or cook gently until beans are nearly done.

Sauté onion and garlic in butter in skillet until soft then add meat and fry until all pink has gone out of meat. Add tomatoes and tomato paste along with salt, pepper and cinnamon. Combine meat mixture with beans in large pan, adding one cup water, cover cook until done. Taste and adjust seasonings as needed.

Stuffed Cucumbers

Khyar Bil Labneh

2 English cucumbers or 2 slim regular cucumbers
8 Tbsp. labneh
1 Tbsp. mint

Wash cucumbers, peel, and cut in half lengthwise. Scoop out the seeds and pulp and fill with Laban. Garnish with mint leaves.

Variation: Put 2 half together and cut into slices.

Lebanese Salad

10 leaves Romaine lettuce
4 green onions
1 English cucumber, sliced in quarters
8–12 grape tomatoes or 3 tomatoes, diced
¼–½ onion, sliced thinly with grain
2 Tbsp. dried mint or 4 Tbsp. fresh mint
Lebanese dressing

Wash and drain lettuce, then cut into pieces and place in large salad bowl. Add remaining ingredients. Toss and serve.

Lebanese Salad Dressing

1 clove garlic
1 tsp. salt
¼ tsp. pepper
¼ cup lemon juice
¼ cup olive oil

In a small mixing bowl, crush garlic and salt together. Add pepper, lemon juice, and oil, mixing well. Pour over salad and toss well.

Cooked Spinach

⅓ cup oil
2 medium onions, chopped
1 lb. fresh spinach, chopped
½ tsp. salt
¼ tsp. black pepper
¼ pine nuts (optional)
¼ cup pomegranate seeds (optional)
Lemon slices

Saute and brown onions in oil. Add spinach, salt, and pepper, and cook over low heat about 20 minutes or until the spinach is tender. Saute pine nuts in oil. Add pine nuts and pomegranate seeds to spinach. Garnish with lemon slices.

Lebanese Cabbage Salad

Susan Rizzo

1 head of green cabbage
3 cloves of garlic
2 tsp. salt
¼ cup olive oil
1–2 tsp. lemon juice
2 tsp. dried mint

Quarter cabbage, shred cabbage very thinly. Put cabbage into a large bowl. Crush 3 cloves of garlic with the salt. Mash garlic until it is a smooth creamy paste. Spoon garlic into a jar, add olive oil and 1–2 teaspoons lemon juice.

Dressing: Add dried mint to jar. Place the lid on the jar and shake. Pour the dressing onto the cabbage. Use only what you will eat in one day as the cabbage becomes soggy.

Lebanese Potato Salad

Susan Rizzo

Serves: 6 people

1½ lb. of small potatoes, fingerlings, such as Yukon Gold etc.
1 large lemon, squeezed
⅓ cup of extra-virgin olive oil
Dash of sea salt and white pepper
6 green onions, chopped

½ cup of parsley washed, dried and chopped fine
2 Tbsp. dried mint

Scrub the potatoes and place them in a pot of water. Boil them gently with the lid open just a crack until the water has evaporated and the potatoes are cooked.

Drop them in a serving bowl and add the parsley, lemon juice, spices and extra-virgin olive oil. Toss gently. Sprinkle mint over dish before serving.

Lebanese Rice
Louise Malouff

¼ small pkg. vermicelli, broken into 1" pieces
1 cup rice (makes 2 cups of cooked rice)
2 cups of water to 1 cup rice
Salt to taste

Wash rice to remove starch, drain and set aside

Brown vermicelli in butter (watch carefully as it will burn quickely after browning).

Add 2 cups of water. When water starts to boil, add washed rice let water return to a boil again, then reduce heat, cover and cook until rice is done.

Lemon Hummus
Susan Rizzo

2 (14 oz.) can chickpeas, drained
1 garlic clove, crushed
5 Tbsp. extra virgin olive oil
2 lemons, zest and juice only
3 Tbsp. Greek yogurt
Good pinch ground cumin (if desired)
Plenty of ground black pepper and salt

Place all the ingredients in a food processor with two tablespoons of hot water and blend until smooth. Season, to taste, and serve chilled.

Lima Bean Salad

½ lb. lima beans
1 tsp. salt
1 clove garlic, minced
¼ cup lemon
2 Tbsp. olive oil

Boil beans until tender and drain. Add salt, garlic, lemon juice, and oil to beans. Thoroughly mix. Serve warm or cold.

Spinach and Rice

Yield: 6 Servings

1 large onion. diced
½ cup oil
2 lb. spinach, cut into small pieces
3 cups parboiled (Uncle Ben's) rice
½–1 tsp. salt (to taste)
6 cups hot water

Brown onion in oil in large frying pan. Wash then cut spinach into small pieces. Add spinach to onion and cook until done. Rinse rice and add to spinach. Mix well. Add salt and pepper, then water. Bring to a boil, then simmer for 15–20 minutes or until water is absorbed.

Rice with Vermicelli

Yvette Hasse

Time: 30 minutes About: 4 cups Prep Time: 10 minutes

1 box vermicelli
2 cups rice
4 cups water
1 Tbsp. unsalted butter
½ to 1 tsp. salt (or to taste)

Melt butter in large saucepan on medium heat. Then add vermicelli, stir to coat and continue cooking until lightly browned in color; watch closely so the vermicelli does not burn. Then add rice, stir for about a minute; add salt and water.   Bring to a boil, then lower heat, and simmer for 20 minutes or until water is absorbed.

Although submitted by Yvette, she feels that the blessed hands that came before us, who taught us and brought it to our table, and used for many events really deserved the credit for this recipe.

Spicy Cabbage and Burghul
Marshoosheh
Susan Rizzo

½ head of green cabbage, thinly sliced
1 large onion, chopped
2 Tbsp. burghul
½ to 1 tsp. hot Chili powder or Cayenne pepper (to taste)
½ tsp. salt
5–7 Tbsp. olive oil

Place the olive oil and chopped onions in a large skillet and lightly fry them for 5 minutes on medium heat. Add sliced cabbage and mix well with onions. Add salt, Cayenne pepper, sprinkle the burghul and mix well.

Add a ¼ cup of water, mix well with ingredients, cover pot and simmer on low-medium heat for 10–15 minutes while occasionally stirring. Serve hot with Pita bread but just as good cold.

Pickled Turnips
(Kabees El Lift)
Susan Rizzo

6 peeled turnips
3 peeled beets
1 cup vinegar
2 cups water
6 tsp. salt
Several garlic cloves

Slice turnips and beets lengthwise into quarter-inch slices. In a large bowl add water, vinegar, and salt and stir well. Using a large jar, alternate layers of turnips, beets, and garlic, repeat layers until jar is full. Pour in vinegar mixture to the top of jar. Gently shake jar to get color of beets flowing. Seal and store container in refrigerator for 10 days to 2 weeks. If you like a spicier turnip you can add one sliced jalapéno to jar.

Pumpkin Dip

Soumaya Diab Doenges

2½ lb. pumpkin
1 cup lemon juice
5 gloves garlic
1 small spoon of salt
⅔ cup of Tahini
Bunch of Parsley

Peel and cut the pumpkin after removing the seeds. Boil until it is soft and done (about 45 minutes to an hour) on medium heat. Drain and squeeze out the water. Peel and cut the garlic. Add salt and mash in pestle and mortar until it is soft. Put the cooked pumpkin with other ingredients in the food processer and blend it until it is like hummus. Taste and add more spices to your liking.

Rice and Spinach

Soumaya Diab Doenges

1 large bag of spinach
1½ pound of meat
1 tsp. salt
1 tsp. cinnamon
1 tsp. allspice

Sauté about 1½ pounds of any kind of meat. Add salt and spices. Add to the pot your wet spinach and no extra water. Flip it around many times until it is done about 8 minutes.

Rice

1 cup of rice
2 cups of water
1 little piece of butter or 1 Tbsp. olive oil
1 tsp. salt

Put all ingredients in a pot and cook until it is done. Serve the dish by putting rice on top of the spinach and enjoy.

Simply Rice

1 cup parboiled rice (like Uncle Ben's)
¼–½ tsp. salt
¼ cup butter
2 cups water

Melt butter in a saucepan, then add rice. Sauté the rice until crispy and slightly browned. Then add salt and water. Bring to a boil, then reduce to a simmer for about 20 minutes or until water is absorbed. Serve.

Shanklish
Soumaya Diab Doenges

One Shanklish ball
1 medium white or red onion, diced (or few spring onions)
2 tomatoes
¼ cup olive oil

Finely chop the tomato and the onion. Crumble the shanklish, then add onion and tomatoes and mix. Drizzle with a generous amount of olive oil and mix. Garnish with tomato.

Serve with Arabic flat bread. Eat like hummus or other dips.

Note: Feta cheese can be used instead of shanklish cheese.

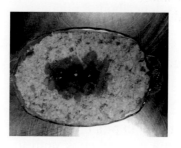

Squash Tops
Kir' at Koossa

Oven: 350°F. Cook time: 30–40 minutes Yield: 4–6 servings

Tops or bottoms of squash remaining after making Koossa
Oil or butter
1 lb. beef chunks
1 large onion, chopped
12 oz. can tomato puree
1 tsp. salt
½ tsp. pepper
¼ tsp. allspice (optional)

Wash squash tops. Saute in oil or butter over low heat until tender. Remove from pan. Add beef to pan and saute until brown.

In casserole dish, place onions on bottom, then squash tops, and then the meat. Add salt and pepper to puree and pour over meat and veggies. Place in 350°F. for 30–40 minutes. Serve.

Shanklish
Jeanette Van Delden

2 shanklish cheese balls (find at middle eastern stores)
½ cup olive oil
3-4 tomatoes, diced small
1 small onion, diced finely

Crumble shanklish balls and spread over a plate. Pour oil over the cheese, cover and allow the cheese to soften for 3 to 4 hours or overnight.

Then cover the cheese with onion and then tomato. Decorate with sliced avocados. Serve with pita bread.

Roast Cauliflower
with Cumin, Sumac and Lemon

Susan Rizzo

Oven: 375°F. Cook time: 45 minutes Yield: 6 servings

2 small or 1 large cauliflower
½ tsp. sumac
½ tsp ground cumin
Lemon juice
2 Tbsp. parsley, chopped
Sea salt

Preheat the oven to 375°F. Separate cauliflower into flowerets. Drizzle the cauliflower liberally with oil, and sprinkle with salt, sumac and cumin. Roast for 45 minutes to an hour, but turn the temperature down if the cauliflowers start to get too dark. They're cooked when they're lightly browned and an inserted fork meets with just a little resistance.

Before serving, drizzle again with good quality olive oil and a fair squeeze of lemon, then sprinkle with parsley and a little more salt.

Roasted Chickpeas

Oven: 375°F. Cook time: 15–20 minutes

1 lb. dry chickpeas (garbanzo beans)
6–8 cups water
1–2 Tbsp. olive oil
3 cloves garlic, finely minced
½–1 tsp. salt
Ground pepper to taste
¼ cup dried mint
Lemon wedges

Rinse and sort beans in a large pot. Add beans and 6–8 cups of cold water. Let stand overnight or at least 6–8 hours. Then drain water from beans and rinse. Then add 6 cups of hot water to the drained beans. Cover and simmer beans until desired tenderness is reached, generally 45 minutes to 1½ hours.

Preheat the oven to 375°F. Mix together the olive oil, garlic, salt, and pepper.

Put chickpeas into baking dish and toss with olive oil mixture until the chickpeas are well coated with oil. Season with salt and pepper. Put chickpeas in the preheated oven and roast for 15 to 20 minutes, until chickpeas are slightly browned and barely beginning to crisp.

Remove from the oven and allow to cool slightly. Transfer to a serving dish and stir in mint. Season with additional salt and pepper as needed. Serve with lemon wedges.

Quinoa Tabbouleh

Eleanor Khattar

Yield: 12 servings

2 large bunches curly parsley
½ cup pearl quinoa
1 cup water
Juice of 2 lemons (about 6–8 Tbsp.)
1 tsp. salt or to taste
½ cup of fresh mint, finely chopped
2–3 large tomatoes, cut in small pieces
3 scallions, finely sliced
4 Tbsp. extra-virgin olive oil
¼ tsp. garlic powder (if desired)

Thoroughly rinse the parsley by dunking it in clean water several times to remove dirt and grit. Lay it out on a clean kitchen towel or microfiber cloth to dry, blotting it with another dry towel, or running the parsley through a salad spinner in batches.

In a small saucepan, bring the cup of water to a boil over high heat. Meanwhile rinse the quinoa in a fine mesh strainer with cold water. Then add to boiling water, cover the pot, reduce the heat to low cooking the quinoa about 15 minutes or until it is tender and the liquid is absorbed. Place the quinoa in a large bowl to cool. Stir in lemon juice and pinch of salt.

While the quinoa cooks, chop the vegetables and leave the parsley to last, so that it is as dry as possible, if it was just washed.

To chop the parsley: Pinch the curly leaves from the stems, discard the stems. Stems can make the tabbouleh bitter. Using a very sharp knife, chop the parsley finely or use a food processor in two batches, pulsing until no large pieces are apparent. Two large bundles of parsley should yield about 10 cups of parsley.

Add the parsley, mint, tomatoes, and scallions to the bowl with the quinoa. Mix the lemon juice, olive oil, and salt in a bowl and add to parsley mixture combining well. Adjust the taste and seasonings, if needed. Combine everything thoroughly, taste, and adjust the seasonings if needed. Let the tabbouleh rest for 15 minutes to several hours to allow the mixture to season in refrigerator. Serve.

Tabbouleh

Rose Trad Ribble

Yield: 6–8 servings

1 cup fine (burghul) wheat
2 cups parsley
1 onion (white or yellow)
1 large tomato
1½ lemons (juice only)
½ cup oil (vegetable or olive)
2 Tbsp. salt
1 cup fresh mint leaves
1 cup fine chopped chives

Soak 1 cup (burghul) wheat for 30 minutes.
Chop parsley, fresh mint leaves and chives into tiny pieces.

Chop onions, tomatoes into very small pieces. Mix all ingredients together in bowl stirring well. Chill about 1 hour before serving.

Note: Use as an appetizer or side to full course Lebanese meal.

Tabbouleh

Louise Malouff

¼ cup #1 burghul wheat (find in middle eastern stores)
½ cup boiling water
1 cup finely, chopped parsley
¼ cup chopped fresh mint leaves
5 tomatoes, diced
2 tsp. olive oil
1 medium lemon, juiced
1 onion, finely diced
Salt to taste (about ½ tsp.)

Place the burghul wheat in a small mixing bowl. Add boiling water, mix and cover with a towel. Let stand for 1 hour, then drain any excess water.

Combine parsley, mint, tomatoes, onions, olive oil, lemon juice, and salt. Add the burghul wheat and mix well. Serve.

Note: Great tasting and easy to make.

Tahini La Cauliflower

1 head cauliflower
2 cloves garlic, crushed
Salt
Tahini
1 lemon (or 2)

Pour salt over garlic and crush until garlic blends with salt in pistil and mortar. Add 4 tablespoons of Tahini. Gradually add water and stir until mixture is the consistency of a medium thick gravy. Stir in lemon juice and mix well. Add ¼ lemon to water and boil cauliflower until tender. Drain. Arrange on platter. Pour sauce over cauliflower. Garnish with parsley.

Mixed Vegetable Dish

Oven: 350°F. Cook time: 30–45 minutes Yield: 8 servings

2 lb. ground beef or lamb
1 large onion, chopped finely
½ cup oil
1 cup tomato juice
1 cup chicken or beef broth
1 tsp. salt (to taste)
½ tsp. black pepper (to taste)
1 cup carrots, sliced
1 cup green peas
1 cup squash, quartered
1 cup cut green beans
1 cup potatoes, sliced

Brown the onions in oil. When onions are half cooked, add ground meat and brown. Add tomatoes juice, broth, salt, and pepper.

To prepare the casserole: Arrange each vegetable in a separate layer, but spread a thin layer of meat mixture between each vegetable. Cover the casserole and cook in a 350°F. for 30 to 45 minutes or until the vegetables are tender. Add more broth if casserole begins to dry out.

Variation: Use a cup of cooked rice in place of potatoes.

Mint Tea
Yield: Large pitcher

3 family size Luzianne tea bags
2 cups hot water
Bunch mint leaves
Extra water
Sugar, if desired

Bring water to a boil, add tea bags and remove from heat. Twist mint leaves slightly to release flavor. Add the bunch of mint. Steep for 10–15 minutes, then remove tea and mint leaves. If you want it sweet, add a cup of sugar while hot; stir to dissolve. Add tea concentrate to a pitcher and fill with water. Serve over ice with a sprig of fresh mint!

Lebanese (Turkish) Coffee
Marie Saleh

2 cups water (demitasse size)
2 Tbsp. coffee (ultra pulverized)
2 cardamom pods (if desired)
1 tsp. sugar (if desired)

Bring water to a boil in a pot. Then add sugar gradually. Stir until mixture comes to a boil and is frothy. Add cardamom, if desired. Remove from fire and stir until froth has receded. Repeat this boiling process twice more. After coffee has foamed and receded for third time, pour into Arabic cups or demitasse. Serve.

Note: Coffee is traditionally made in a brass pot called Rakweh. But you can use a saucepan instead. Coffee is served in a demitasse cup and saucer. Coffee is sipped slowly.

Lebanese Breads

Easter Bread
Phillip La Monica
Oven: 375°F. Time: about 45–50 minutes
(depending on size of loaf pan)

5 lb. flour
24 eggs
1 lb. sugar
1 lb. shortening
2 pkg. yeast
1 water glass of milk
1 Tbsp. salt

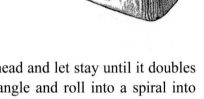

Mix all ingredients together. Knead and let stay until it doubles in size. Then roll out into rectangle and roll into a spiral into loaves of bread. Let bread rise again. Paint with egg yolks and bake at 375°F. until golden brown.

Lebanese Bread

½ oz. dried yeast or 1 oz. fresh yeast
2 ½ cups warm water
1 tsp. sugar
8 cups plain flour
2 tsp. salt
3 Tbsp. oil

Dissolve yeast in warm water, add sugar and set aside until it foams about 10–15 minutes. Sift flour and salt into bowl; mix well add yeast mixture and knead until smooth. Place bowl in warm area and let rise about 1 hour. Pinch off golf ball size pieces, roll out on floured surface. Bake in very hot oven or griddle, turn once while cooking. Bread will puff up while cooking and flatten out as it cools, stack under towel until serving or place in plastic bags.

Fried Dough
Louise Malouff

4 cups flour
1 tsp. salt
1 pkg. yeast
1⅞ cup warm water (½ of ¼ less than 2 cups)

Pour water over yeast to dissolve. Mix flour and salt. Put yeast water on the side of the flour mixture, then mix together. Knead dough. Oil top and sides of dough, slightly, and cover. Let rise until double in size.

When ready, cut or pull off pieces, stretch out in your hands (or roll out if you prefer), and fry in hot oil. Serve with butter and honey.

Note: Experiment with your own favorites. Try a little of each!!
Variation: Put cinnamon and sugar on top OR Cut into strips and fry, then season with either onion powder or garlic powder. (I used to use Onion Salt and Garlic Salt, or plain.)

Fried Dough
(Zalabee)
Janie Ashmore

2 cup flour
1 Tbsp. oil
½ tsp. salt
½ pkg. yeast dissolved in ½ cup warm water + 1 Tsp. Sugar
Oil for frying

Mix flour, salt, and oil in a bowl. Add dissolved yeast to flour mixture. Mix with hands until smooth. Cover well. Let dough rise for about an hour.

Roll dough ⅛" thick onto floured cutting board. Cut into strips 2" x 6" inches long. Various shapes can be made. Heat oil in skillet and fry strips until golden brown on both sides. Drain on paper towel and serve. Can sprinkle with powdered or granulated sugar. Can use syrup. Can add cinnamon sugar. Best eaten hot, but also eat cold.

Pita Bread

Suzanne and Danny Karam

Oven: 500°F. Time: 5 minutes Yield: 20 pieces

2 lb. white or wheat flour
1½ tsp. salt
2 tsp. sugar
1½ Tbsp. dry yeast
3 Tbsp. vegetable oil
3 cups water

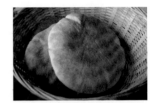

Sift the flour into a large mixing bowl, then add the sugar, salt and yeast; stir until a sticky dough forms. Add the water and oil and keep mixing on low speed for eight minutes. Sprinkle a little bit of flour on the top of the dough, cover with a clean cloth or plastic wrap and let the dough rise until it's doubled in size (about 1 to 2 hours).

Gently deflate the dough and turn it out onto a lightly floured work surface. Divide the dough into 20 equal pieces. Cover the round pieces of dough with a dishcloth and start to flatten one at a time. With a floured rolling pin on a floured counter, roll the dough into a circle about 6" wide and 1" thick. *Don't make the pita circles too thick or thin. Make sure that all the pieces are an even thickness so you get the desired pocket pita you want.* Cover the rolled-out pitas with a dish cloth for an additional 15 minutes. While waiting, heat the oven to 500°F. Put the pitas on a parchment lined baking sheet and place it on the middle rack. Bake for about five minutes, until the pitas start to puff and become fully bloated. Take the pitas out of the oven while they are still pale and not too brown and immediately cover them with a dish cloth. Wait until the pitas are fully cooled, then slice at one end to form a pocket. Now they're ready to stuff with your favorite fillings and serve!

Note: At room temperature the pitas last for one day, but they can be frozen for up to a month if wrapped and sealed properly.

Syrian Bread

Louise Malouff

Oven: 550°F. Bake Time: 2 to 3 minutes

4 cups flour
Approximately 1⅔ cups lukewarm water
1 package yeast
1 Tbsp. sugar
1 Tbsp. salt (may want less salt)

Preheat oven to 425 to 550°F. (preferably gas). Take out shelves and use bottom of oven to bake.

Mix salt, flour, and sugar. In another bowl, dissolve yeast in lukewarm water. Then pour yeast water slowly into flour mix. Blend and knead. Make sign of the cross over whole batter. Cover and let rise for 20 to 30 minutes.

Put saran wrap or wax paper on cookie sheets. Scoop out and make into baseball sized balls. Place on cookie sheet, cover, and let balls rise for another 10 to 20 minutes.

When you take a ball out, punch down edge lightly, then roll out as thin as possible. Cook for 1 to 3 minutes on bottom of oven.

Note: It doesn't take but a minute. By the time you roll out one, the first one is done in oven. Use large wooden paddle and place inside a towel in oven to keep warm. When each loaf is done, place between 2 to 3 towels. Cool. Place in plastic bags to keep fresh. Bread may be frozen as it keeps well. Enjoy!

Zaatar

Normally buying zaatar is easier than making it yourself. But one of the benefits of making it yourself is that you can alter the proportions of the ingredients to suit your taste. Here are two variations.

Aromatic and Tart Zaatar

⅓ cup dried thyme
3 Tbsp. sumac
1½ tsp. sesame seeds

Mix all ingredients. Makes about ½ cup.

By adjusting quantities just a little, the taste becomes much different.

Nutty and Crunchy Zaatar

¼ cup dried thyme
2 Tbsp. sumac
1 Tbsp. sesame seeds

Mix all ingredients. Makes about ⅓ cup.

Note: A great idea would be to make zaatar, wrap in a beautiful bottle or glass; decorate and give either or both as gifts. Not everyone is aware of this spice. It is great in many dishes, and gives a nice exotic flavor.

Zaatar

Oven: 350°F. Time: 5 minutes

1½ cups zaatar
Juice 1 lemon
Vegetable oil
Pita bread

Combine zaatar, lemon juice, and enough oil to liquefy. Cut pita bread in half and spread with zaatar mix. Cut each half into quarters, then each quarter in half again. Bake 5 minutes at 350°F.

Note: Zaatar spice mix can be found in middle eastern grocery stores.

Zaatar Bites
(Krass zaatar)

Susan Rizzo
Oven: 400°F. Prep Time: Several Hours
Cook Time: 10 Minutes Yield: 36 servings

3 cups semolina flour (can replace with cornmeal or regular flour)
1½ cups all-purpose or bread flour (can switch to semolina or cornmeal)
1 tsp. salt
1 tsp. sugar
1 Tbsp. rapid dry yeast, dissolved in ½ cup warm water with sugar
¼ tsp. mahlab (optional)
1 cup olive oil
3 cups (3 ounces) fresh Zaatar or oregano, washed and air-dried
1½ cup warm water

Place the semolina, flour, salt and mahlab (if using) in a mixing bowl; mix to combine and add the olive oil. Mix to combine then add the Zaatar or oregano leaves. Finally, add the proofed yeast and enough warm water to get a moist but compact dough. Leave it to rest a few hours or overnight.

Scoop out walnut-sized balls of dough and place in mini-muffin tins or on a baking sheet lined with paper. Bake in a preheated 400°F. oven for about 10 minutes until golden and dry. Cool and serve. Store in a tightly closed box for up to a week.

Note: These bites are super crunchy; if you would rather eat soft and chewy ones, switch to regular flour and a bit of semolina instead.

Zaatar Bread
(Manaiesh Bi Zaatar)

Susan Rizzo
Oven: 450°F. Prep: 1 hour Cook Time: 10 minutes Yield: 6

2 tsp. active dry yeast
1 egg, beaten
7 Tbsp. olive oil
2 Tbsp. sugar
2 tsp. salt
3 cups unbleached white flour
2–3 Tbsp. zaatar spice mix, to taste (homemade is best)
8 oz. tepid water (more or less depending on your bread
    machine and or the type of flour you use)

Manual: Dissolve the yeast in 3 tablespoons tepid water. Next add the egg, 4 tablespoons olive oil and the sugar. In large bowl combine the flour and salt. Gradually stir in the yeast mixture and add the tepid water using enough to make a dough ball. On a floured surface, knead the dough until it is smooth and elastic. Put dough in an oversized bag and allow to rise in a warm place for about 45 minutes. *Proceed with recipe where indicated.

Bread Machine: Add all ingredients to the bread machine according to manufacturer's instructions *EXCEPT* for the zaatar and add *ONLY* 4 tablespoons of the olive oil. Once dough is done, remove from bread pan and place dough in an oversized plastic bag in a bowl. Allow to proof in a warm area for about 45 minutes.

Divide the dough into six pieces. On a floured cutting board shape each piece of dough to form an oblong. Arrange the oblongs on a baking sheet lined with parchment paper. Cover with plastic (cling) wrap and leave for 15 minutes. In a small bowl combine the remaining 3 tablespoons of olive oil and the zaatar. Brush the mixture evenly over each bread loaf, pressing gently into the dough making "dimple" patterns with your fingers. Serve warm.

Lebanese Desserts
& Sweets

Homemade Filo (Phyllo) Dough

Louise Malouff

Yield: 5 lb.

5 lb. flour
1 egg white
½ cup olive oil
2 cups lukewarm water
1 tsp. salt
Cornstarch
Orange blossom Water

Pour flour in a large bowl and make a well in the center. Place egg white, oil, water, and salt in well; stir.

Gradually mix in flour and knead dough until smooth and elastic. Cover and set in warm place for 4 hours. Cut dough in sections (size of a orange) and dip in cornstarch. Let set another 2 hours covered with a cloth. Roll dough as thinly as possible on floured board. Place a cloth on table.

Start pulling the rolled piece of dough on the cloth toward you until tissue-thin. In just a few minutes the dough will be dry and begin to feel like paper. Cut into lengths to fit baking pan. Cover with heavy wax paper. Continue to roll and pull dough, covering each sheet with wax paper.

For a smaller amount:

2 cups flour
1 Tbsp. oil
⅔ cup lukewarm water
½ tsp. salt

Note: For extra-thin pastry sheets, sprinkle the board with cornstarch when rolling dough.

Phyllo or Filo dough is now commonly found in the freezer section of your larger grocery stores. Homemade has been included for the more adventurous.

Baklawa #1

Louise Malouff

Oven: 250°F. Time 2 hours Yield: 2 dozen

2 pounds pastry sheets (Filo Dough)

Filling #1

4 cups ground English Walnuts
½ cup sugar
1 tsp. rose water
1 Tbsp. butter

Combine all ingredients. Brush baking tray with melted butter. Place pastry sheet on bottom of pan and brush with butter. Repeat until you have piled up 15 pastry sheets, each one brushed with butter. Distribute the nut mixture (about ½ " thick) over bed of pastry tissues. Then add 15 layers of pastry sheets on top of nut mixture, brushing each sheet with butter as before.

With a sharp knife, cut into diamond shapes. A clove bud may be placed in center of each diamond if desired. Place pan on second rack in oven. Bake in slow oven (250°F.) for 2 hours until top turns a light golden brown.

While pastry is baking, prepare syrup.

Syrup:

3 cups sugar
2 cups water
1 tsp. rose water
Juice of 1 lemon

Mix sugar, water, and rose water. Boil and then add lemon juice. When syrup is cool, pour very slowly over Baklawa.

Syrup for Pastries
Marie Saleh
Yield: about 2 cups

2 cups sugar
1 cup water
½ lemon (about 2 tsp.)
1 Tbsp. orange blossom (Mazaher) or rose water (Maward)

Mix sugar and water. Slowly bring to a boil, then lower heat and simmer for 10–15 minutes. Allow to cool, then add lemon and orange blossom or rose water.

Note: Pour into glass container with tight-fitting lid to store. Syrup lasts for at least 6 months.

Baklawa #2

Louise Malouff

For a slightly different taste, try this filling:

Filling #2

2 lb. chopped walnuts or pistachios
2 tsp. cinnamon
1 tsp. cloves
1½ lb. rendered butter

Combine chopped walnuts, cinnamon, and cloves.

Follow directions above.

Syrup #2

2 Tbsp. honey
½ tsp. lemon extract
3 cups sugar
Juice of 1 lemon

Boil together honey, lemon extract, sugar and lemon. Cool and, with a spoon, pour very slowly over Baklawa.

Baklawa

(*Egyptian Style*)
Sue Guergues

Oven: 325°F. Time: 45 minutes Yield: 60 diamond triangles

Filling

4 cups walnuts chopped
½ cup sugar
1 tsp. ground cinnamon
1¾ cup margarine or butter melted
16 oz. pkg., frozen phyllo dough thawed

Syrup

1 cup water
1½ cups sugar
¼ cup honey
½ tsp. shredded lemon peel
2 Tbsp. lemon juice
2 sticks cinnamon

For filling: In a large mixing bowl stir together walnuts, ½ cup sugar, and ground cinnamon. Set aside.

Brush bottom of a 15" x 10" baking pan with melted butter. Unfold phyllo dough, generously brushing each sheet with melted butter, after using ½ of the phyllo, sprinkle with 1½ cups of the filling. Repeat layering the phyllo sheets using the rest of the filling before finishing the sheets. Drizzle any remaining butter over the top. Using a sharp knife cut through all layers to make 60 diamond triangles.

For syrup: Using a saucepan, stir together 1½ cups of sugar, water, honey, lemon peel and juice, and cinnamon sticks; bring to a boil, then reduce heat, and simmer uncovered 20 minutes. Pour honey mixture over slightly cooled Baklawa.

Baklawa
Reggie Raba
Bake 300°F. 1 hour/30 minutes plus
Yield: Large Baking Tray 11" x 17" x 2" Deep

Syrup

2 cups water
3 cups sugar
1 tsp. orange flower water
Lemon juice

Filling:

8 cups pecans, coarsely chopped
2 lb. sugar
2 Tbsp. rendered butter
1 tsp. orange blossom water

Dough

2 boxes phyllo dough (about 28 sheets per box)
2 lb. rendered butter

Syrup Preparations: Combine water, sugar, and orange flower water and bring to a boil. Then add lemon juice and boil for an additional 10 minutes. Syrup should feel sticky; touching fingers together should feel pretty sticky. You can make the syrup a few days before. Allow to cool and leave on counter top covered.

Filling: Combine pecans, sugar, rendered butter, and orange flower water. Set aside.

Dough: Butter baking sheet before putting down the first phyllo sheet. Put 1st phyllo sheet and butter with rendered butter using a pastry or paint brush. Continue until entire box is used, buttering each sheet. Then put the pecan filling mix and continue with the second box as before with phyllo and butter until you reach the last sheet. Do not butter the last phyllo sheet on top. Cut into triangles or squares, then sprinkle rendered butter over the last sheet. Bake for 1½ hours at 300°F. oven. After baking, broil the top brown watching closely not to burn. Pour syrup over the top of Bak-lawa after you remove it from the oven. Make sure syrup is cool.

Clarified (Rendered) Butter
(Ghee)
Yield: 2 lb. butter makes 2 lb. clarified butter
Cooking Time: 20 minutes

2 lb. butter
2 Tbsp. burghul (#2)

In a large saucepan, place butter and allow to melt. Add a couple tablespoons of burghul. Bring it to a boil slowly, and boil for several minutes, but watch closely so it does not burn. As soon as the foam (froth) begins to emerge, remove the pan from the heat and allow to cool. Skim off the rest of the foam.

Pour into a glass or stoneware jar, being careful not to pour in the sediment from the bottom of the pan. Use a fine mesh colander to help keep the sediment from pouring into the jar. If you do not have a fine mesh colander, use a cheesecloth.

Note: Unlike butter, clarified butter keeps *indefinitely* unrefrigerated.

Ghraybe
Azizi Karam
Oven: 300°F. Time: 20 minutes

2 cups rendered butter
2 cups sugar
4–5 lb. flour as needed
Almonds or chocolate sprinkles

Mix the rendered butter and sugar. Add flour until you have soft dough and not sticky. Roll into small balls and flatten slightly. Press an almond into each cookie or top with chocolate sprinkles. Bake 300°F. for 20 minutes.

Knaafeh
(String Pastry Sweets)

Cathy Van Delden

Oven: 350°F. for 45 minutes, then 450°F. for 10–15 minutes

Syrup

3 cups sugar
1½ cups water
1 Tbsp. lemon juice
1 tsp. rose water or orange blossom water or 1–2 tsp. almond extract

Boil sugar, water, and lemon juice about 10 minutes until the syrup thickens slightly. Then add flavoring. Let stand to cool. Refrigerate, if not using the same day.

Dough

16 oz. box shredded phyllo dough (Kataifi)
1 cup unsalted butter, melted
¾–1 cup Pistachio nuts, finely chopped + reserve for garnish

In a large bowl, separate the phyllo dough strings as much as possible. Pour in melted butter and work in with your fingers until all of the pastry is well-coated.

Spray a 15½" x 9" pan with cooking spray. And press half of the phyllo dough mixture on the bottom of the pan. Reserve the other half.

Filling

1½ cups corn starch
2 cups half and half
2 cups cream
3–4 tsp. vanilla extract

Heat cream and Half & Half; then remove some of the cream mixture to dissolve cornstarch in a bowl. Add dissolved cornstarch into cream mixture, stir and heat until it thickens. If mixture is lumpy, use an egg beater to smooth. Once it thickens add some vanilla and remove from stove. Mixture is pourable until it is baked, then it thickens. *Hint*: I use a double-boiler and make half of mixture at a time.

Pour warm mixture over layer of phyllo dough. Top with remaining phyllo dough strings and press down slightly into cream mixture.

Bake in a preheated 350°F. oven for 45 minutes; then turn oven to 450°F. for 10 to 15 minutes until light golden brown. Remove from oven. Pour syrup mixture over the warm pastry and sprinkle with ¾ to 1 cup of finely chopped pistachio nuts.

Note: Find shredded phyllo dough in middle-eastern groceries.

Variations: Ricotta cheese can be used instead of cream filling.

Keefler

Carrie Lyons

Oven: 375°F. Time 18–20 minutes Yield: 16 wedges

2½ cups flour
1 egg yolk
½ cup butter
¾ cup sour cream
¾ cup sugar
¾ cup pecans, chopped
2 tsp. cinnamon

Cut butter in flour thoroughly. Add egg yolk and blend more. Add sour cream, making sure it is well blended. (I use food processor, but it can be done by hand.) Shape into 4 equal balls. Roll each ball and wrap in waxed or saran wrap. *Chill overnight.*

Combine sugar, pecans, and cinnamon for filling.

Roll each ball into a 10" circle. Spread with one-fourth of sugar nut filling. Cut into 16 pie wedges. Roll from wide side to center. Place on a sprayed cookie sheet. Bake at 375°F. for 18 to 20 minutes or golden brown.

Note: Old family recipe

Lebanese Butter Cookies

(Ghraybeh)

Oven: 325°F. Bake 15–25 minutes Yield: 36 cookies

1 cup butter, chilled
1½ cups powdered sugar
2½ cups flour
Dash cinnamon
Blanched almonds for garnish

Cream butter until fluffy; add sugar and cinnamon, cream well. Add flour, slowly ½ cup at a time. Test to see if too soft by rolling a ball in palm of your hands; if too soft, add more flour until it rolls easily. Cover and let rest 30 minutes.

Shape into walnut sized balls and place on parchment paper or ungreased cookie sheet. Make indentation in the middle of the cookie with your thumb. Place ½ blanched almond in indentation, if desired or dust with powdered sugar after baking. Bake at 300°F. for about 20 minutes until the cookies are baked through but still pale. The cookies should not be browned except for a small amount on the bottom of the cookie. Let stand overnight to cool before removing from pan. Carefully remove the cookies with a spatula.

Variation:

1) Use 1 tsp. orange blossom water instead of cinnamon

2) Don't use any flavoring for a butter taste.

3) Take a large handful of the dough and shape it into a log about ½" crosswise on a lightly floured work surface. If the dough is crumbly, gently push it together. Use a sharp knife to cut ½" pieces diagonally. Place these diamonds on a parchment covered heavy sheet pan. Cookies will spread slightly when baked. Dust with powdered sugar, if desired.

Note: Store in an airtight container for up to 2 weeks or freeze to keep longer.

Maamoul
Elmosa Herrera and Adriana Khalife
Oven: 350°F. Bake: 25 minutes Yield: about 24

Dough:

2 cups flour
1 cup rendered butter (unsalted)
2 Tbsp. sugar
1 Tbsp. milk

Filling:

1 cup ground walnuts, pecans or pistachios
¼ cup sugar
1 Tbsp. rose water
1 Tbsp. butter

Topping:

Powdered sugar
Cooking spray

Combine flour, sugar, and butter. Add milk and knead well. Form dough into small balls (smaller than golf balls or ping pong ball size for date filling). Poke an indent into the ball or flatten into a small patty. Fill with 1 tablespoon of walnut filling or grape size date ball and close the opening until all of the filling is concealed. Spray mold with Pam and press prepared ball into the mold pressing down to fit. Then tap out the cookie by hitting the mold on the side or top. Place the cookies on baking sheet and bake at 350°F. until bottoms are light brown (about 25 minutes). Then broil until tops are very light brown (about 1 minute). When cool, sprinkle with powdered sugar.

Variation: Alternative filling is prepared dates.

Maamoul

Azizi Karam

Oven: 350°F. Bake: 20 minutes Yield: 80 cookies

2 cups rendered butter
2 eggs
½ cup sugar
1 Tbsp. whiskey
2 lb. flour, as needed

Mix rendered butter, eggs and sugar together; add whiskey. Then add flour until dough is soft yet not sticky. Roll into a ball about 1½" to 1¾" in size depending on the size of your mold. Keep dough covered to keep from drying out. Make an indent in middle, and fill with date or nut mixture; close the dough around the filling. Then place in mold with filled side up. Press into mold. Hit mold on the edge of the table with a folded towel. Place on parchment paper. Bake about 20 minutes at 350°F. Sprinkle with powdered or granulated sugar while hot. Allow maamoul to cool completely before removing from tray and place in air tight container.

Note: Maamoul freezes well.

Nut Filling

4 cups ground pecans or walnuts
1 to 1½ cups of sugar (or to taste)
Add 1 tsp. orange blossom water (mazaher)

Mix ground nuts with sugar. Add orange blossom water. Mix. Use about 1 teaspoon per cookie for filling.

Date Filling

Pitted date paste is available at middle eastern stores in 13 to 35 oz. package. Date paste can be used immediately and rolled into ¾" to 1" balls.

Maamoul

Gloria Benson

Oven: 325°F. Bake: 15–20 minutes Yield: about 15 dozen

8 cups rendered butter
8 eggs
8 tsp. whisky
2 cups sugar
6 lb. flour
Powdered sugar

Cream butter until light and fluffy. Add sugar gradually and beat.
Add whiskey and 1 cup of flour and continue to mix. Add eggs,
then add remaining flour slowly, until you get a workable dough.
If necessary, knead by hand. Dough has to be the consistency to
where you can shape it into a ball about 1½" in diameter. Add
more flour if dough is too soft.

Indent ball with finger in middle and add about a teaspoonful of
nuts or a 1" date ball to fill. Press dough together over opening.
Shape back into a ball. Keep filled side up. Press into a cookie
mold to shape. Then place on a parchment covered baking sheet.
Bake at 325°F. for 15 to 20 minutes. Let cool completely. Sprinkle date filled with powdered sugar. Store in an air tight tub.

Note: Traditionally, the date maamoul are put in a round mold
and the nut maamool are shaped into an oblong mold.

Mamoul (Maamoul)
Elmosa Herrera and Adriana Khalife
Oven: 450°F. Bake: 20 minutes

Dough

2 cups all purpose flour
1 cup semolina flour (fine)
2 Tbsp. sugar
1 tsp. baking powder
¼ cup milk
2 sticks butter (room temperature)
1 tsp orange blossom water

Nut Filling

1 cup ground walnuts
¼ cup sugar
¼ tsp. cinnamon
1 tsp. orange blossom water

Date Filling

8 medjool dates, pitted or buy date paste
1 tsp. orange blossom water
Pam spray or vegetable oil for mold so dough releases easily
Powdered sugar
1 Maamoul mold

Preheat oven to 450°F. Combine flour, semolina, and baking powder in a large bowl, and mix well. Add butter, milk, orange blossom water to flour mixture and combine until dough is formed.

In a food processor, blend walnuts until fine and crumbly, pour walnuts into bowl and add sugar, cinnamon and orange blossom water. Next, put the dates into the food processor and blend until it is formed into a fine ball, remove and add orange blossom water, set aside. To form maamoul cookies, roll dough into balls, smaller than golf balls, poke an indent into the ball and place some of the filling inside, close the opening until all of the filling is concealed. Next, wipe down the maamoul mold with some Pam or vegetable oil so that dough does not stick; press ball into the maamoul mold and then tap out the cookie by hitting the mold on the side. Place the cookies on a non-stick baking sheet and bake for 20 minutes, until bottom of the cookie is light brown. Remove cookies and let cool completely. Dust cookies completely with powdered sugar and store in an airtight container for up to 2 weeks.

Moghli/Meghli
Susan Rizzo
Prep Time: 25 min. Cooking Time: 20 min. Servings: 12

1 cup rice flour
1½ cups sugar
9 cups water
1 Tbsp. caraway powder
1 tsp. cinnamon powder
½ Tbsp. aniseed (anise) powder
¼ tsp. fennel powder

For garnishing:

1 cup coconut powder
1 cup raw almonds, or walnuts
¾ cup raw pine nuts or pistachios chopped

In a pot, put the rice flour with 2 cups of water. Stir them for 3 minutes. Add the remaining 7 cups water, the spices, and sugar to the pot and put it on high heat. Start stirring immediately as you put the pot on heat.

Continue stirring until the mixture thickens. Turn off heat. Pour in small serving cups and wait until the meghli cools completely before placing the cups in the refrigerator.

To serve, garnish with a layer of coconut powder, pine nuts, pistachios, and almonds or walnuts.

Note: Lebanese spicy pudding is prepared for newborns and Christmas.

Rice Pudding
Riz B'haleeb

Susan Rizzo

Prep Time: 10 minutes Cooking Time: 30 minutes Servings: 8

1 cup rice, soaked in 1 cup of water for 3 hours
2 cups milk
2 tsp. meske (Gum Mastic)
2 Tbsp. sugar
2 Tbsp. rose water
2 Tbsp. orange blossom water
Pistachios ground
1 cups water

In a bowl, crush the meske by either using the bottom of a bottle or a pestle and add in a pinch of sugar.

In a pan mix the milk, sugar, rose water, and orange blossom water together with 1 cup of water. Stir over medium heat until the mixture starts boiling.

Meanwhile, drain the rice and set aside. Reduce the heat and add in the drained rice slowly while constantly stirring until the whole mixture starts to boil and thicken.

Add the crushed meske to the rice mixture while still stirring to prevent the mouhalabieh from sticking to the pan. Turn off the heat and pour the warm mouhalabieh into serving bowls. Allow to cool at room temperature for about 30 minutes then refrigerate for several hours. Garnish with pistachios and serve cold.

Maamoul
Sandy Nasif
Oven: 325°F. Time: 35 minutes

2 cups butter
2 eggs
2 tsp. whisky
7 to 8 cups flour

Cream butter. Add eggs and whisky. Add enough flour until dough is soft and pliable.

Form into large golf ball sized balls, then work dough into cup, fill with date or nut filling (see previous recipes for fillings). Press dough together and press into maamoul mold. Then put onto a parchment covered baking sheet. Bake at 325°F. for 15 to 20 minutes. Let cool completely. Sprinkle nuts filled with powdered sugar. Store in an air tight container.

Rice Pudding
Minnie Mery
Yield: 7 to 9 servings

1 cup rice
3½ cups water
3 cups whole milk
1½ cups sugar
1 Tbsp. rose water

Wash rice well, drain and place into a saucepan. Add water and simmer on medium for 15 to 20 minutes. Add milk to rice, stir continually. When mixture begins to thicken, add sugar and rose water. Continue to stir constantly until rice is soft and well done. Mixture should be consistency of a cream filling. Remove from burner and pour into dessert dishes.

Variation: Use 2% milk for less fat.

Cardamom Rice Cookies

Nan-e Berenji

Susan Rizzo

Oven: 350°F. Time: 10–15 minutes

Syrup:

1½ cups sugar

½ cup water

1 tsp. rose water

Batter:

3 egg yolks

1 Tbsp. sugar

1 cup clarified (rendered) butter or ghee

½ cup corn oil

1½ tsp. cardamom

3 cups rice flour

2 Tbsp. poppy seeds or roughly chopped pistachios

Combine the sugar and water in a pot. Bring to a boil and simmer for 4 minutes, being careful not to let the mixture boil over. Remove from the heat, add the rose water, and set aside to cool. This syrup should be room temperature and not too thick. Set aside 1 cup, and bottle the remainder for future use.

In a warm mixing bowl, combine the egg yolks with 1 tablespoon sugar and beat well, until creamy.

In another mixing bowl, combine the clarified butter, oil, cardamom, and rice flour. Mix well for a few minutes, then add the egg yolk mixture and mix a few seconds. Add the 1 cup syrup created earlier and knead well for a few seconds, or until the dough no longer sticks to your hands. This creates a snow-white dough. Allow the dough to cool for 30 minutes at room temperature. Then preheat oven to 350°F. Line a cookie sheet with parchment.

Take a spoonful of dough, roll it into a ball the size of a hazelnut, flatten it slightly, and place it on the cookie sheet. Repeat, leaving

2½" between each ball. With a fork or the edge of a cookie cutter, draw geometric patterns on the cookies and sprinkle them with poppy seeds or chopped pistachios. You may also use a cookie press (readily available in most cookware stores) to stamp a design in the dough.

Place the cookie sheet in the center of the preheated oven and bake the cookies 10 to 15 minutes. Keep in mind that the cookies should be white when they are done. Remove the cookies from the oven and cool.

Baked Rice Pudding
Violet Winkler

2 cups cooked rice
¼ cup sugar
½ tsp. cinnamon
2 Tbsp. margarine
2 cups milk
½ tsp. vanilla

Combine all ingredients. Bake at 350 degrees for 20 minutes, then stir gently. Then bake 20 minutes longer or until creamy and thick.

Pudding

1 quart milk
⅔ cup sugar
3 Tbsp. cornstarch + 2–3 tsp. water
1 tsp. orange blossom water or vanilla

Bring milk to a boil over low heat heating until a crust forms on surface. Add sugar and continue stirring until it boils. In a small jar mix 2–3 teaspoons of water to cornstarch to make a paste; when smooth add to milk. Continue heating over low heat stirring constantly until pudding starts to thicken. Cook 1 minute longer. Add orange blossom water, stirring well. Pour into a large bowl or individual cups.

Sambooski

Azizi Karam
Oven: 350°F. Bake: 20 minutes Yield: 94 cookies

Dough

4 cups flour
1¼ cups rendered butter
¾ cup water

Filling

4 cups ground pecans
1–1½ cups sugar
2 tsp. orange blossom water

Syrup

10 lb. sugar
7–8 cups water
½ cup lemon juice
Orange blossom water

Dough: Heat butter and water until hot. Add flour to make into a ball. Dough should not be sticky. Roll into a ball and then flatten into 2" circles.

Filling: Place filling on half of dough leaving about ¼" from the edge open. Fold dough over and use tweezers to close edge tightly. Bake 20 minutes at 350°F.

Syrup: Place sugar in a saucepan. Add water and lemon; mix. Bring mixture to a boil, and turn to simmer for about an hour. Skim off any foam that forms. Allow to cool for 10–15 minutes; add orange blossom water. Pour into a glass container with a tight fitting lid.

Sambooski

Louise Malouff

Oven: 400°F. for 15–20 minutes,
then 425°F. for another 15 minutes

1 lb. good butter, lightly salted
4½ cups unsifted flour (may need more)
Few shakes salt
Orange blossom water
3 or 4 oz. nuts, chopped (1 pkg.)
Granulated white sugar

Mix together 4 oz. nuts, 2 oz. sugar, and orange-blossom water, just enough to moisten (maybe ½ tsp.). If filling is too damp, it will harden. Set aside.

Measure flour, add salt.

Melt butter and have boiling (bubbling) pour over flour immediately. Add about 3 tablespoons orange blossom water. Mix well. It will be oozing with butter while still hot. If it starts breaking apart, keep on top of stove to keep warm.

Roll into ball. Press into a round/oval disc or shell. Stuff with the filling (not too much). Pull up sides to make it a half-moon shape. Press edges together and pinch. (Sito Latify used a tweezer to clamp together and for decoration.)

Bake at 400°F. for 15–20 minutes, then at 425°F. for another 15 minutes on ungreased cookie sheet until slightly brown. Cool very slightly. Roll in regular sugar.

Sambooski
Sandy Nasif (from her mother and other LAS members)
Oven: 400°F. Time: 20–30 minutes

7½–8½ cups flour
3 cups rendered butter
Water

Add warm water and mix until dough holds together (as pie dough).

Filling

4 cups ground pecans
1 cup sugar
2 Tbsp. orange blossom water

Combine pecans and sugar. Add orange blossom water and mix thoroughly. Roll dough like biscuit dough. Use biscuit cutter and fill. Bake until lightly browned. Pour syrup over while hot.

Syrup

2 cups sugar
1 cup water
1 Tbsp. lemon juice
1 Tbsp. orange blossom water

Combine sugar and water. Boil for 10 minutes or until soft boil stage. Take off fire and add orange blossom water and lemon. Syrup must be cool or chilled before dunking Sambuski.

Stuffed Dates (Ajwee)
Minnie Mery

1 package pitted dates
3 Tbsp. sugar
3 Tbsp. shelled walnuts, finely chopped

Gently open date at slit where pit was removed. Combine sugar and walnuts, then stuff date with small amount (⅛ to ¼ tsp.) of mixture. Press closed after filling.

Yellow Anise Cake
Sfoof

Oven: 350°F. Time 30 minutes Yield: 9" x 13" pan

3 cups flour
3 cups semolina
2½ cups sugar
1 tsp. turmeric (curcumin)
1 cup oil
3 tsp. baking powder
3 tsp. anise powder
2 cups milk
1 Tbsp. orange blossom water
2–3 Tbsp. almonds
2–3 Tbsp. Tahini
Water (if needed)
Preheat oven. Grease the bottom of a 9" x 13" pan with Tahini.

In a large bowl mix together flour, baking powder, anise, and turmeric. Add sugar; mix. Then add oil; mix well. Add milk and blend until well mixed. Batter is thicker than cake batter. If batter is too thick, add some water.

Pour into the prepared pan. Soak hands in water to flatten and smooth top. Dot the batter with almonds. Bake at 350°F. oven for 55–60 minutes until browned. After baking cut into squares or diamonds. Serve or store in a tightly covered container separating each layer with wax paper.

Spoon Doughnuts

2 medium potatoes
2 cups flour
1 Tbsp. rapid rise yeast (about ½ envelope)
⅓ cup lukewarm water

Syrup for Doughnuts

1 cup water
1 cup sugar
¼ cup lemon juice
Drop of orange blossom water

Peel the potatoes, cube, and boil until tender. Remove from heat. Drain, and mash. Allow potatoes to cool to about 120°F. or until you can touch for 10 seconds comfortably. While cooling, dissolve the yeast in the water, then add to potatoes along with flour. Knead dough, leaving the mixture soft. Cover and grease top of dough, then place in a warm place to rise for about an hour. Meanwhile, fill a heavy skillet about two-thirds full of oil and set aside. Allow 5–10 minutes for the oil to heat, then after the dough has risen, pick up small portions of the dough with a spoon and drop into the skillet. Allow to brown in oil, then remove and dip in cold syrup immediately. Serve.

Syrup: Combine all of the ingredients together and bring to a boil. Simmer for 10 minutes, then remove from burner and add orange blossom water. Place syrup in a glass jar and chill.

Mouhalabieh
Susan Rizzo

Prep Time: 10 min. Cooking Time: 20 minutes Servings: 6

5 cups milk
3½ Tbsp. cornstarch, dissolved in 1 cup milk
½ cup sugar
1 tsp. vanilla sugar
1 Tbsp. rose water
1 Tbsp. orange blossom water

For garnish:

1 cup raw ground pistachios

In a non-stick or stainless steel pot, put the milk, the dissolved cornstarch and vanilla sugar together. Place the pot on medium heat and stir until the mixture starts boiling. Reduce the heat, add the sugar and continue stirring for 10 more minutes. Turn off the heat then add the rose water and orange blossom water. Pour the mouhalabieh in serving bowls. Allow them to cool at room temperature for about 30 minutes, then refrigerate for several hours. Garnish with raw ground pistachios and serve cold.

Easter Sweet Bread

Kaak B'Haleeb

Susan Rizzo
Oven: 425°F. Bake Time: 8–10 minutes Yield: 25–30 buns

4 cups all-purpose flour, plus some for kneading
½ pkg. dry yeast
3¼ cup milk
½ cup oil
1¾ cup granulated sugar
3 sticks unsalted butter
¾ cup sesame seeds
1 Tbsp. ground mahlab
1 Tbsp. ground anise seeds
½ tsp. salt

Mix together all flour and dry ingredients including yeast, set aside. Scald milk, take off stove. Add butter and oil then let cool until you can place little finger in liquid and hold for 10 seconds. Using dough hook, add wet to dry ingredients, mix well then turn onto floured surface and knead 5–10 times. Cover and set in warm place until doubled in size. Pinch off pieces of dough about the size of a walnut; cover and let rise again about 30 minutes. Place on ungreased sheet pans. You can cut cross on top of each ball or flatten using the bottom of fancy cut glass bowl or mold. Bake until nicely browned. Ice when cool with following icing.

1 cup milk or light cream
1 tsp. orange blossom water
1½ cup sugar
½ cup confectioners' sugar
4 Tbsp. butter

Heat all ingredients except orange flower water until warm, then stir in the orange flower water. Dip each bun into icing and set aside to cool. Do not layer buns as they will stick together. Freezes well.

Appetizers & Snacks

Artichoke Balls

Irene Rodriquez

13 oz. can artichoke hearts
2 eggs
4 cloves garlic, minced
1½ cups Italian bread crumbs
2 Tbsp. Romano cheese
6 Tbsp. olive oil
Dipping sauce
½ cup butter, melted
1 lemon, juiced

Drain and mash the artichoke hearts. In a separate bowl, mix 1 cup of bread crumbs, eggs, and cheese. Add artichoke hearts. Preheat oven to 375°F.

Meanwhile, sauté garlic in olive oil until tender, but not brown. Add to artichoke mixture. Hand roll into 1 inch balls followed by rolling in remaining bread crumbs. Place into oven for 15 minutes or until brown.

Basic Cream Cheese Fruit Dip

Susan Rizzo

Yield: Makes 2 to 3 cups

8 oz. pkg. cream cheese softened
3 Tbsp. sugar
1 cup sour cream or Mascarpone
1 tsp. vanilla extract

Combine all ingredients and beat until smooth and creamy.

Almond Fruit Dip:

Add 3 tablespoons of finely chopped almonds and 1½ teaspoons of almond liqueur to the basic recipe. Garnish with 1 tablespoon of finely chopped almonds, if desired.

Raspberry Fruit Dip:

Puree 1 cup sweetened raspberries (approximately a 10 oz. pkg.) Spoon half the basic recipe into a serving dish and smooth. Top with half the raspberry puree and smooth. Repeat.

Lemon Fruit Dip:

Add zest of 1 lemon, a tablespoon of lemon juice, and 1 extra tablespoon of sugar to the basic cream cheese fruit dip recipe.

Marshmallow Fruit Dip:

Add a half cup marshmallow creme to the basic recipe.

All recipes: Chill and serve with assorted fruit dippers such as bananas, grapes, kiwi, apple, pineapple, strawberries, raspberries, and papaya, cut into bite-size pieces, if necessary. Bagel bites are good too.

Best Spinach Dip Ever

Susan Rizzo

1 cup mayonnaise
16 oz. container sour cream
1.8 oz. pkg. dry leek soup mix
4 oz. can water chestnuts, drained and chopped
½ (10 oz. pkg.) frozen chopped spinach, thawed and drained
1 lb. loaf round sourdough bread

In a medium bowl, mix together mayonnaise, sour cream, dry leek soup mix, water chestnuts and chopped spinach. Chill in the refrigerator 6 hours, or overnight.

Remove top and interior of sourdough bread. Fill with mayonnaise mixture. Tear removed bread chunks into pieces for dipping.

Calavo Fresh Guacamole

Helen Antonelli

4 ripe Calavo avocados, peeled, seeded and mashed
2 vine-ripe tomatoes, chopped
1 onion, diced
2 jalapeño or Serrano chilies, minced
½ cup fresh cilantro, chopped, stems discarded
1 tsp. dried oregano
1 fresh garlic clove mashed or minced or ⅛ tsp. garlic powder
Juice from 1 fresh lime
Hot pepper sauce, salt and pepper to taste

Combine all ingredients. Cover and refrigerate approximately 1 to 2 hours. Serve as a dip with chips, or use as a spread or topping on sandwiches, burgers or Mexican entrees.

Calavo Salsa Fiesta

Helen Antonelli

4 ripe Calavo avocados, peeled, seeded and chopped
4 medium vine-ripe tomatoes, chopped
1 red onion, diced
4 jalapeño or Serrano chilies, minced
1 bunch fresh cilantro, chopped, stems discarded
15 oz. can black beans, drained and rinsed
8 oz. can yellow corn drained and rinsed
Juice of 2 fresh limes
Salt and pepper to taste

Combine all ingredients. Cover and refrigerate approximately 2 hours or more. Serve as a dip with chips or as an accompaniment to grilled chicken, fish, Mexican entrees, or as a side dish salad.

Cheese Log

8 oz. pkg. cream cheese
8 oz. bleu cheese (2–3 oz. pkg.)
8 oz. sharp cheddar cheese

Let cream cheese get soft.

Shred cheddar cheese. Grate bleu cheese.

Mix all together (with hands). Make it fluffy. Do not pack. Roll into ball. Put into a plastic bag and roll into a log.

Refrigerate. Roll into ground pecans.

Cream Cheese Dip

8 oz. cream cheese
Mayonnaise (to taste)
Garlic salt (to taste)
Tabasco sauce (to taste)
Worcestershire sauce (to taste)
Onion (if desired)

Combine all of the ingredients and serve.

Cream Dip

Nancy Nasif

8 oz. cream cheese
1–2 green onions, chopped finely
8 oz. crushed pineapple, drained
¼ of a green pepper
3 oz. pecans, chopped

Mix all together with a mixer or food processor. Serve with crackers or chips.

Cocktail Sauce

1 cup mayonnaise
1 tsp. mustard
½ cup ketchup
4 drops Tabasco sauce
¼ cup Half and Half

Blend all of the ingredients except the Half and Half. Then mix Half and Half in, blend well. Serve.

Blila

Susan Rizzo

A warm chickpea appetizer seasoned with garlic, lemon juice, olive oil and cumin. Blila is also served as part of an elaborate Lebanese breakfast!

**Prep Time: 5 minutes Cook Time: 5 minutes
(unless using dry chickpeas) Yield: 4**

2 cups canned chickpeas
1 clove garlic, crushed
8 Tbsp. lemon juice
⅓ cup olive oil
1 tsp. cumin
1 tsp. salt

Empty the chickpeas and the water into a pot and put over low heat until warm. Drain the chickpeas and put them in a serving bowl. Keep half a cup of the water for the dressing.

To prepare the dressing: Combine the lemon juice and olive oil with the reserved water. Add the crushed garlic, salt and ½ teaspoon of cumin.

Mash three tablespoons of chickpeas and add them to the dressing and mix well. Pour the dressing over the chickpeas and stir.

Sprinkle the rest of the cumin on the blila and garnish with 1 tablespoon of parsley, chopped. Serve warm with pita bread.

Deviled Eggs

Regina Aune

12–15 hard-boiled eggs
½ cup sour cream
½ cup mayonnaise
⅓ cup Dijon mustard
1 tsp. horseradish
Small can sliced black olives (optional)
Sliced green olives (optional)
Paprika

Bring the eggs to a boil and simmer for 10 minutes, then put in ice cold water to cool. Peel the eggs , then separate the egg yolks from the egg whites. Place the yolks in a small bowl and mash thoroughly with a fork. Add the sour cream, mayonnaise, mustard, and horseradish to the yolks. Blend until creamy. Using a pastry bag or plastic bag (with a corner snipped off) pipe the yolk mixture into the egg whites. Top each egg with either a black olive slice or a green olive slice. Sprinkle paprika on the eggs.

Energy Nuggets

Yield: 4 bite size servings

½ cup peanut butter
½ cup nonfat dry milk
½ cup honey
4 graham cracker squares, finely crushed
½ cup quick cooking oatmeal

Mix together peanut butter, nonfat milk, and honey in a large bowl. Add crushed graham crackers and oatmeal and mix with wooden spoon.

Roll dough into balls with your hands. Store in airtight container in the refrigerator.

East Asian Snack Mix

Susan Rizzo

Oven: 250°F.   Prep Time: 30 Minutes   Yield: 8 Servings

2 cups Rice Checkerboard cereal
2 cups Wheat Checkerboard cereal
2 cups Wasabi Rice crackers
2 cups Sesame crackers
1½ cups East Asian Spiced nuts

Toss roasted nuts with Rice and Wheat Checkerboard Cereals, Wasabi Rice Crackers and Sesame Crackers to serve. Store in an airtight container.

Spiced Nuts

2 Tbsp. soy sauce
1 tsp. rice vinegar
1 tsp. sesame oil
2 Tbsp. dark brown sugar
½ tsp. cayenne
1½ cups roasted cashews and peanuts

For Spiced Nuts:

Combine the first 5 ingredients in a large bowl. Toss nuts in mixture to coat. Spread nuts onto a parchment or silicone lined baking sheet. Roast nuts in oven 35–40 minutes, being careful not to burn. Then remove and let cool.

Pinwheels

Tortillas
Cream cheese
Green chiles
Black olives

Chop chiles, and olives, then combine. Spread mixture on flour tortillas. Roll up tortillas. Slice through tortillas about every ⅛" or ¼" as desired.

Ham & Swiss Puff Pastries

Theresa Birkner

Oven: 400°F. Prep time: 20 minutes Total Time: 1½ hour
Yield: 72 appetizers

Pastry

½ (17.3-ounce pkg.) =1 sheet frozen puff pastry sheets, thawed
1 egg, slightly beaten
1 Tbsp. water
1 tsp. poppy seeds

Filling

3 (¾ oz.) slices Swiss cheese, finely chopped
½ cup deli ham, finely chopped
¼ cup mayonnaise
1 tsp. Dijon-style mustard
2 Tbsp. chopped green onions

Preheat oven to 400°F. Place waxed paper onto cutting board then unfold 1 pastry sheet onto waxed paper. Using a pizza cutter or knife, cut pastry sheet into 1½" squares. Place squares onto ungreased baking sheet. Repeat with remaining pastry sheet.

In a small bowl, combine egg and water. Brush tops of pastry squares with egg-water mixture; sprinkle with poppy seeds. Bake for 8 to 10 minutes or until pastry is puffed and golden brown. Allow to cool completely.

Combine all of the filling ingredients in medium bowl. Split each square horizontally with small serrated knife. Fill with about 1 teaspoon filling mixture, then replace square top. Serve.

Note: Easy to make appetizers with puff pastry.

Hot Crab Meat Dip

Regina Aune

Oven: 350º F.   Yield: About 1½ cups

1 Tbsp. milk
8 oz. pkg. cream cheese
8 oz. pkg. crab meat (can use fresh)
1 Tbsp. horseradish
1 Tbsp. onion, finely chopped
3 oz. pkg. almond slivers
plain crackers

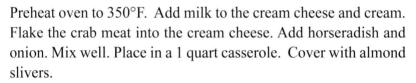

Preheat oven to 350°F. Add milk to the cream cheese and cream. Flake the crab meat into the cream cheese. Add horseradish and onion. Mix well. Place in a 1 quart casserole. Cover with almond slivers.

Bake for 30 minutes or until hot and bubbly. Serve with crackers.

Red Pepper Hummus

Susan Rizzo

15 oz. can chickpeas, or garbanzo beans

2 whole red bell peppers – see below on how to roast (or substitute about ¾ cup chopped char-roasted roasted red peppers)

¼ cup fresh lemon juice, about 1 large lemon

¼ cup Tahini

Half of a large garlic clove, minced or more to taste

2 Tbsp. olive oil, plus more for serving

½ to 1 tsp. Kosher salt, depending on taste

1 tsp. ground cumin

2 to 3 Tbsp. water

Dash of ground paprika for serving

To Roast Peppers: Move an oven rack so that it is about 5" from the broiler. Turn oven broiler on. Remove core of peppers then cut into large flat pieces. Arrange pepper pieces, skin-side up, on a baking sheet. Broil 5 to 10 minutes until the peppers skin has charred. Add peppers to a sealable plastic bag; seal then wait 10 to 15 minutes until cool enough to handle. Or, add peppers to a bowl, then cover with plastic wrap and wait 10 to 15 minutes. Gently peel away the charred pepper skin and discard. Reserve 1 to 2 pieces to use as a garnish when serving then roughly chop the rest.

In the bowl of a food processor, use hand pulser to combine Tahini and lemon juice. Process for 1 minute. Scrape sides and bottom of bowl, then turn on and process for 30 seconds. The extra time helps *whip* or *cream* the Tahini, making smooth and creamy hummus possible.

Add olive oil, minced garlic, ground cumin, and the salt to whipped Tahini and lemon juice. Process for 30 seconds, scrape sides and bottom of bowl then process another 30 seconds.

Open can of chickpeas, drain liquid then rinse well with water. Add half of the chickpeas to the food processor, then process for 1 minute. Scrape sides and bottom of bowl; add remaining chickpeas and process for 1 to 2 minutes or until thick and quite smooth. Add peppers to hummus and continue to process for 1 to 2 minutes or until smooth. If the hummus is too thick or still has tiny bits of chickpea, slowly add 2 to 3 tablespoons of water until the consistency is perfect.

Finely chop reserved pepper from earlier. Then, scrape the hummus into a bowl, and make a small well in the middle, add finely chopped peppers. Serve with pita chips.

Store homemade hummus in an airtight container and refrigerate up to one week.

Russian Eggplant Caviar

Helen Antonelli

2 purple-globe eggplants (1½ lb. each)
2 plum tomatoes, chopped
¼ cup minced onion (about 4 oz.)
¼ cup roughly chopped fresh flat-leaf parsley
½ cup extra virgin olive oil
1½ tsp. freshly squeezed lemon juice
Salt and pepper to taste
Pita or rye bread

Place eggplants on a shallow baking pan, and place under the broiler. Broil, turning eggplants every five minutes, until skin is blackened all over and the flesh is falling apart tender, 20–30 minutes.

Take roasted eggplants and peel away blackened skin.

Place eggplants in a food processor; pulse until pureed. Transfer to large bowl; stir in the remaining ingredients. Serve warm or at room temperature with pita or rye bread.

Italian Bread Appetizer

Oven: 350°F. Prep Time: 20 Total Time: 90 minutes
Yield: 16 servings

1 Tbsp. butter, melted
1 tsp. finely chopped fresh garlic
1 lb. loaf frozen bread dough, thawed
¼ lb. thinly sliced deli ham or Genoa salami
6 (1 oz.) slices Provolone Cheese, cut into strips
¼ cup sliced black olives
2 green onions, cut thinly
1 egg, beaten
1 tsp. water
Poppy seeds, if desired

In a bowl, stir together butter and garlic. Roll out bread dough on lightly floured surface to 12" square. Place on lightly greased baking sheet; brush with butter mixture.

Layer ham or salami, cheese, olives and onions in 3 inch strip down center of dough to within one-half inch (½") of top and bottom, leaving 4½" of dough on each side of filling.

Cut twelve 3" long strips, 1" apart, along both sides of filling. Fold strips across filling at an angle, alternating sides to give a braided effect. Pinch dough at bottom and top to seal.

Cover; let rise in warm place 30 to 45 minutes, or until almost double in size. In a bowl, combine egg and water, and brush over braid. Sprinkle with poppy seeds, if desired.

Heat oven to 350°F. Bake 25–35 minutes or until golden brown. Remove from baking sheet; allow to cool 10 minutes, then cut into slices.

Italian appetizer bread is stuffed with salami, cheese, and olives that produce a fabulous warm appetizer for a gathering.

Mexican Fiesta Cubes

Prep Time: 25 minutes Total Time: 2½ minutes Yield: 72 pieces

½ cup fat free sour cream
8 oz. pkg. light cream cheese, softened
1 cup Mozarella cheese, shredded
2 oz. jar diced pimentos, drained
2–3 Tbsp. sliced green onions (about 1–2 green onions)
2 Tbsp. chopped mild green chiles, drained
2 Tbsp. chopped ripe olives, drained
¼ tsp. cilantro spice
10 (8 inch) whole wheat flour tortillas
Paprika OR chili powder
Jalapeño pepper rings, if desired

Combine sour cream and cream cheese in small bowl. Beat at medium speed, scraping bowl often, until smooth. Stir in cheese, pimentos, green onions, chiles, cilantro, and olives.

Spread about ⅓ cup sour cream mixture over 1 tortilla. Top with another tortilla; then spread with about ⅓ cup sour cream mixture. Continue layering two more times ending with tortilla; wrap in plastic food wrap. Repeat with remaining tortillas and cheese mixture. Refrigerate at least 2 hours or overnight.

Cut tortillas into 1 inch cubes to serve; sprinkle tops with paprika or chili powder. Garnish with jalapeño pepper rings. Serve with toothpicks.

Salsa, Your Way

Christina Valenzula

Yield: One batch makes about 32 oz. of Salsa

3 lb. can of tomatoes (I use S&W tomatoes. Find at Costco)
16 oz. can of jalapeños (I use La Costena. Find at Vallarta)
Salt
Cilantro (Use 1 to 3 bunches, to taste)
½ onion (or to taste)
A lot of Tortilla Chips

Spice monitor:

Just a hint of spice: Add ¼ can of jalapeños.

Mild: Add ½ can of jalapeños

Spicy to the Extreme: Add the full can.

Chop the cilantro. Chop the onion. Place chopped cilantro and onion into a container.

Drain the tomato juice. Drain and de-stem the jalapeños.

Mix the tomatoes and jalapeños in the blender, add salt. Pour mixture into the container.

Repeat mixing in blender until all tomatoes and jalapeños are used. Mix all the ingredients together, and enjoy with tortilla chips.

Stuffed Jalapeños

Susan Rizzo

1 pkg. cream cheese
1 jar pimento cheese spread
1 pkg. dry Italian dressing
½ tsp. garlic powder

Alternate: Make or purchase tuna salad. Serve with stuffed jalapeños.

Santa Fe Salsa

Anne Molina

16 oz. can whole tomatoes, undrained and coarsely chopped
¾ tsp. cayenne pepper
4 tsp. fresh lime juice
4 tsp. cider vinegar
4 cloves garlic finely chopped
½ tsp. leaf oregano crumbled
½ tsp. ground cumin
1 tsp. crushed coriander seeds
½ tsp. salt

Combine tomatoes, cayenne pepper, lime juice, vinegar, garlic, cumin, coriander seeds, oregano, and salt in a glass or pottery bowl. Let stand 30 minutes at room temperature before serving.

Spinach Rolls

Regine Aune

Yield: About 80 appetizers

2 (10 oz. pkg.), chopped spinach, thawed and squeezed dry
6 green onions, chopped fine
1 oz. pkg. Ranch dressing mix
1 cup mayonnaise
1 cup sour cream
½–1 cup bacon bits or ham
8 flour tortillas, regular (use thinnest ones)

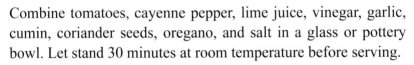

Mix together all the ingredients except for the tortillas. Spread mixture on the tortillas and roll up.

Chill at least 3 hours. Slice diagonally into ⅓" slices.

May be made the day before.

Shrimp Cocktail aLa Mexicana
Magda Irene Rodriquez

1 lb. cocktail shrimp (small)
3 avocados (large)
2 tsp. salt
1 bunch cilantro
4 jalapeño peppers, diced (or less)
2 large tomatoes, diced
1 large onion, diced
8 oz. orange juice
1 cup catsup
5 lemons, juiced
1 lb. corn chips

Dice tomatoes and onion; mix with the shrimp.

Chop cilantro and add to mixture.

Juice the lemons. Add salt, lemon and orange juices and catsup.

Dice the jalapeños and add to your taste.

Dice the avocado. Mix into mixture and refrigerate for about 2 hours. Serve with large corn chips.

Sweet Hot Pickles
Susan Rizzo
Yield: 5 quarts

1 gallon sliced hamburger dill pickles
4 lb. sugar
4–6 cloves of garlic sliced (or as desired)
1 pt. sliced jalapeño peppers (or as desired)

Drain vinegar from pickles and discard. Put sugar, peppers, and drained pickles in layers to fill in the large jar. Every other day, turn the jar over to mix contents. When all sugar dissolves and looks crunchy. Keep refrigerated.

Supreme Pizza Dippers

Susan Rizzo

Oven: 425°F.

2 lb. pizza dough
1½ cups shredded Mozzarella Cheese
1 cup freshly grated Parmesan Cheese (divided)
1 tsp. dried oregano
1 tsp. dried parsley
Olive oil
Salt and pepper
Marinara Sauce for dipping
Anchovies to serve (optional)

Fillings:

½ lb. hot Italian sausage (casing removed)
16 miniature meatballs (your favorite meatball recipe)
½ lb. sliced pepperoni (chopped)
⅓ cup diced red and yellow bell peppers

Place a 10" cast iron pan in an oven and preheat oven to 425°F.

In a small bowl, stir together ½ cup of the Parmesan cheese with the oregano, parsley, and season with salt and pepper.

For the Fillings: In a medium sauté pan heat a few tablespoons of olive oil over medium heat. Add the sausage and cook until crispy, breaking up with a wooden spoon as it cooks. Transfer to a paper towel-lined plate and allow to cool. Add the bell peppers to the pan and sauté for 2 minutes just to soften. Use a slotted spoon and transfer to a plate. In the same pan with the sausage drippings remaining, add the meatballs and cook on all sides until dark golden brown and cooked through, about 10 minutes. Remove to a paper towel-lined plate and allow to cool. Toss the filling ingredients (sausage, pepperoni, and peppers) plus shredded mozzarella together to combine.

On a lightly flour surface, with a floured rolling pin, roll out dough to ½" thickness. Use a floured 3" biscuit cutter to cut circles out of the dough. Place a small amount of filling into the center of each circle.

Remove the hot pan from the oven and drizzle with a few tablespoons of olive oil. Place the sealed balls with seam side down into the pan. Brush the top with olive oil and sprinkle with the cheese mixture. Bake for 15 minutes or until deep golden brown on top. Remove from oven and allow to cool for a few minutes before serving. Garnish with the remaining Parmesan cheese, anchovies and warm marinara sauce for dipping.

Pour salt onto a spill in the oven, then remove spill with a spatula when oven is cool.

Salads

Apple Salad
Kathy Birkner

3 Fuji apples, cored, and cut into chunks
1 cup celery, chopped
½ cup walnuts, chopped
¼ tsp. cinnamon (if desired)
¾ cup mayonnaise

Combine all ingredients. Cover and refrigerate, if not serving immediately.

Lime Salad

Bea Russell

1 small pkg. lime or lemon Jello
1 cup hot water
½ cup small curd cottage cheese
¼ cup nuts, chopped
1 cup crushed pineapple
½ pint whipping cream, sweetened (whipped)
1 dozen marshmallows, cut up
2 Tbsp. lemon juice

Mix jello in hot water. Let Jello cool, but not gel. Fold in cottage cheese, nuts, pineapple, whipping cream, marshmallows, and lemon juice. Enjoy!

Broccoli Salad
Susan Rizzo

1¼ crown of fresh broccoli
⅝ cup red onion
5 oz. bacon
½ cup raisins
½ cup sunflower seeds
⅔ cup mayonnaise
⅓ cup white sugar
1 Tbsp. and 1 tsp. wine vinegar
Salt and pepper to taste

Cook bacon over a medium high heat until evenly brown and crisp. Cool and crumble.

Cut the broccoli into bite-size pieces. Cut the onion into thin bite-size slices. Combine bacon, raisins and nuts, mix well.

Dressing: Mix the mayonnaise, sugar, and vinegar together until smooth. Pour dressing over the salad, let chill and serve.

Cucumber-Yogurt Salad
Yield: 6 servings

2 large cucumbers
2 cloves garlic or 1 tsp. garlic powder
¼ tsp. salt or to taste
1 quart yogurt
1 tsp. pulverized dried mint or 1 Tbsp. chopped fresh mint

Peel and quarter lengthwise, then slice the cucumbers, or use without peeling. Mash garlic with salt in a pestle and mortar, then add cucumbers, garlic, and mint to yogurt.

Carrot Salad

From Luby's

Susan Rizzo

2 lb. carrots (peeled and shredded)
1 cup drained crushed pineapple
1 cup mayonnaise
1 cup raisins (plump in hot water for 30 minutes, then drain)
¼ cup powdered sugar

Combine all ingredients. Mix well and chill.

Caesar Salad with Salmon

Helen Antonelli

½ cup olive oil
3 or 4 cloves garlic, minced
1 Tbsp. freshly squeezed lemon juice or
    to taste
2 tsp. Worcestershire sauce
2 tsp. Dijon-style mustard
1 small head romaine lettuce, rinsed and dried
1 small head green leaf lettuce, rinsed and dried
¼ cup grated Parmesan cheese
1 cup smoked salmon (about 4 oz.)
½ cup croutons
Salt and freshly ground black pepper

Combine the olive oil, garlic, lemon juice, Worcestershire sauce, mustard, and salt and pepper to taste in a jar with a tight fitting lid and shake well to mix.

Tear romaine and green leaf lettuce into large pieces and put them in a large bowl. Add the Parmesan cheese, smoked salmon and croutons and toss. Shake the dressing to mix, then drizzle it over the salad, and toss to coat well. Serve immediately.

Corn Bread Salad

Lila Dustin

Left over corn bread, crumbled
2 medium tomatoes, diced
1 bunch of green onions, diced
1 large green pepper, diced
1 cup bacon bits
8 oz. bag of mild shredded cheese
1 cup real mayonnaise
½ cup white sugar

Crumble leftover corn bread in bottom of casserole dish. Add diced tomatoes, green onions, and green peppers.

In a separate medium bowl add mayonnaise and sugar and mix well. Pour the mixture over top of the corn bread and vegetables.

Add shredded cheese and bacon bits to garnish. Chill in the fridge for at least an hour before serving.

Four Bean Salad

1 can red kidney beans
1 can white kidney beans
1 cup green string beans
1 can yellow wax beans
4 green onions, diced
¼ cup fresh parsley, chopped
1–1½ cups Italian dressing

Combine four beans, onions, and parsley.

Pour the dressing over the bean mixture and toss. Cover and refrigerate for at least 3 hours, mixing occasionally. When ready to serve, sprinkle parsley over beans.

Cranberry Salad
Alice Casillas
Yield: 6 Servings

3 oz. pkg. raspberry Jello
1 cup boiling water
1 envelope unflavored gelatin
1 Tbsp. cold water
1 Tbsp. lemon or lime juice
1 can crushed pineapple, drained
1 can whole cranberries
1 cup chopped celery
½ cup chopped pecans or walnuts
Juice of 1 orange
Grated peeling of 1 orange

Dissolve Jello in boiling water. Soften gelatin in cold water, and add to dissolved Jello mixture. Add remaining ingredients to Jello mixture.

Pour into cooking sprayed mold. Refrigerate until set.

German Potato Salad
Mary Louise Goreczny

1 small onion
5 small potatoes
1 cucumber
2–4 Tbsp. vinegar
2–3 Tbsp. oil
Salt and pepper to taste

Boil potatoes until done. Slice potatoes and cucumbers thinly. Chop onions in small pieces. Add vinegar and oil to perfection. Salt and pepper to taste.

Note: Bratwurst is good with it.

Gel-Yo
Yield: 6 ½ cup servings

3 oz. pkg. cherry gelatin
8 oz. non-fat or low-fat yogurt

Prepare gelatin as directed on the package. Chill until almost set. Add yogurt, stirring to mix well. Chill until set. Serve.

Seven Layered Salad
Regina Aune

1 head iceberg lettuce (or any other lettuce that you prefer)
1 cup mayonnaise or Miracle Whip Salad Dressing
1 cup carrots, either sliced or shredded
1 cup sliced cucumbers
1 cup sliced radishes
1 or 2 containers (depending on size) of grape tomatoes
16 oz. bag of frozen peas
6 hard-boiled eggs, sliced
3 strips crisp bacon cut in pieces or 1 jar of bacon pieces or bits
2 Tbsp. sugar

Tear the lettuce into pieces and line the bottom of a glass bowl. Spread the cup of sliced cucumbers, carrots, radishes, frozen peas, and tomatoes in layers on the lettuce. Next, place the egg slices on top. Mix 2 tablespoons of sugar with the mayonnaise or Miracle Whip and spread the mixture on top of the eggs. Lastly, spread the bacon pieces or bacon bits on the top. Chill for several hours or overnight.

Variations: You can substitute any of your favorite salad vegetables such as mushrooms, cauliflower, broccoli, zucchini, etc., for any of the ingredients, except the lettuce. You can also add sliced onions as an additional layer. If you do not want to use the bacon bits, you can top the salad with your favorite shredded cheese.

Greek Pasta Salada
Helen Antonelli

8 oz. rotini or any sturdy pasta
⅔ cup + 2 tsp. olive oil, divided
3 Tbsp. white wine vinegar
1½ tsp. dried oregano
1 large clove garlic, minced
½ tsp. salt
Pepper to taste
1 sweet onion, sliced thin
1 medium cucumber, peeled, seeded, cut in coarse chunks
1 green pepper, sliced in ribbons
4 large tomatoes, peeled, seeded, cut in coarse chunks
16 black oil-cured olives (such as Greek Kalamata), pitted
6 oz. feta cheese, cut in 1" cubes

Cook pasta according to package directions, al dente. Be sure water is well salted. Drain, rinse with cold water. Drain again. Toss with 2 teaspoons of olive oil.

In a small bowl, place vinegar and with a fork or whisk, beat in oregano, garlic, salt and pepper. Beat in ⅔ cup olive oil. Taste and add more vinegar, salt or pepper, if needed.

In a large bowl, combine onion, cucumber, green pepper, tomatoes, olives, feta cheese, and pasta. Pour dressing over all ingredients and toss gently until everything is well coated. If the salad stands a short while before serving, the flavor improves. Serve at room temperature.

Hearts of Palm Salad

with Grape Tomatoes and Avocado

Helen Antonelli

8 oz. can of Hearts of Palms (do not drain)
2 lb. pkg. sweet grape tomatoes
¼ cup fresh lime juice
1 Tbsp. fresh oregano, minced
1 Tbsp. cilantro sprigs, minced
¼ cup olive oil
Salt and pepper to taste
3 whole avocados
1 bag fresh salad greens (Italian Blend)
Sprigs of parsley for garnish

Place palm slices in a bowl, add the lime juice, oregano, cilantro and olive oil. Season with salt and pepper, mix and let stand for 15 minutes. Drain and reserve liquid. Cut avocados in half, remove seed, and cube. Add the grape tomatoes and the cubed avocados to the marinated hearts of palms. Divide the salad greens among four plates. Add the marinated mixture on top of each plate of salad greens. Sprinkle ¼ cup of reserve liquid over each salad. Garnish with parsley.

Jo's Jello Salad

Jo Tompkins

1 large carton cottage cheese
1 small pkg. lemon or orange jell-o (orange preferred)
Drained, crushed or chunked pineapple (to suit you)
½ small carton Cool Whip (2¼ cups = 34 Tbsp.)

Mix well. Serve.

Larb Gai - Spicy Thai Chicken Salad
Susan Rizzo

1 lb. boneless skinless chicken breast, minced in food processor (do not substitute ground chicken, it's too fatty!)

1 Tbsp. roasted rice powder (available in Asian markets or make your own by roasting raw rice in a dry skillet till brown, then grinding in food processor)

3 Tbsp. chopped fresh cilantro

2 green onions, chopped

2 Tbsp. chopped shallots

½ cup shredded carrots

½ cup shredded red cabbage

3 Tbsp. chopped mint leaves

2 Tbsp. lime juice

1½ Tbsp. fish sauce

1 tsp. garlic and red chili paste

Lettuce leaves, for serving

Fresh cilantro stem, for garnish

Heat nonstick skillet over medium heat, no oil necessary. Add chicken, stir until cooked through. Remove from heat, drain excess liquid. Add fish sauce and lime juice. Toss all together with cilantro, onion, shallots, mint, carrots, cabbage, rice powder, and ground chili/garlic paste. Adjust seasoning to taste. Serve immediately in lettuce leaves. Garnish with cilantro sprigs.

Orange Jell-O

Jo Ann Reed

1 can fruit cocktail
1 small can mandarin oranges, cut oranges in half
1 can of crushed pineapple, drain overnight in refrigerator
1 small package of orange Jell-O
12 oz. container of Cool Whip
Coconut for garnish

Mix Jell-O and cool whip after fruit has drained. Stir in fruit with cool whip and sprinkle top with coconut.

Pea Salad

Arlene Coury

10 oz. pkg. frozen peas
½ cup + diced cheddar cheese
2 hard-boiled eggs, sliced
¼ cup chopped celery
2 Tbsp. chopped onion
⅓ cup mayonnaise
½ tsp. salt
¼ tsp. Tabasco sauce
⅛ tsp. pepper

Mix the peas, cheese, sliced eggs, celery, and onion together.

Combine the mayonnaise, salt, pepper, and Tabasco.

When you are ready to serve, stir the mayonnaise mixture into the pea mix and serve.

Keep refrigerated.

Pineapple Delight
Yield: Serves 8

¾ cup evaporated milk in ice tray until almost frozen around edges

3 oz. pkg. gelatin (any flavor)

½ cup boiling water

½ cup cold water

8 marshmallows, finely cut

9 oz. can undrained crushed pineapple

½ cup chopped nuts

Chill evaporated milk along with quart sized bowl and mixer beaters in freezer.

In a 2 quart bowl, dissolve a package of gelatin in a half cup (½ cup) boiling water. Stir in cold water. Then add marshmallows, pineapple, and chopped nuts. Set aside at room temperature.

Whip evaporated milk in the cold quart bowl until stiff using the cold beaters. Fold into gelatin mixture. Cover and chill.

Potato Salad

Regina Aune

5 lb. of red potatoes
8 hard-boiled eggs
2 cups of chopped celery
1 cup chopped radishes
10 oz. jar of salad olives
1 cup sour cream
2 cups mayonnaise
⅓ cup Dijon mustard
1 small onion, chopped
1 Tbsp. garlic, minced
1 Tbsp. fresh cilantro
1 Tbsp. horseradish
½ tsp. salt
¼ tsp. pepper
Paprika

Wash and slice the red potatoes, then boil until tender and drain. While potatoes are boiling, mix together the celery, radishes, salad olives (with the olive juice), onion, and the cilantro.

In another bowl mix together the sour cream, garlic, mayonnaise, mustard, horseradish, salt, and pepper.

Chop 4 of the eggs and add to the celery mixture. Mix together thoroughly the celery mixture and the dressing mixture. Pour over the potatoes and mix thoroughly. Place salad in a prepared bowl. Slice the 4 remaining eggs and place on top of the salad. Sprinkle paprika over the top of the salad. Chill overnight.

24 Hour Salad

1 can Mandarin oranges, drained
8 oz. can chunk pineapple, drained
Small jar maraschino cherries, drained and cut in half
16 oz. can fruit cocktail, drained
1 cup coconut
1 cup nuts
1 cup sour cream
Small pkg. miniature marshmallows

Combine all of the ingredients except marshmallows and sour cream in a bowl. Add marshmallows, then fold in sour cream. Cover tightly and refrigerate for 24 hours. Serve.

Dressings, Marinades, Sauces, & Stuffings

Apple Cranberry Stuffing
Susan Rizzo
Oven: 350°F. Prep Time: 15 minutes
Cook Time: 30–40 minutes Yield: 8–10 servings

2 cups chicken broth
1 cup dried cranberries
¼ cup butter
1 onion, chopped
1 green bell pepper, chopped
1 cup celery, chopped
2 baking apples, cored and finely chopped
3 large eggs
½ tsp. salt
¼ tsp. ground black pepper
10.75 oz. can cream of chicken or celery soup
½ tsp. ground cinnamon
8 cups bread, cubed and toasted

Combine chicken broth and cranberries; let soak.

In a large skillet, melt butter over medium heat. Add onion, pepper and celery; cook for 5 minutes stirring frequently or until tender. Add apples and cook for 5 minutes, stirring frequently. Remove from heat and place in a large bowl.

Beat 3 eggs in a separate bowl. Add salt and pepper. Set aside.

In the large bowl with vegetables, stir in chicken broth mixture, celery soup, and cinnamon. Add toasted bread, stirring gently to combine. Add eggs.

Preheat oven to 350°F. Lightly grease a 13" x 9" x 2" baking dish.

Spoon mixture into prepared dish and bake for 30 to 40 minutes or until center is set.

Avocado Dressing

Helen Antonelli

1 ripe Calavo avocado, peeled, seeded, and mashed
1 bottle prepared red wine vinaigrette or Caesar salad dressing

Combine ingredients until smooth. Cover and refrigerate until needed. Serve as a dressing to salads, cabbage slaw or vegetable marinade. Use as a dip or spread by incorporating additional avocados into the recipe.

Dried Cranberry Mustard

Susan Rizzo

Yield: 1½ cups

Scant ¼ cup (1¼ oz.) brown mustard seeds
About 1 cup plus 2 Tbsp. (3¾ oz.) mustard powder
½ cup water
¾ cup unsweetened cranberry juice
1½ tsp. Kosher salt
½ cup sugar
½ tsp. ground cinnamon
¼ tsp. ground cloves
½ cup chopped dried cranberries

Soak the mustard seeds: Place the mustard seeds and powder in a medium glass or ceramic bowl along with the water and cranberry juice. Set aside, covered (but not sealed airtight) for 24 hours.

Place the mixture in a food processor along with the salt and sugar and process for 1 to 2 minutes until the seeds are coarsely ground. Stir in cinnamon, cloves, and dried cranberries. This makes about 1½ cups mustard.

The mustard may be very pungent at first and *very, very hot.* Cover and refrigerate for at least a day or two before using.

Marinade for Chicken or Beef Fajitas
Martha Doenges

¼ cup lime juice
2 Tbsp. extra virgin olive oil
4 cloves garlic, crushed
2 tsp. soy sauce
1 tsp. sea salt
½ tsp. liquid smoke
½ tsp. cayenne pepper
¼ tsp. black pepper

2 Tbsp. water
1 tsp. soy sauce
½ tsp. lime juice
1 dash salt
1 dash black pepper

1 Tbsp. olive oil
1 Spanish onion, thinly sliced
½ of a green bell pepper, ½ of a red bell pepper, and ½ of a yellow bell pepper, remove seeds and thinly sliced
1 lb. sirloin steak or skinned, boned chicken breast

Combine the first 8 ingredients plus meat in plastic container with cover or plastic bag and refrigerate for at least 2 hours or overnight. Discard leftover marinade.

Grill meat over medium flame, 4–5 minutes each side (or grilled to your preference). Wait 20 minutes to let meat rest (in order to seal in juices). Cut meat into thin strips; set aside and keep warm.

Combine the 2 tablespoons of water, soy sauce, lime juice, salt and pepper. Set aside.

Cook onion and peppers in oil until brown. Remove from heat. Pour reserved mixture over onions and peppers. Combine meat, onions, and peppers. Serve with tortillas, cheese, salsa, sour cream and chopped lettuce.

Minted Lamb Marinade

Susan Rizzo

1 cup (packed) fresh mint leaves, coarsely chopped
¾ cup orange juice
½ cup (packed) golden brown sugar
¼ cup dry sherry
¼ cup apple cider vinegar
3 garlic cloves, chopped
1 Tbsp. finely grated orange (or blood orange) peel
1 Tbsp. chopped and peeled fresh ginger
2 tsp. black and red peppercorns (wild peppercorns)
1 tsp. sesame oil
1 tsp. soy sauce
1 tsp. peppercorns, crushed

1½ lb. 1" cubes trimmed leg of lamb
Salt (to taste)
Pepper (to taste)

Combine all ingredients except lamb, salt, and pepper in medium bowl for marinade. Place lamb into plastic bag, pour marinade over and make sure all lamb is well-coated. Marinate overnight or longer for greater marinade flavor. Thread lamb onto metal skewers. Transfer lamb skewers to baking sheet. Pour marinade into small saucepan.

Prepare barbecue (medium–high heat). Sprinkle lamb with salt and pepper. Grill to your desired doneness, turning, about 8 minutes for medium–rare. Transfer to platter.

Boil marinade 5 minutes. Strain, then spoon over lamb and serve.

Italian Dressing
Kathy Birkner
Yield: 1½ cups

1 cup olive or canola oil
½ cup vinegar
2 cloves garlic, crushed
2 Tbsp. onions, pulverized
1 tsp. sugar
1 tsp. Dijon mustard
½–1 Tbsp. dry basil
¼ tsp. pepper
½ tsp. salt

Combine all and allow to mingle flavorings for 30 minutes. Use as wanted.

Mint Sauce
Susan Rizzo

Large bunch of mint
Pinch salt
4 Tbsp. boiling water
4 Tbsp. white wine vinegar
1 Tbsp. sugar

Strip off the mint leaves, sprinkle with salt and chop finely.

Place into a jug, add the sugar and pour over the boiling water over the mixture; stir and leave to cool. Stir in the vinegar and taste.

Add more water or vinegar and adjust seasoning to suit your taste. Serve with Roast Lamb, chops, etc.

Plum Sauce
Yield: 4 cups

2 lb. ripe plums
¼ cup honey
1 Tbsp. grated fresh ginger
1 Tbsp. water
1 Tbsp. minced fresh garlic
½ tsp. red chili paste, or more to taste
¼ cup soy sauce

Pit and chop the plums.

Place them in a medium-size saucepan along with the honey, ginger, water, garlic and chili paste. (I use Chinese Hot Bean Paste, flavorful, but hot.). Bring to a boil, then reduce the heat and simmer until the plums are soft, about 15 minutes.

Remove from the heat and stir in the soy sauce. Purée the mixture in a blender or food processor.

Note: If sauce is too thin, mix 2 teaspoons of cornstarch to 2 tablespoons of water together, then add to thicken. What you don't use after a few days, freeze for up to a year.

Poppy Seed Dressing
From Joske's of San Antonio
Yield: 3 cups

1½ cup sugar
2 tsp. dry mustard
2 tsp. salt
⅔ cup vinegar
2 tsp. onion juice
2 cups salad oil
1 Tbsp. poppy seeds

Combine sugar, mustard, salt, and vinegar and beat. Add onion juice, beat. Add salad oil slowly. When thick, add poppy seeds. Chill before serving.

Santa Fe Salsa

Anne Molina

16 oz. can whole tomatoes, undrained and coarsely chopped
¾ tsp. cayenne pepper
4 tsp. fresh lime juice
4 tsp. cider vinegar
4 cloves garlic, finely chopped
½ tsp. leaf oregano, crumbled
½ tsp. ground cumin
1 tsp. crushed coriander seeds
½ tsp. salt

Combine tomatoes, cayenne pepper, lime juice, vinegar, garlic, leaf oregano, cumin, coriander seeds, and salt in a glass or pottery bowl. Let stand 30 minutes at room temperature before serving.

Shrimp Butter

Jeanne Girardi

Yield: 48 crackers

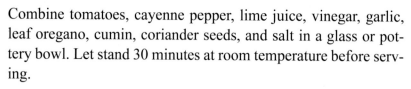

8 oz. pkg. cream cheese
1 stick butter
1 lb. fresh shrimp, cooked
1 tsp. onion or garlic powder
1 package Ritz crackers

Let cheese and butter come to room temperature. Then combine butter and cheese, beating until smooth. Add onion or garlic powder and shrimp; whip until shrimp are smooth in cheese-butter mixture.

Lightly coat each Ritz cracker with a light coat of butter, then add shrimp-cheese butter. Put back in refrigerator to cool. Serve.

Smoky Chipotle Barbecue Sauce
Helen Antonelli

2 (18 oz.) bottles of barbecue sauce
2 of the canned chipotle chile peppers
2 Tbsp. brown sugar
1 tsp. chili powder

Process all ingredients in blender until smooth. Pour into saucepan and bring to boil over medium high heat. Reduce heat and simmer 30 minutes.

Great with baby back pork ribs. To make ribs more tender, rub with cut side of citrus fruit (lime or orange) before cooking. Wrap tightly in plastic wrap and chill for 8 hours.

Tartar Sauce
Yield: 1 cup

1 cup mayonnaise
4 Tbsp. sweet relish
½ tsp. onion (optional)

Combine ingredients. Keep refrigerated until served. Serve with fish.

Tzatziki Sauce
Yield: 1¼ cups

½ cup plain Greek yogurt
½ cup sour cream
½ cup peeled cucumber, grated, then squeezed dry
1 tsp. garlic, minced
1 Tbsp. extra virgin olive oil
1 Tbsp. mint, chopped or fresh chopped dill
Juice of ½ lemon (about 2 Tbsp.) + 1 tsp. lemon zest
Salt, as needed
Black pepper, as needed

Combine the yogurt, sour cream, cucumber, and garlic in food processor and purée until smooth.

Transfer to a bowl and fold in olive oil, mint, lemon juice and lemon zest. Stir until combined and season to taste with salt and pepper. Keep refrigerated.

Breads

Applesauce Nut Loaf

Viola Kolos Doenges ("Mama D")

Oven: 350°F. Bake: 1 hour Yield: 1 loaf (9" x 5" x 7")
Prep Time: 10 minutes

1 cup sugar
1 cup applesauce
⅓ cup vegetable oil
1 tsp. baking soda
½ tsp. baking powder
½ tsp. ground cinnamon
2 eggs
3 tsp. milk
2 cup sifted flour
¼ tsp. salt
¼ tsp. ground nutmeg
¾ cup chopped pecans

Topping

¼ cup brown sugar, packed
¼ cup chopped pecans
¼ tsp. ground cinnamon

In a large mixing bowl, thoroughly combine sugar, applesauce, oil, eggs and milk. Sift together flour, soda, baking powder, cinnamon, salt, and nutmeg. Add to applesauce mixture and beat until well combined. Stir in pecans. Turn batter into well-greased loaf baking pan.

For topping: Combine brown sugar, cinnamon and pecans. Sprinkle evenly over batter. Bake at 350°F. for 1 hour. Cap loosely with foil after the first 30 minutes of baking. Remove from pan, and cool on rack.

Note: Bake nut and fruit breads the day before serving so the flavors mellow and the bread slices easier.

Apricot Bread

Regina Aune

Oven: 350°F. Cook Time: 1 hour Yield: 1 large loaf

2 (3 oz.) packages cream cheese, softened
⅓ cup sugar
1 Tbsp. all-purpose flour
½ cup dried apricots, chopped
2 eggs
1 tsp. orange peel, grated
½ cup orange juice
½ cup water
17 oz. package quick nut bread mix

Combine cream cheese, sugar, and flour. Add apricots.

Beat in 1 egg and the orange peel. Set aside.

Combine the second egg, slightly beaten with the orange juice and water. Add this to quick bread mix, stirring until moistened.

Turn ⅔ of the bread batter into greased and floured 9" x 5" x 5" loaf pan.

Pour cheese mixture over top. Spoon on remaining batter.

Bake for 1 hour. Cool 10 minutes, then remove from pan.

When cool, wrap in foil, and refrigerate or freeze until ready to serve.

Note: When using glass pans for baking, set the oven temperature 25° degrees lower than specified. Glass heats faster than metal and holds the heat longer.

Banana Nut Bread
Kathy Birkner

Oven: 350°F. Time: 55–60 minutes Yield: (2) 9" X 5" loaf pans

4 cups spelt flour (or use 2 cups whole wheat and 2 cups all purpose flour)
2 eggs + 2 whites, beaten lightly
1½ cups buttermilk
5 ripe bananas (medium), mashed
2 tsp. baking powder
1 tsp. baking soda
5 tsp. canola oil
1 cup Splenda or sugar
1 tsp. salt
½ to 1 cup walnuts, chopped finely

Combine all ingredients, but don't overmix. Pour into 2 (9" x 5" x 5") well-greased loaf pans. Bake until toothpick inserted into bread comes out clean.

Red Lobster Biscuits
Cathy Van Delden

Oven: 375°F. Time: 10 minutes Yield: 12 biscuits

2 cups Bisquick
⅔ cup milk
½ cup shredded cheddar
¼ cup butter, melted
½ tsp. garlic powder (or to taste)

Mix baking mix, milk and cheese until soft dough forms. Beat vigorously for 30 seconds. Drop by spoonful onto a greased cookie sheet. Bake at 375°F. for 10 minutes.

Mix butter and garlic powder. Brush over warm biscuits before removing from tray.

Banana Bread

Rosebud

Oven: 300°F.   Time: 1 hour 15 minutes
Yield: 2 large loaves OR 1 large Angel Food Pan OR 4 small loaf pans (4" x 8") OR 1 large Bundt pan

Cream in mixer

1½ cups sugar
1 cup Crisco

Add: 2 eggs, mix well.

Mix together and add to above:

3 cups unsifted flour
1½ tsp. baking soda
½ tsp. salt

Add:

½ cup buttermilk (or 1 tsp. vinegar to ½ cup milk to make sour milk)
3 mashed ripe bananas
Nuts, if desired

Bake at 300°F. for 1 hour 15 minutes or until done.

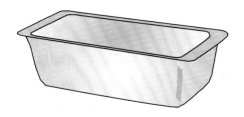

Banana Salsa Bread

Louise Malouff

Oven: 350°F. Bake: 1 hour Yield: 1 loaf pan

½ cup butter or margarine
1 cup sugar
3 medium ripe bananas (mashed)
1 cup Pace chunky salsa
2 eggs
2 cups all purpose flour
1 tsp. baking soda
pinch salt

Preheat oven to 350°F. Spray 9" x 5" x 3" loaf pan with vegetable cooking spray.

Cream together butter, sugar until light and fluffy, using electric mixer on medium speed.

Add bananas, salsa, and eggs; mix well. Add flour, baking soda, and salt; mix well.

Pour mixture into a prepared loaf pan. Bake 1 hour or until done. Cool in pan on wire rack for 15 minutes. Removed from pan and cool completely on rack.

Blueberry Muffins

Theresa Birkner

Oven: 400°F. Time: 20 minutes Yield: About 16–18 muffins

2 cups spelt flour
1 cup sugar or Splenda
2 tsp. baking powder
½ tsp. baking soda
¾ tsp. salt
Dash nutmeg
½ tsp. cinnamon
2 eggs
1 cup plain Greek yogurt
½ cup milk
⅓ cup canola oil
2 cups blueberries
½ cup walnuts, chopped

Mix flour, sugar, baking powder, baking soda, salt, and spices. Beat eggs, add yogurt, milk, and oil to eggs.

Add flour mixture to egg mixture. Add blueberries and nuts; fold in gently. Fill paper-lined muffin cups about ¾ full. Bake until toothpick inserted comes out clean or about 20 minutes.

Blueberry Muffins

Frances Jerome

Oven: 375°F. Time: 30 minutes Yield: 12 muffins

2 cups flour
1 cup sugar
2 tsp. baking powder
½ cup butter (cold)
½ cup milk
1 tsp. vanilla
2 eggs
2½ cups blueberries

Preheat oven to 375°F. Grease a muffin tin.

In a medium bowl, combine all dry ingredients with pastry blender. Cut in butter until mixture resembles crumbs. In another bowl combine milk, eggs, and vanilla. Add to dry ingredients all at once, stirring just until moistened. Do not over mix. Fold in berries. Spoon into muffin pan. Sprinkle with sugar. Bake 30 minutes or until toothpick comes out clean. Cool 5 minutes.

Broccoli Cheese Corn Bread

Arlene Coury

Oven: 350°F. Cook Time: 45 minutes to 1 hour

4 eggs, beaten
2 sticks butter, melted
1 medium onion, finely diced
2 oz. cottage cheese
1 pkg. (10 oz.) chopped broccoli, thawed
2 boxes corn muffin mix (such as Jiffy)

Preheat oven to 350°F. Combine eggs, butter, onion, cottage cheese and broccoli. Add corn muffin mix. Pour into a greased 12" cast-iron skillet. Bake for 45 minutes to 1 hour. Cut into wedges to serve.

Corn Bread

Kathy Birkner

Oven: 425°F. Time 20 minutes Yield: 8–9 or 16–18

Full recipe

¾ cup cornmeal
1 cup spelt flour
6 Tbsp. sugar
3 tsp. baking powder
½ tsp. salt
Dash cinnamon
1 cup milk or buttermilk
2 eggs, well beaten
2 Tbsp. canola oil

Preheat oven to 425°F. Grease 8" square pan or 9 muffins tins. Mix dry ingredients in a large bowl. Set aside.

Mix the wet ingredients (milk, eggs, oil) and blend well. Combine wet and dry ingredients mixing only until blended.

Spoon into square pan or muffin tin filling about ⅔ full. Cook about 15 minutes for muffins or until toothpick inserted comes out clean. If using square pan, cool and cut into squares.

Note: I divide the recipes in two and make one and put the other in a plastic bag so that I have one ready to go…..all I add is the wet ingredients, put in a pan and bake for quick corn bread like a pre-packed from the store, but with your ingredients. You save money and control the ingredients *without* added preservatives.

Half recipe

6 Tbsp. cornmeal
½ cup spelt flour
1½ tsp. baking powder
¼ tsp. salt
Dash cinnamon

Put dry ingredients in a plastic bag until read to mix. Then add:

½ cup milk or buttermilk
1 egg, well beaten
1 Tbsp. canola oil

Kolaches

Viola Kolos Doenges ("Mama D")

Oven: 400°F. Bake 20–30 minutes Yield 48 kolaches
Prep Time: 1½–2 hours

Dough

1 envelope (1¼ oz) dry yeast
¼ cup warm water
2 cups scalded milk
1½ tsp. salt
4 Tbsp. sugar
6 cups flour
1 stick butter
1 egg
2 cans (12 oz.) pastry filling (Various fruit fillings are available in cans: apricot, cherry, pineapple, plum /prune, or poppy seed)

Topping

⅓ stick butter
4 Tbsp. sugar
½ cup flour

To make dough: Melt butter in milk, stirring over low heat in large saucepan. Add sugar and salt. Let cool (test on wrist) so milk is slightly warm but not hot (110–120°F.). Add yeast dissolved in warm water. Add and mix in about half flour, then egg, then rest of flour. Cover and let dough rise to double in size. While dough is rising, prepare topping by blending together with knife or pastry cutter butter, sugar, and flour. Mix until crumbly.

Knead dough on floured pastry cloth, adding flour to keep from sticking to hands. Separate dough into four balls. Shape each quarter into a long cylinder about an inch in diameter and slice into 12 pieces. Shape each piece into a rounded mound and place on a baking sheet. Depress a cavity in the center of each piece using your thumb. Add filling to each cavity. Sprinkle topping over each kolache. Cover with a cloth, and let rise in a warm place until double in size.

Bake at 400°F. for 20 to 30 minutes until light tan. Brush with melted butter after removing from oven.

Note: Two cans are enough for entire recipe. If more flavors are desired, use more cans and freeze leftovers to use for another batch

.

Lemon Blueberry Muffins

Regina Aune

Oven: 375°F. Time: 20–25 minutes Yield: 24 large muffins

2 cups all-purpose flour, unsifted
⅔ cup sugar
1 tsp. baking powder
1 tsp. baking soda
½ tsp. salt
Pinch of ground cloves
2 cups fresh blueberries
½ stick butter
8 oz. container plain, low-fat yogurt
1 large egg
2 tsp. lemon rind, grated
1 tsp. lemon extract
1 tsp. vanilla extract

Combine flour sugar, baking powder, baking soda, salt and cloves. Add blueberries and toss to coat with flour mixture. Set aside.

Melt butter and let cool. Mix butter, yogurt, egg, lemon rind, and extracts. Combine with dry ingredients.

Stir until moistened. Do not over mix. Fill well-greased large muffin pans and bake for 20–25 minutes. Sprinkle with granulated sugar and remove from pan when cool.

Cinnamon Rolls

Mildred Seck

Oven: 375°F. Time: 30 minutes Yield: 3 dozen rolls

1 potato, peeled and diced
2 cups potato water (makes rolls softer)
½ cup sugar
½ cup margarine
1½ tsp. salt
2 pkg. quick-rising yeast, (dissolved)
½ cup lukewarm water (110–120°F.)
2 eggs
6–8 cups flour to make soft dough

Pare and dice a medium potato, cook until tender. Beat potatoes in the water to make a soupy mixture. Add enough water to make 2 cups. Pour over sugar, margarine and salt. Cool.

Add yeast dissolved in ½ cup lukewarm water, add potato water, some flour, eggs, and beat well with mixer. Then add flour a little at a time to make dough thickened but soft. Turn onto floured board kneading just enough to form a soft ball. Let rise until double in size.

Roll out and sprinkle with following mixture:

1 cup white sugar
1 cup brown sugar, well packed
2 tsp. cinnamon
½ tsp. nutmeg
Or just use cinnamon-sugar mixture

Roll up and cut for cinnamon rolls. Let rise again. Place on parchment covered pan or greased pan. Bake.

Mom's Cinnamon Rolls
Louise Malouff
Oven: 375°F. Time: 1 hour

2 cups sugar
⅓ cup shortening (maybe more)
1 Tbsp. salt

Mix in mixing bowl. Pour 1 cup hot water over
that and let shortening dissolve.

In a small dish, put
1 cup lukewarm water
1 Tbsp. sugar
1 envelope dry yeast

When shortening is dissolved, add 1 cup cold water and some flour.
Add yeast mixture and beat very well. Add flour to make dough
(about 7– 8 cups flour). May add 2 eggs, beaten, if desired, at the
time you put yeast in. Let rise till double in size.

*To make cinnamon roll*s: In a small bowl, mix 1 cup sugar with 1
tablespoon of cinnamon; set aside. Roll out dough into a rectangle
with a rolling pin; spread with butter, then cinnamon-sugar mixture. Roll up and cut in about 1" slices. Put rolls on a parchment
lined pan leaving 1" between each roll, then set aside and let rise
till double in size. (about 1 hour) Bake at 375°F. for ½ hour or until
nicely browned. (see below for topping)

To make coffee cake: Roll out dough into a rectangle, then spread
with butter. Cover with pineapple, add brown sugar. Roll up as for
Cinnamon Rolls. Cut rolls in half, place ½ on one side of pan, ½
on other side of pan. Cut in 1" pieces with scissors. Lay slices
overlapping on one another. Let raise till double in size (approx.
1 hour). Bake at 375°F. for ½ hour or until good and brown. Be
sure middle is cooked.

Topping: Mix 1 cup powdered sugar and enough milk (a little bit
at a time) to make right consistency for topping or add butter, sugar
and cinnamon and/or nuts.

Peppy's Pita Bread

Louise Malouff

Oven: 500°F. Prep Time: 15 minutes + rising Yield: 8 servings

1⅛ cup warm water (110°)
3 cups all purpose flour
1 tsp. salt
1 Tbsp. vegetable oil
1½ tsp. white sugar
1½ tsp. active dry yeast

Place all ingredients in bread pan of your bread machine, select dough setting and start. When dough has risen long enough machine will beep.

Turn dough onto a lightly floured surface. Gently roll and stretch dough in to a 12" rope. With a sharp knife divide into 8 pieces. Roll each into a smooth ball. With a rolling pin, roll each ball into a 6" circle. Set aside on a lightly floured counter top. Cover with towel. Let bread rise about 30 minutes or until slightly puffy.

Preheat oven to 500°F. Place 2 or 3 pitas on a wire cake rack. Place cake rack directly on oven rack. Bake pitas 4–5 minutes until puffed and tops begin to brown. Remove from oven and immediately place pitas in a brown paper bag or cover them with a damp towel until soft.

Once pitas are softened, either cut in ½ or split top edge for a ½ or whole pita. Store in a plastic bag.

Note: Store the bag in refrigerator for several days or in freezer for 1–2 months.

Pumpkin Bread

Louise Malouff

Oven: 325°F. Time: 1 hour Yield: 2 loaves

1 cup shortening
3 eggs
#303 can Pumpkin
2½ cups sugar
3½ cups flour
½ tsp. baking powder
1 tsp. baking soda
1 tsp. cinnamon
1 tsp. nutmeg
1 tsp. allspice
1 tsp. cloves
½ cup chopped nuts

Mix shortening, sugar and pumpkin; then add eggs and mix. In a separate bowl, combine dry ingredients; add to pumpkin mixture and blend well. Add nuts and stir. Pour into 2 greased and floured loaf pans and bake at 325°F. for one hour. Let cool before removing from pan.

Quick Sweet Dough
Kathy Birkner
Oven: 375°F. Time: 25 to 30 minutes Yield: 24 rolls

2 pkg. active dry yeast
½ cup warm water (110–120°F.)
2 cups sweet potatoes, cooked, peeled, and mashed
1¼ cups buttermilk
2 eggs
½ cup butter or margarine, softened
½ cup sugar or Splenda
1 Tbsp. cinnamon
2 tsp. baking powder
2 tsp. salt
5–6 cups of flour (I use spelt or kamut flour.)

In large mixing bowl, dissolve yeast in warm water. Add sweet potatoes and combine well. Then add buttermilk, eggs, sugar (or Splenda), butter, cinnamon, baking powder, salt, and 2½ cups flour. Blend ½ minute on low speed, scraping bowl frequently. Beat 2 minutes at medium speed, scraping bowl intermittently. Stir in enough remaining flour to make dough easy to handle. (Dough should remain soft and slightly sticky).

Turn onto a floured board and knead 5 minutes or 200 turns. Shape dough immediately into desired rolls. Cover; let rise in warm place until double, about an hour. (Dough is ready if impression remains when touched.) Bake as desired in a 375°F. oven.

Cinnamon Apple Rolls

1 recipe of Quick Sweet Dough
⅓ cup butter, melted
1 cup Splenda or sugar
4–5 large apples, diced
1 Tbsp. cinnamon
½ cup walnuts, finely chopped

Core apples with skins on. Cut into smaller pieces and chop in food processor. Pour apples into a small bowl, then add Splenda, cinnamon, and walnuts, combine well.

Roll dough into a rectangle about 15" x 9", then spread with melted butter. Spread apples over dough. Roll up starting at wide side, pinch edge of dough into rolled dough. Pinch end of dough into roll and seal well. Cut into ¾" to 1" inch thick slices. Place slightly apart on a parchment prepared pan (or use greased pan or muffin cupped pan). Let rise until double. Bake as above. While still warm, frost roll with icing, if desired.

Southern Biscuits
Theresa Birkner
Oven: 450°F. Time 10–15 minutes Yield: 12–18 biscuits
(depends on size)

2 cups flour
4 tsp. baking powder
½ tsp. salt
2–3 Tbsp. sugar
½ tsp. cream of tartar
½ cup shortening
1 egg, beaten
¾ cup milk

Preheat oven to 450°F. Sift dry ingredients together, place in food processor. Add shortening and pulse to mix. Add egg and milk. Pulse only until it forms a stiff dough. Turn onto flat surface, then roll dough to 1" thickness. Dip biscuit cutter or glass into flour, then cut dough into rounds. Place on parchment paper or a greased baking sheet. Bake 10 to 15 minutes. Serve with butter.

Sweet Potato Biscuits
Kathy Birkner

Oven: 425°F. Time: 10–12 minutes Yield: 12 biscuits

1 big sweet potato, peeled and mashed after cooking
1¾ cups unbleached all purpose flour
4 Tbsp. sugar
1½ tsp. baking powder
1 tsp. salt
½ tsp. baking soda
6 Tbsp. cold unsalted butter, cut into small pieces
⅓ cup chilled buttermilk

Prick sweet potato with a fork and microwave until soft and tender. Remove peel and mash in a large dinner plate to facilitate cooling. Allow sweet potato to cool to room temperature.

Place oven rack in the center of the oven and preheat the oven to 425°F. Line a jelly roll or shallow pan with parchment paper.

In a large mixing bowl, or a food processor, whisk for a minute or pulse five times, the flour, sugar, baking powder, salt, and baking soda. Cut in the butter or pulse it in just until it resembles small peas.

Mix the buttermilk with the sweet potato puree in a small bowl and add it to the flour-butter mixture, stirring or pulsing in a food processor just until combined.

Turn the dough out onto a lightly floured table and gently kneading enough so dough holds together. Roll the dough out to about a rectangle 1½" thick. Flour a 2½" biscuit or round cutter and cut the biscuits out near each other. Place the biscuits about 1" apart on the prepared pan. Bake the biscuits for 10 to 12 minutes or until light golden. Serve warm with softened butter.

Variation: To make a buttermilk substitute, squeeze a teaspoon of lemon into milk (whole or 2%) and let it sit for 10 minutes. The sweet potato puree can be made a day ahead.

Zucchini Pineapple Bread

Louise Malouff

Oven: 325°F. Time: 1 hour Yield: 2 loaves

3 eggs
1 cup oil
2 cups sugar
3 tsp. vanilla
2 cups grated zucchini
1 tsp. baking soda
3 cups flour
1 tsp. baking powder
1 tsp. salt
1 tsp. cinnamon
½ cup raisins
1 cup chopped nuts
8 oz. can crushed pineapple, drained

Beat eggs till fluffy. Add oil, sugar, vanilla and zucchini. Mix well. Add dry ingredients; mix well. Add raisins, nuts and pineapple. Blend all together.

Bake in 2 greased and floured loaf pans for 1 hour in 325° F. oven. Cool 10 minutes; remove from pan to cooling rack.

Del Monte Pumpkin Bread

Louise Malouff

Oven: 350°F. Time: 1½ hours Yield: 2 loaves

3 cups sugar
1 cup salad oil
4 eggs, beaten
16 oz. can Del Monte Pumpkin
3½ cups flour
2 tsp. baking soda
2 tsp. salt
1 tsp. baking powder
1 tsp. nutmeg
1 tsp. allspice
1 tsp. cinnamon
½ tsp. cloves
⅔ cup water

Cream sugar and oil together, add eggs and pumpkin. Mix well.
Sift together dry ingredients. Add dry ingredients alternately with
water. Pour into two well-greased floured 9 x 5 loaf pans. Bake
at 350°F. for 1½ hours or until tests done. Let stand 10 minutes.
Remove from pans to cool.

Main Dishes

Albondigas (Tuna Patties)
Adriana Khalife
Yield: 10 to 12 patties

2 medium russet potatoes, diced or mashed
4 green onions, sliced thin
3 eggs
2 cans tuna fish, drained
¼ cup cilantro, chopped
Salt and pepper to taste

Boil potatoes for about 10–15 minutes or until you can easily pierce with a fork. Drain, cool and remove skin.

In a medium bowl, combine potatoes, canned tuna, green onions and cilantro. Add salt and pepper and season to taste.

In two smaller bowls, separate three egg yolks from their whites. Reserve the yolks. Whisk the whites until slightly foamy. Add in the yolks and whisk to incorporate. Add the eggs to the potato mixture. The mixture will be slightly wet and loose.

In a non-stick sauté pan, over medium-high heat, use a ¼ cup measuring cup to spoon out some of the batter into the pan. Use the back of the cup to flatten out the patties. Cook about 3–4 minutes per side, or until firm and golden brown. Remove from pan and keep warm.

Optional Additions:

Make patties with a little dried shrimp powder.

Deep fry them.

Don't peel potatoes to add fiber.

Use ¼ package of Lipton Onion and Mushroom mix instead of salt and pepper.

Make a sauce by blending red peppers, garlic, tomatoes, parsley, and oil, or use ketchup or tartar sauce.

Beef Shawarma
Susan Rizzo
Oven: 350°F. Prep Time: 120 minutes
Cooking Time: 60 minutes Yield: 6 servings

2 lb. beef roast, cut into thin fajita-like strips
2 white or yellow onions, cut in slices
1 tomato, cut in slices

Marinade

3 tomatoes, cut in slices
1 cup apple cider vinegar
¼ cup olive oil
2 tsp. 7 spices
½ tsp. cinnamon
¼ tsp. ground nutmeg
¼ tsp. black pepper
1½ tsp. salt

Tahini sauce

½ cup Tahini (sesame paste)
1 clove garlic, crushed (or more if you like your tahini garlicky)
½ cup water
4 Tbsp. lemon juice
½ tsp. salt

Garnish

1 cup chopped parsley
1 tsp. sumac

In a bowl, place the meat strips and all the marinade ingredients together. Mix well and marinade in the refrigerator for at least 2 hours.

Transfer the beef and its marinade onto a baking tray, mix in the onion slices and layer with the tomato slices on top.

Cover the tray with aluminum foil and place it in the oven on medium heat for 1 hour or until the meat is well done.

To prepare the tahini sauce: With a spoon, mix the tahini with water until you get a smooth texture. Add the crushed garlic, lemon juice, and salt. Mix again until you get a fluid sauce. Adjust lemon and salt to taste.

Beef shawarma is served with chopped fresh parsley sprinkled with sumac, along with tahini sauce and pita bread.

Note: You can replace ¼ cup of the apple cider vinegar with ½ cup of red wine.

Broccoli Quiche

Kathy Birkner

Oven: 350° F. Time: 40 minutes Yield: 6 servings

1 whole wheat pie crust 9" or 10" (see Never Fail Pie Crust, p. 337)
1 cup broccoli, cooked and chopped
½ cup onion, chopped and sautéed
3–4 oz. ham, finely chopped
6 oz. Swiss cheese, shredded
2 eggs + 2 egg whites
8 oz. can fat-free evaporated milk or 1 cup Half and Half

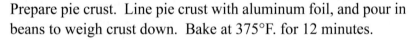

Prepare pie crust. Line pie crust with aluminum foil, and pour in beans to weigh crust down. Bake at 375°F. for 12 minutes.

Meanwhile prepare broccoli, then put in a medium bowl; then add ham and cheese. Sauté onion until translucent, then add to broccoli mixture and mix well. Spoon into pie crust.

Beat eggs and egg whites together. Add milk. Mix well; then pour over broccoli ham mixture.

Place quiche on a piece of foil in 350°F. oven for about 40 minutes or until middle is no longer liquid. If crust begins to get too brown, cover crust with foil. Serve with a salad.

Belgian Beef
Susan Rizzo
Prep Time: 30 minutes Cooking Time: 120 minutes
Yield: 6 servings

4.5 lb. stewing beef, cut into medium cubes
6 onions, thinly sliced
1 tsp. salt
½ tsp. black pepper
4 cups dried prunes
6 tablespoons olive oil, or more if needed
Red wine or water to cover meat (really much better using wine)
3–4 slices of white bread
Several Tbsp. of stone ground spicy mustard
Cooked rice or egg noodles (enough for 6 servings)

In a large saucepan heat olive oil, add meat cubes and fry on medium heat until meat starts changing color. Add onions, salt, and pepper. Pour enough water or red wine to cover meat and stir.

Bring to a boil, then cover and lower the heat to a gentle simmer. Cook until the meat is tender and the liquid has thickened and reduced. This could take up to 2 hours; add more water or red wine, if needed. When the meat has cooked for about 1 hour, add the prunes and stir well.

Cook until the prunes get very soft. Butter slices of bread with the mustard and place mustard side down on top of meat. Continue cooking while preparing rice or egg noodles.

To serve: Stir meat, prunes and bread together in pan. Place the meat mixture on top of rice or noodles on individual plates.

Braised Lamb Shanks

Susan Rizzo

Oven: 400° F. Total Time: 4 hours Cook: 3 hour Yield: 4 servings

Extra virgin olive oil
4 lamb shanks (each about 1¼ pounds; 1 shank is a portion)
Kosher salt
1 large Spanish onion or 2 small yellow onions, diced into 1" pieces
3 carrots, peeled and cut into ½" diced
3 celery ribs, cut into ½" diced
4 cloves garlic
12 oz. can tomato paste
2 cups hearty red wine
2 Tbsp. finely, chopped rosemary leaves
10 to 12 thyme branches tied together in a bundle
3 to 4 cups water
4 bay leaves

Coat a large Dutch oven generously with olive oil and bring to a high heat. Season the shanks generously with salt, and then add them to the pan. Brown well on all sides. This is an incredibly important step; do not rush it.

Meanwhile, purée the onions, carrots, celery, and garlic in a food processor until it becomes a coarse paste. Remove and set aside.

Remove the shanks from the pan to a sheet tray. Discard the excess fat from the pan. Add a little more oil to coat the bottom of the pan and add the puréed veggies. Season with salt, to taste. Sauté the veggies until they are very brown and aromatic, about 20 minutes. The brown veggies should form a sort of crust on the bottom of the pan. Do not let this burn; it is where a lot of the flavor is! Don't rush this step either, since this is where you will develop the brown color and flavor.

Add the tomato paste and brown for 5 minutes. Stir in the wine, chopped rosemary and thyme bundle. Stir frequently and cook until the wine has reduced by about half. *(continue on next page)*

Add the shanks back to the pot and pour in 3 to 4 cups of water. The shanks should be submersed. If they are not, add more water. Add the bay leaves to the pan, cover with a lid or foil, and put in the preheated oven. The cooking time will be about 2½ to 3 hours. Turn the shanks over about halfway through the cooking time. Check the shanks every 45 minutes or so. If the liquid has reduced too much, add more water. De-fat as you go.

Remove the lid or foil the last 30 minutes of cooking time for maximum browning. When the shanks are done the meat should be incredibly tender and flavorful. Transfer to serving plates and serve with Lebanese Rice or Iraqi Biryani.

Cathy's Shrimp Creole

Cathy Van Delden

Yield: 3–4 servings

1 lb. of medium to large shrimp, peeled and de-veined
4 Tbsp. butter
½ cup bell pepper, diced
½ cup green onions, chopped
1 cup celery, chopped
½ tsp. sage
1 tsp. salt
¼ tsp. tabasco
1 cup tomato sauce or V8 juice
4 cups of steamed rice

Sauté the vegetables in butter until tender. Add salt, sage, Tabasco, and tomato sauce. Bring to a boil, then add shrimp. Cook until pink in color or about 2 minutes (Overcooking the shrimp makes them tough.) Serve over rice immediately.

Note: Serve extra Tabasco sauce on the side for those who like it spicier. Enjoy!

Pecan Chicken

Kathy Birkner

2–3 cups chicken, cooked and diced
½ cup pecans, coarsely chopped
1 cup grapes, cut in half, if large
2–3 stalks of celery, coarsely chopped (1 per cup of chicken)
1–2 tsp. poppy seeds
½ cup mayo (preferably olive oil or canola), more if needed

Combine all ingredients. Serve with crackers or bread.

Cheese Stuffed Chicken Wraps

Regina Aune

Oven: 350°F. Bake: 30–40 minutes Yield: 12 servings

6 whole chicken breasts, halved, skinned and boned
⅓ cup lemon juice
8 oz. cream cheese
½ cup green onions
½ tsp. dried tarragon
½ tsp. salt
12 slices bacon (8 oz. pkg.)
toothpicks or small skewers

Preheat oven to 350°F.

Flatten chicken pieces by pounding between slices of wax paper. Dip in lemon juice.

Combine cheese, onions, tarragon, and salt.

Place about 2 tablespoons of this mixture on each piece of chicken. Roll like a jelly roll and wrap with a slice of bacon. Secure with toothpick or skewer.

Place in a shallow 9" x 13" buttered baking dish and bake, uncovered, for about 30 to 40 minutes in 350°F. oven.

Chicken Pecan Quiche

Cathy Van Delden
Yield: 9" pie

Crust

1 cup flour
1 cup cheddar cheese, finely shredded
¾ cup pecans, finely chopped
½ tsp. salt
¼ tsp. paprika
⅓ cup vegetable oil

Filling

3 eggs or 2 eggs and 2 egg whites, beaten
8 oz. carton sour cream
¼ cup mayonnaise
½ cup chicken broth
2 cups cooked chicken
⅔ cup cheddar cheese, shredded
⅓ cup onion, minced
¼ tsp. dry dill weed
3 drops Tabasco hot sauce

Preheat oven to 350°F. Combine flour, 1 cup cheddar cheese, pecans, salt, paprika in a bowl; stir in oil and mix well. Set aside ¼th of the mixture. Press remaining mixture into the bottom and sides of a 9" quiche pan to form the crust. Prick bottom and sides of crust with a fork. Bake 10 minutes; remove from oven and set aside.

Reduce oven to 325°F. In a medium bowl combine eggs, sour cream, mayo, and chicken broth; stir to blend. Add chicken, ¼ cup cheddar cheese, onion, dill weed, and hot sauce; stir then pour mixture into prepared crust. Sprinkle remaining crumb mixture over the filling. Place pan on a foil-lined cookie sheet (in case filling spills over) and bake 45 minutes.

Note: Fill custard cups, and bake if there is too much filling.

Cheese-Mexican Soup
Candy Monsour

1 lb. ground beef
1 large onion, chopped
1 can regular corn
1 can Ranch style beans
1–2 cans chicken broth
1 can cream of chicken soup
1 can Rotel tomatoes with green chillies
1 large can diced tomatoes
1 lb. Velvetta cheese

Garnish Topping

Cream cheese. sliced or diced
Avocado, diced
Cilantro sprigs

Brown 1 pound ground beef and 1 large chopped onion. Then add corn, beans, broth, cream of chicken soup, Rotel tomatoes, and diced tomatoes; mix to combine and heat. Then add one pound of Velvetta cheese. Garnish the bowls with cream cheese, avocado, cilantro.

Note: I use large can of tomatoes instead of a regular can and another can of chicken broth so it is more soup and not so thick. You can add more broth to thin further.

Variation: You can play with the ingredients.

1) Use 2 pounds of Velvetta, so it is more cheesy.

2) Add a can of black beans.

Chicken Scallopini

Lorraine Taylor

Yield: 4 servings

2 cooked chicken breasts, cut in half
¼–½ cup all-purpose flour
1 tsp. garlic salt
½ tsp. paprika (or to taste)
¼ cup butter or margarine
3 Tbsp. water
1 Tbsp. lemon juice
¼ tsp. instant chicken bouillon
4 thin lemon slices
Parsley, snipped

Remove skin and bones from chicken breasts. Mix flour, garlic salt, and paprika. Coat chicken with flour mixture. Brown chicken in butter in 10" skillet. Remove chicken from skillet to serving platter and keep warm. Stir water, lemon juice, and instant bouillon in skillet, loosening brown particles on bottom. Add lemon slices, and heat over low heat 1 minute. Pour broth on chicken; garnish with the lemon slices and snipped parsley.

Chicken Skewers

with Lemon-Mint Vinaigrette

Helen Antonelli
Time: 30 minutes Yield: Serves 6

1 Tbsp. hot paprika
1½ tsp. minced garlic
½ tsp. dried oregano
½ tsp. ground cumin
½ cup plus ⅓ cup extra-virgin olive oil
Salt and freshly ground pepper
2 Tbsp. chopped parsley
2 Tbsp. chopped fresh mint
2 Tbsp. fresh lemon juice
2 tsp. grated lemon zest
⅛ tsp. cayenne pepper

2 lb. skinless, boneless chicken thighs cut into 1½" pieces
1 large red onion, sliced crosswise ½" thick
8 cups loosely packed washed arugula or spinach
Lemon wedges, for serving

Light a grill or preheat a grill pan. In a small bowl, mix the paprika with 1 teaspoon of the garlic, the oregano, and cumin. Whisk in ⅓ cup of the olive oil and season the paprika oil with salt and pepper.

In another small bowl, combine the parsley, mint, lemon juice, lemon zest, cayenne pepper, and the remaining ½ tsp of garlic. Whisk in the remaining ½ cup of olive oil and season the vinaigrette with salt and pepper.

Thread the chicken pieces onto 6 skewers. Brush the chicken and onion slices all over with the paprika oil and arrange on the grill. Cook the onions for 4 minutes, turning once, until they are slightly softened. Grill the chicken for 12 minutes, turning occasionally, until it is cooked through.

Arrange the arugula on a platter. Spread the onions and chicken on top, drizzle with the vinaigrette, and serve with lemon wedges.

Deep Dish Pizza
Susan Rizzo
Oven: 450° F. Cook time: 45 minutes

3½ cups flour
¼ cup cornmeal
1 pkg. (¼ oz.) active yeast
1–1½ tsp. sugar
½ tsp. salt
1 cup water
⅓ cup olive oil
4 cups of mozzarella cheese shredded
Pizza sauce (homemade or store bought)
Favorite pizza ingredients

Combine 1½ cup flour, cornmeal, yeast, sugar, and salt in large bowl. Heat water and oil to 120–130°F. (hot enough to hold little finger in water to the count of 10). Add to dry ingredients and beat until moistened. Add remaining flour to form a stiff dough. Knead 6 to 8 minutes, then place into a greased bowl; spin so oil covers dough all over. Let rise until doubled about 30–45 minutes depending on temperature of kitchen.

Divide dough in half, roll each half into a circle large enough to fit greased bottom and sides of spring-form pan.

Place 2 cups mozzarella cheese on bottom crust. Next place all your favorite pizza toppings: sausage, peperoni, olives, onions, mushrooms, green pepper etc. Spoon pizza sauce over toppings, cover with second circle of dough, seal sides and top together with fingers. Place in hot oven for 35 minutes. Check to see that the crust is browning nicely and sides are pulling away from pan. Add another cup or two of mozzarella on top place in oven again until cheese is bubbling and brown. Remove and let set for a few minutes. Then release spring form, remove bottom pan, and place on cutting board. Enjoy!

Devils' Chicken

Susan Rizzo
Prep time 1 hour 30 minutes Servings: 6

¼ cup olive oil
4 (4 oz.) boneless skin-on chicken thighs (pounded to a ¼" thickness)
Kosher salt
Freshly ground black pepper
2 garlic cloves, sliced
1 red bell pepper, thinly sliced
1 jalapeño, sliced into rings
Pinch salt
14 oz. can San Marazano crushed tomatoes (drained, but reserve
    liquid)
2 Tbsp. capers, rinsed and drained
½ cup water
½ cup roughly chopped fresh flat-leaf parsley leaves

Put a Dutch oven or deep cast iron skillet over medium-high heat. Add the olive oil to the preheated pan. Season both sides of the chicken with salt and pepper. Put the chicken skin-side down in the pan and cook until golden brown, about 2 minutes. Flip the chicken and cook for another 30 seconds. Add the garlic, bell pepper, jalapeño, and a pinch of salt, and cook for another 30 seconds.

Add ½ cup water and deglaze the pan, scraping with a wooden spoon to get up the browned bits on the bottom of the pan. Cook until the liquid is reduced by half, another minute. Add the tomatoes with juices and capers. Cover the pan, and cook for 2 minutes. Remove the pan from the heat and stir in the parsley. Taste and adjust the seasoning, adding salt and pepper as needed. Serve immediately.

Eggplant and Lamb Stew
Cook time: 2 ¼ Hours Yield: 6 servings

2 Tbsp. butter
1½ lb. lamb shoulder
2 large eggplants, peeled and chopped
2 large tomatoes, chopped
2 large onions, chopped
2 green bell peppers, chopped
10 cloves garlic, chopped
1 Tbsp. tomato paste
½ cup water
1 tsp. allspice
2 tsp. salt
1 tsp. ground black pepper

In a large pot, melt the butter over medium heat, and brown the lamb on all sides. Mix in the eggplants, tomatoes, onions, green bell peppers, and garlic. Cook and stir until tender and lightly browned.

In a small bowl, blend the tomato paste and water. Mix into the pot with the lamb. Season lamb with allspice, salt, and pepper. Reduce heat, and simmer about 1½ hours, stirring occasionally, until the meat shreds easily with a fork. Add a little water as necessary to keep the ingredients moist.

Eggplant Parmigiana

Peggy Saleh

Oven: 400° F. Cook time: 15–20 minutes or until heated through
Yield: 6 Servings

½ cup chopped onion
¼ cup finely chopped celery
1 small clove of garlic, minced
2 Tbsp. cooking oil
16 oz. can tomatoes, cut up
⅓ cup tomato paste
1 bay leaf
1 tsp. dried parsley flakes
½ tsp. salt
½ tsp. dried oregano, crushed
¼ tsp. pepper
¼ cup all-purpose flour
½ tsp. salt
1 medium eggplant, peeled and cut crosswise into ½" slices
1 beaten egg
¼ cup cooking oil
⅓ cup grated Parmesan cheese
6 oz. sliced mozzarella cheese

For tomato sauce: In saucepan cook onion, celery, and garlic in 2 tablespoons oil until vegetables are tender. Stir in undrained tomatoes, tomato paste, bay leaf, parsley, salt, oregano, and pepper. Bring to boiling; reduce heat. Boil gently, uncovered, about 15 minutes or until desired consistency, stirring occasionally. Discard bay leaf.

Combine flour and ½ teaspoon of salt. Dip eggplant slices into beaten egg, then into flour mixture. In large skillet brown eggplant, half at a time, in ¼ cup cooking oil about 3 minutes on each side, adding additional cooking oil as needed. Drain well on paper towels. (Continue on next page.)

Arrange a single layer of eggplant in bottom of 10" x 6" x 2" baking dish, cutting slices to fit. Top with half of the Parmesan cheese, half of the sauce, and half of the mozzarella cheese. Cut remaining mozzarella into triangles. Repeat the layers of eggplant, Parmesan, tomato sauce and mozzarella. Bake uncovered in 400°F. oven for 15 to 20 minutes or until heated through.

Fresh Mushroom Bisque

½ stick butter (about 4 Tbsp.)
1 clove garlic, minced
½ cup minced onion
5 Tbsp. flour and blend into a béchamel sauce
1 can chicken broth
2 boxes fresh sliced mushrooms
1 pint (16 oz.) heavy cream
Salt and pepper to taste
Parsley, minced
1 Tbsp. olive oil

Melt better, then sauté onion, then add garlic until clear. Add the flour and blend into a béchamel sauce; set aside.

Sauté the mushrooms in a little oil until soft. Then add chicken broth, stir together. Add the reserved béchamel sauce mixture, and heavy cream; mix. Add salt and pepper to taste. Sprinkle with minced parsley before serving.

Fusilli Pasta
in Balsamic Vinaigrette

Helen Antonelli

1 Tbsp. Dijon mustard
2–3 cloves garlic, minced
Red pepper flakes to taste
¼ cup balsamic vinegar
1 tsp. sugar
Salt and freshly ground black pepper, to taste
¾ cup olive oil, divided

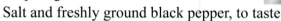

1 lb. fusilli
1 sweet yellow or red pepper, chopped
6 green onions, sliced thin
1–2 small zucchini, cut in small cubes
½ cup Greek olives (such as Kalamata), cut in small pieces
½ cup small artichoke hearts (not marinated), cut in bite size pieces
¼ cup sun-dried tomatoes in oil, drained and chopped
¾ cup Parmesan cheese, freshly grated
1 cup chopped fresh basil leaves, or 1 Tbsp. dried basil
½–¾ cup pine nuts

In a jar with a tightly fitting lid, place mustard, garlic, red pepper flakes, balsamic vinegar, sugar, salt, pepper, and one-half (½) cup of olive oil. Cover and shake hard. Set aside.

Cook fusilli as directed on package, al dente. Drain and toss with one-fourth (¼) cup olive oil. Cool to room temperature, stirring occasionally.

To the cooled pasta: Add yellow or red peppers, green onions, zucchini, olives, artichoke hearts, tomatoes, Parmesan cheese and basil. Add the vinaigrette sauce and toss gently but thoroughly. Cover and let stand at room temperature for at least 2 hours.

To serve: Garnish with more Parmesan cheese, a handful of pine nuts, strips of sweet peppers, olives—whatever strikes your fancy.

Note: A cold specialty that is delightful for lunch.

Goldrush Brunch

Regina Aune

Yield: 8 servings

Oven: 350°F. Cook Time: 20 minutes & 10–12 minutes

5½ oz. pkg. dry hash brown potatoes with onions
4 Tbsp. butter or margarine
¼ cup all-purpose flour
½ tsp. salt
⅛ tsp. pepper
2 cups of milk
1 cup sour cream
2 Tbsp. snipped fresh parsley (dry parsley works too)
8 (¼") slices of Canadian bacon
8 eggs

Prepare potatoes according to the package directions and set aside.

In a 3-quart saucepan, melt the butter and blend in the flour, salt, and pepper; add flour, mixing well. Add milk all at once; cook and stir until thick and bubbly. Remove from heat. Stir in sour cream, parsley, and hash browns. Turn mixture into a 13" x 9" x 2" dish.

Arrange bacon slices in a row down the center, overlapping slightly. Bake uncovered at 350°F. for 20 minutes.

Remove from oven and make four depressions on each side of the bacon; slip one egg into each depression.

Sprinkle with salt and pepper. Return to 350° F. oven for 10–12 minutes or until eggs are set.

Fried Fish or Chicken
Kathy Birkner

Buttermilk (to cover)
Chicken or fish in quantity desired
½ cup self-rising flour *per piece of chicken or fish*
¼–½ tsp. salt (to taste)
¼ tsp. black pepper (to taste)
Oil

Place your prepared fish or chicken in a glass bowl. Cover with buttermilk and let marinade for at least 2 hours. The buttermilk tenderizes and freshens the fish or chicken.

Preheat oil to 400°F. When ready to fry, depending on the amount of chicken or fish you are preparing, use about a ½ cup of self-rising flour per piece of chicken (like chicken breast) or fish along with ¼ to ½ teaspoon of salt and black pepper or to taste; place flour seasoning in a large plastic bag. Remove chicken or fish from buttermilk and place into plastic bag, shake to cover. Fry until done.

Jo's Meat Paste
Jo Tompkins

Chunk bologna (to your taste)
Chunk cheese (to your taste)
Pickle relish or sweet pickles (to your taste)
Mayonnaise (to your taste)
Put into blender and mix.

Scaling a fish is easier if vinegar is rubbed on the scales first. When grilling fish, the rule of thumb is to cook 5 minutes on each side per inch of thickness. Before grilling, rub with oil to seal in moisture.

Hamburger Casserole

Louise Malouff

Oven: 350° F. Yield: 8–10 Servings

2 pkg. mixed vegetables
1 lb. ground beef
¼ cup onion, minced
1 can mushroom soup
½ cup milk or water
Bread crumbs, crushed potato chips or mashed potatoes.

Cook 2 packages of mixed vegetables, according to package directions.

Fry ground beef, mashing into small pieces. Add minced onion. Add 1 can mushroom soup and ½ cup milk or water. Simmer for a few minutes and add cooked vegetables. Leave in skillet or turn into greased casserole. Top with buttered crumbs, potato chips or mashed potatoes.

Heat thoroughly in moderate oven 350° F. until top is browned.

Homemade
German Noodles with Cabbage
Susan Rizzo
Prep time 30–60 minutes Servings: 6

Noodle Batter

3 cups all-purpose flour
4 whole eggs
½ cup milk
2 Tbsp. whole grain mustard
Salt
Freshly ground black pepper (to taste)

Beat the eggs, mustard, and milk together; then season well with salt and pepper. Add the flour and bring together to form a sticky batter. Dampen a small cutting board with water, then spread the noodle batter in a 2" wide line down the board. (If it spreads some during resting process, it's okay.) Place in refrigerate and let it rest for two hours.

Cabbage Mix

4 Tbsp. butter
1 head green cabbage, cored and diced
1 yellow onion, diced
Flat leaf parsley, chopped for garnish

Bring a large pot of salted water to a boil. Place a large sauté pan over medium heat. When the pan is hot, add the butter along with the onion and a pinch of salt cooking until soft and trans-lucent, about 10 minutes. Add the cabbage and mix to coat with the onions and butter. Add another pinch of salt and some freshly ground black pepper then cook until the cabbage is soft. While the cabbage is cooking, start to cook your noodles.

Hold the cutting board over the pot of boiling water, and with a scraper, cut one-fourth (¼") wide strips from the line of batter into the boiling water. Cook until the noodles floats, then another

30 seconds more. Remove the noodles from the water with a slotted spoon and add them to the cabbage mixture. Continue this process until all of the batter is used. Thoroughly mix everything together and serve, garnished with freshly chopped parsley.

Helpful Tips: The dough should be tacky because this type of noodle or spaetzle is wetter than a regular pasta dough. If you live in a German community, you may even be able to find a spaetzle press in order to make true spaetzle. Keep your hands wet so the dough doesn't stick.

Honey Juice Chicken

Regina Aune

Time: 1 hour+ Yield: Serves 8

8 boneless and skinless chicken breasts
1 cup pancake mix
1 tsp. salt
½ tsp. pepper
¼ cup shortening or vegetable oil
½ cup honey
6 oz. orange juice

Mix dry ingredients together then coat chicken pieces. Brown chicken pieces in frying pan using the shortening or vegetable oil. As soon as the pieces are browned (20–30 minutes), mix the honey and orange juice together and pour over the chicken pieces. Cover the pan and cook the chicken over low heat for 45 minutes, basting the pieces with the sauce and turning periodically. Remove from heat and garnish with fresh parsley and orange slices.

Note: If a thicker sauce is wanted, use more honey; for thinner sauce, use more orange juice.

Variation: Pineapple chunks can be added to the sauce.

Manicotti (Crepe Style)

with Spinach Filling
Margaret Mauriello Perillo
Bake: 350°F. Time: 20 minutes Yield 16-18 Crepes

Crepes:

3 eggs
1 cup water
1 cup sifted flour
Pinch of salt

Beat eggs slightly; add water, salt and flour gradually. Whisk gently until batter is smooth without lumps or excessive bubbles.

Grease a 5" or 6" iron skillet with a ½ teaspoon of oil. Use a paper towel to coat the pan evenly. Continue to oil skillet to avoid sticking. You may try a spray oil. (If you have a crepe pan, follow manufacturer's directions for a 5–6" crepe) Heat pan to medium high heat.

Drop 1½ tablespoons of batter into pan. Spread batter evenly by lifting the pan by the handle and swirling the batter until it coats the surface completely creating a thin even pancake. Cook until set and lightly brown. Do not overcook. Cook only on one side.

Let pancake cool briefly. Place pancake on a plate separating each pancake with waxed paper. Repeat until all batter is finished.

The pancakes may be kept in refrigerator covered with plastic wrap until ready for filling. Before filling, let pancakes stand at room temperature for about 1 hour. Batter for crepes may be made ahead of time and frozen until ready for use.

Spinach Filling

2 boxes frozen chopped spinach or 2 lb. fresh spinach chopped
1¾ lb. ricotta or small curd cottage cheese
5 Tbsp. grated Parmesan cheese
1 tsp. salt
2 whole eggs
5 Tbsp. Italian flavored bread crumbs

Boil or microwave spinach as directed on package, or steam fresh spinach about 10 minutes. Drain spinach thoroughly. Set aside briefly to cool before adding to other ingredients.

When cool add spinach, eggs, bread crumbs, and salt to the cheese. Mix well, but gently to combine all ingredients. Let mixture rest for two hours before filling the crepes.

Tomato base

2 cups of prepared tomato or tomato-meat sauce

Spread tomatoes or meat sauce on the bottom of baking pan.

To fill the crepes: Put 2–3 tablespoons of the cheese mixture on the cooked side of the pancake and roll crepe over filling, placing the seam side down in pan.

Spoon tomato sauce generously over the pan of crepes covering well to avoid burning or drying out during the cooking process. Sprinkle Parmesan over the crepes before serving.

Variation: For a lower salt option, try a grated mozzarella.

Note: Adapt this batter for dessert crepes by adding 2 tablespoons of sugar and dash of vanilla extract to batter. Cook to light brown on both sides of the crepe. Allow to cool and fill with fresh fruit, cream cheese, Nutella, or other filling of your choice. Crepes are light, yet durable, and can be used on short notice.

Monterey Beef Rice Skillet

Louise Malouff

Time: 30 minutes

1 lb. ground beef
1 cup Uncle Ben's Rice (Converted)
2½ cups water
2 tsp. salt
1 cup chopped onion
3 oz. pkg. cream cheese, cubed
15 oz. can tomato sauce
1 tsp. chili powder

Brown beef in 10" skillet, then drain. Stir in rice, water, salt and onion. Bring to boil, reduce heat. Cover. Cook over low heat until water is absorbed, about 25 minutes. Stir in cubed cream cheese till softened. Combine tomato sauce and chili powder and stir into the rice mixture. Cover and heat 5 minutes or until hot.

Sprinkle beef with Hungarian paprika after piercing with a fork to tenderize meat plus the beef will turn golden brown when cooked.

Moroccan Lamb Kabobs
Preheat outdoor grill Yield: 6 servings

2 lb. ground lamb
1 cup raisins
5 oz. goat cheese
⅓ cup mayonnaise
1 red onion, finely chopped
1 clove garlic, finely chopped
2 Tbsp. fresh cilantro, chopped
¾ Tbsp. ground cayenne pepper
½ tsp. ground cumin
½ tsp. ground coriander
Salt to taste
Coarsely ground black pepper to taste

Preheat outdoor grill for high heat and lightly oil grate.

In a medium bowl mix together ground lamb, raisins, goat cheese, mayonnaise, red onion, garlic, cilantro, cayenne pepper, cumin, coriander, salt and black pepper.

Divide the mixture into approximately 6 even portions and press around skewers.

Place skewers on grill. Cook approximately 4 minutes per side or until the cheese has melted, the raisins are tender and lamb reached desired doneness.

Note: This is a magnificent sweet and spicy lamb recipe. Serve with warm pita bread with a mixed greens (use some strongly flavored ones) and fresh herbs. Drizzle with lemon and herb yogurt sauce or a tzatziki sauce. Increase cayenne and other spices to suit individual tastes.

Northern Pork Roast

Theresa Birkner

Oven: 300°F. Time: 2–3 hours

1½–2 lb. pork roast
2 (15 oz.) cans sauerkraut, undrained including juice

Place roast in a deep dish oven-proof baking pan. Pour sauerkraut over top. Bake at 300°F. for 2–3 hours until pork is completely done. Thermometer temperature should be 165°F.

Allow to rest 15 minutes after removing from oven, then slice. Serve with sauerkraut with juice ladled over pork and mashed potatoes.

Chicken Cutlets

4 boneless, skinless chicken breasts
½ tsp. salt or to taste
¼ tsp. pepper or to taste
2 Tbsp. flour
1 Tbsp. olive oil
½ cup slivered almonds
½ cup chicken broth or dry white wine
4 Tbsp. unsalted butter
¼ cup green onions, chopped

Pound each chicken breast between 2 sheets of plastic wrap with a meat mallet or rolling pin until ½" thick. Season with salt and pepper.

Place flour in a shallow dish and dredge both sides of each cutlet in flour. Heat oil in large sauté pan over medium-high. Arrange cutlets in pan and sauté until browned on each side about 5–7 minutes total. Remove cutlets from pan, and keep warm. Add almonds to pan and sauté until toasted, about 3 minutes. Deglaze pan with wine, scraping browned bits from bottom of pan. Simmer until wine thickens slightly or about 3 minutes. Stir in butter until melted and sauce thickens, then add green onions to sauce. Pour the sauce pouring evenly over chicken pieces. Serve with rice.

Oven Fried Chicken Parmesan
Regina Aune
Oven: 350°F. Yield: 3-4 servings

½ cup (2 oz.) grated or shredded Parmesan cheese
2 lbs. chicken breast tenderloins
1 egg, slightly beaten
1 Tbsp. milk
¼ cup squeezable margarine
½ tsp. salt
⅛ tsp. pepper
1 tsp. paprika

Combine the cheese and salt and pepper. Combine the egg with milk; dip chicken pieces in the combined egg and milk mixture, and then coat with the cheese mixture. Place in a baking dish and pour the margarine over the chicken. Sprinkle paprika on the chicken. Bake at 350°F. for one hour or until tender.

Paella

Candy Monsour
Oven: 350° F. Time: 60 minutes

Olive oil
2 cloves garlic, chopped
1 onion, chopped
½ of green pepper, chopped
3 cups rice
1 pkg. cut-up chicken breasts
1 lb. pork, cut up
1 lb. smoked sausage cut on diagonal
6 cups chicken broth
2 Tbsp. lemon juice
2 pkg. Goya Sazons seasoning
1 small jar pimentos, diced
10 oz. pkg. frozen green peas
3 lemons, cut in 6 wedges

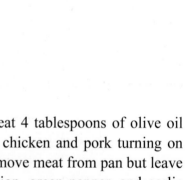

In a large stove top paella pan, heat 4 tablespoons of olive oil over medium high heat, then add chicken and pork turning on all sides sautéing until brown. Remove meat from pan but leave drippings. In same pan, sauté onion, green pepper, and garlic until soft. Add the 3 cups of rice and sauté until rice starts to look clear. Take off fire, and spread rice mixture evenly in the pan. Arrange the reserved chicken and pork on top of the rice.

In separate bowl mix chicken broth, Goya seasoning, and 2 tablespoons of lemon juice; heat. Pour mixture over the meat and rice. It may only take 5 cups and you can add the rest later while cooking. Cover tightly with foil and bake for about 40 minutes or until liquid is absorbed. Remove from oven and arrange the sliced sausage, peas and pimento over it. Cover again and bake for 15 more minutes.

Remove from oven and let set 10 min. Garnish with lemon wedges around the sides of pan and serve.

Pasta Shells with Meat Sauce
Mary Ann Karam

1 lb. lean gound beef
¼ of a large or 1 small onion, diced
8 oz. can tomato sauce
12 oz. pkg. medium or large shells
2 Tbsp. allspice
3 cans or 24 oz. water
Salt and pepper to taste

Dice and sauté onions, brown meat, then mix all together in 3-5 qt. pot adding tomato sauce, water and spices, bring to a boil on high heat then lower to low-medium heat for sauce to thicken a bit. In the meantime, boil the pasta shells, drain and add to meat and sauce mixture on medium heat for about 15 minutes; turn off and remove from burner so that pasta and meat sauce mixture will have a chance to blend well before serving.

Pumpkin Crab Bisque
Patricia Magazzu

5 cups chicken broth
2 Tbsp. butter
1 cup onion, chopped
2 cups mashed pumpkin or squash
2 cups Half & Half
2 cups or 1 lb. crab meat
Pinch cayenne pepper
Nutmeg
Salt and pepper to taste

Sauté onion in butter in large saucepan. Add mashed pumpkin and chicken broth. Simmer 30 minutes. Cool slightly; blend. Slowly add half and half, crab meat, and seasonings. *Do not boil*...just heat well.

Sausage Rice Casserole

Kathy Birkner

Yield: About 1½ quarts

1 1b. low fat sausage (use HEB blue pkg.)
1 cup converted (parboiled) rice, uncooked (Like Uncle Ben's)
1 can whole green chiles, chopped
8 oz. light sour cream
8 oz. Monterrey jack cheese, shredded
Anaheim pepper, chopped (optional)

Cook sausage in frying pan until thoroughly cooked. If adding Anaheim pepper, add to sausage when sausage is about half-cooked. Drain sausage and remove excess fat with paper towel. Then, put sausage in a large glass bowl.

While sausage is cooking, add 1 cup of rice to 2¼ cups of water. Microwave for about 20 minutes or until done, then add to sausage.

While rice is cooking, open can green chiles, chop finely, and add to large glass bowl. Then add sour cream and cheese.

After all of the ingredients are added, mix thoroughly. Put large glass bowl in microwave and heat about 6–8 minutes until melted. Serve while hot.

Granulated Kelp is an alternative for salt. Kelp is low in sodium, and gives foods the taste of salt.

Sergio's Spaghetti
Susan Rizzo

1 bulb garlic, peeled and chopped fine (yes, one whole bulb)
1 can crushed tomatoes (26–28 oz.)
1 can diced tomatoes (14–16 oz.)
1 box spaghetti noodles (16 oz.)
Olive oil
Sugar to taste

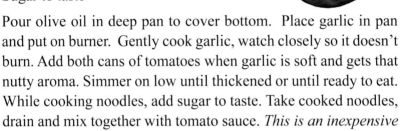

Pour olive oil in deep pan to cover bottom. Place garlic in pan and put on burner. Gently cook garlic, watch closely so it doesn't burn. Add both cans of tomatoes when garlic is soft and gets that nutty aroma. Simmer on low until thickened or until ready to eat. While cooking noodles, add sugar to taste. Take cooked noodles, drain and mix together with tomato sauce. *This is an inexpensive dish to make, is fast, and feeds many for very little.*

Shrimp and Grits
Regina Aune
Yield: Serves 5

1 lb. shrimp, peeled and cleaned
1 cup herb and garlic marinade (or enough to cover shrimp)
¾ cup extra-sharp Cheddar cheese, cubed
5 cups boiling water
1¼ cups grits
1½ tsp. salt
¼ stick butter

Place shrimp in a container, then cover with commercial herb and garlic marinade, refrigerate for several hours or overnight.

Mix grits, salt and butter in boiling water and cook mixture until almost serving consistency. Stir in cubed extra-sharp Cheddar cheese. Cook until cheese is partially melted.

Add drained shrimp, and cook only until the shrimp are heated through.

Shredded Chicken
Yield: 6 servings

3 boneless, skinless chicken breasts (best if slightly frozen)
4 tsp. cornstarch
3 tsp. soy sauce
1 Tbsp. white wine
1 egg white, slightly beaten
5 Tbsp. olive oil
3–4 carrots, shredded
1 bunch green onions, cut in ½" slices
½ tsp. powdered ginger
1 tsp. sugar
2 Tbsp. cold water

Slice the chicken breasts horizontally and paper thin with a very sharp knife. Place in a bowl. Combine 2 teaspoons soy sauce, 2 teaspoons cornstarch with wine and egg white, then pour over chicken and let stand for 30–45 minutes.

Heat 1 tablespoon of oil, then sauté carrots for 30 seconds. Add green onions, sauté 30 seconds; then remove vegetables from pan. Add rest of oil to pan. Remove chicken from marinade, then add to pan cooking until the chicken turns white and shreds. Add ginger, sugar, reserved vegetables, and teaspoon of soy sauce cooking until heated through.

Mix 2 teaspoons cornstarch with 2 tablespoons of cold water. Stir into chicken until all ingredients are coated with a clear glaze. Serve with rice.

Shrimp Pasta Salad

Elmosa Herrera

1st Day:

1 pkg. foot long (12 oz.) vermicelli

Cook, drain and dice vermicelli. Toss with 2 teaspoons minced garlic. Cover and refrigerate overnight.

2nd Day:

Add to the vermicelli:

1 stalk celery, diced
1 bunch green onions, died
1½ lb. boiled shrimp, peeled and diced
2 cups mayonnaise (thinned with 1 tsp. lemon juice & 1 Tbsp. milk)
1 small pkg. frozen peas, thawed and drained (cook per package
      directions or use canned peas.)
Salt and pepper to taste.

Serve on lettuce with crackers or crisp bread sticks.

Homemade Mushroom Soup Stock

2 c. frozen mushroom stems
2 c. frozen vegetable scraps (onion /shallot skins, carrot and
      celery trimmings, etc.)
3 sprigs parsley, chopped
1 garlic clove, minced
1 bay leaf
8 c. water

Combine all ingredients in large Dutch oven or stock pot. Bring to a boil, then reduce heat to low. Simmer partially covered for 45 minutes; remove lid and simmer uncovered for 30 minutes more. Allow stock to cool, then pour through a fine mesh strainer into a bowl. Press vegetable scraps against the strainer with a wooden spoon in order to extract as much stock as possible. Discard solids and store stock in a plastic container or freezer bag.

Shrimp Creole
Thelma L. O'Shaughnessy

2 cups shrimp, more or less
1 can OR ½ lb. mushrooms, sliced
1 medium onion, minced
¼ cup celery, minced
1½ Tbsp. bell pepper, diced
1 can tomatoes
1 small bottle stuffed olives
1 tsp. butter
2 tsp. flour
½ tsp. salt
¼ tsp. paprika
1 tsp. Worchestershire Sauce
¾ cup liquid (mushroom soup stock juice, store bought or see
    previous page for homemade mushroom soup stock)
Dash red pepper flakes

Melt butter, then cook celery, onions, and bell pepper until onions are clear. Add flour, then the liquid. Stir until it thickens, then add other ingredients and simmer for one-half hour.

Serve with well-cooked rice. The above seasoning is fairly mild and should be adjusted to taste.

Spaghetti

with Chickpeas & Roasted Cauliflower

Susan Rizzo

Oven: 425°F. Prep Time: 1 hour Serves: 4–6

1 head cauliflower, cut into florets
Olive oil, for drizzling plus about 4 Tbsp.
Salt and pepper
3 Tbsp. rosemary, chopped
1 lb. spaghetti
4 flat filets of anchovies
5 to 6 cloves garlic
1 tsp. crushed red pepper flakes
28 oz. can chickpeas, rinsed and drained, divided
1 cup chicken stock
½ cup flat-leaf parsley, chopped
Freshly grated Parmigiano-Reggiano cheese

Heat oven to 425°F. Toss the cauliflower with a little olive oil and season with salt, pepper, and rosemary (my family likes less rosemary and more garlic and anchovies). Transfer to oven and roast until caramelized at edges and tender, 25 minutes.

Bring a large pot of water to a boil for the pasta. Salt water and cook the pasta to al dente. Reserve ½ cup starchy cooking water just before draining.

Heat 4 tablespoons olive oil, 4 turns of the pan, over medium heat. Melt anchovies into oil. Add the garlic and lower heat a bit; stir in red pepper flakes.

In a blender or food processor purée half the chickpeas with the stock. Add to the pan with the anchovies and garlic. Add remaining whole chickpeas to the sauce.

Toss pasta in starchy water and chickpea sauce. Add roasted cauliflower to pasta and serve on warm dishes topped with cheese.

Tikki Chicken

Candy Monsour

Active Time: 20 minutes Total Time: 1 hour Yield: 4 servings

Put some spice in your life:
An Indian classic without all the work, but kept the fun.

Chicken

1 cup plain yogurt
2 Tbsp. lemon juice
1 tsp. cinnamon
1 tsp. paprika
½ tsp. cayenne pepper
¼ tsp. black pepper
1 tsp. salt
1½ lb. boneless, skinless chicken breast, cut into 2" pieces

Sauce

2 tsp. minced garlic
2 Tbsp. butter
1 tsp. cumin
1 tsp. paprika
1 tsp. salt
8 oz. can tomato sauce
1 cup heavy cream
1 box frozen green peas

Garnishes

3 Tbsp. chopped cilantro
Jasmine rice
Naan (Indian flatbread)

Whisk yogurt, lemon juice, cinnamon, paprika, cayenne, pepper, and salt. Add chicken, stir, and set aside for 30 minutes. Discard marinade. Oven broil chicken until done. While chicken is broiling, make sauce.

To make sauce: Melt butter in a frying pan, then add garlic, cook garlic in butter for 2 minutes. Add cumin, paprika, and salt, continue cooking about 1 minute. Stir in tomato sauce and cream, then simmer, stirring, until the sauce is thick. Add frozen green peas, and cook for a couple of minutes. Set aside until chicken is done.

Stir into sauce. Top with cilantro. Serve with jasmine rice and naan.

Tortilla Soup
Dora Cuellar

2 chicken breasts with bone
2 chicken bouillon cubes
1 tsp. salt
¼ tsp. black pepper
¼ tsp. garlic powder
¼ tsp. onion powder or 3–4 green onions, chopped
¼ bundle of fresh cilantro, using only the leaves
Mozzarella cheese, shredded (to taste)
Avocado
Tortillas

Cook chicken in 3–4 quarts of water and add a chicken bouillon cube. Cook until done. Take chicken out and allow to cool. Save chicken stock. Debone the chicken and cut into cubes. Add to stock. Add salt, pepper, cilantro, garlic powder, and onions to the stock.

Cut tortillas into strips. Sprinkle the tortillas with mozzarella cheese. Add chicken and broth. Put slice of avocado to garnish with a few tortilla strips.

Turkish Ravioli

Helen Antonelli

Oven: 350°F. Time: 20–30 minutes Serves: 6

2 cups yogurt
4–5 cloves garlic
Salt to taste
2 large onions, finely chopped
11 Tbsp. butter, divided
1 lb. ground lamb or beef
Pepper to taste
40 wonton skins (available in Oriental foods or produce section
    at your grocery)
2 Tbsp. tomato paste
2 tsp. paprika, divided
Pinch or more of cayenne pepper

In a small bowl mix yogurt, garlic, and salt to taste. Set aside.

In a 10" frying pan over medium heat, sauté onion in 2 tablespoons of the butter until wilted. Add lamb and stir until the pink
is gone. Add salt and pepper to taste. Drain in a colander. Set
aside 1 cup of lamb.

Moisten edges of a wonton skin with water. Place 1 teaspoon of
lamb filling in the center. Pinch together two opposite corners.
Repeat with the other two corners. Securely seal the four sets of
facing edges to make a neat package with star-line seams.

Slide the ravioli into a large pan of salted, simmering water and
poach for 6–7 minutes (8 minutes, if you put them in frozen).
Lift out with a slotted spoon to a shallow 9" x 13"ovenproof casserole that can go to the table. Keep warm.

In a small pan, place the reserved lamb filling and 4 tablespoons
of butter, tomato paste, and 1 teaspoon paprika. Stir over medium
low heat for 10 minutes. Spoon it over and between the ravioli,
distributing it evenly.

In a small pan melt 5 tablespoons of butter with 1 teaspoon paprika and the cayenne pepper. Keep warm. If the yogurt mixture is cold, warm it to room temperature and then spread it over the hot ravioli. Drizzle hot paprika butter over all. Serve hot.

Advance preparation tips:
To freeze: Freeze filled, uncooked ravioli on a cookie sheet, then package in a freezer bag. Package reserved cup of lamb and freeze. Poach frozen ravioli for 8 minutes. Defrost lamb earlier in day and add to pan when making tomato paste sauce.

To prepare early in the day: Poach 2–4 hours ahead and place ravioli in the casserole with the meat sauce. Hold at room temperature unless the kitchen is very hot. To finish, cover loosely with foil and heat in a preheated 350°F. oven for 20–30 minutes or until bubbling at the edges and heated through. Top with yogurt sauce and paprika butter and serve hot.

Venison Stroganoff
Cathy Van Delden

1 pkg. Lipton onion soup mix
4 oz. can whole mushrooms
½ stick butter
1½ to 2 lb. venison ham steak, cut into cubes
8 oz. small carton sour cream

Brown venison in butter. Stir in onion soup mix and mushrooms with water to barely cover. Simmer about 45 minutes.

Just before serving, stir in sour cream. Serve over rice or noodles. Enjoy!

Note: *Do not salt...salt in onion mix is enough.*

Water Street's Shrimp Picayune
Candy Monsour
Yield: 3-4 servings

2 lb. large shrimp

Sauce

1 cup olive oil
¾ cup clarified butter (directions follow)
½ cup liquid brown sugar
2 Tbsp. Worcestershire sauce
3 bay leaves
½ cup lemon juice
½ cup dry vermouth
4 tsp. oregano leaves
4 tsp. granulated garlic
4 tsp. salt
4 tsp. pepper
2 tsp. cayenne pepper
1 tsp. ground rosemary
1½ tsp. Tabasco sauce
¾ tsp. poultry seasoning

Position oven rack on top level. Preheat broiler. Rinse shrimp in cold water and drain well. Peel shrimp and place in broiler-safe pan. In bowl, combine all sauce ingredients and stir well. Pour sauce over shrimp and place under broiler. Cook for approximately 5 minutes or until shrimp are cooked through. Serve immediately. Makes 3-4 servings.

To Clarify Butter: Melt butter in a heavy pan over low heat. Skim off froth and carefully pour clear liquid into another container, being careful to leave the milky residue behind.

Weeping Lamb and Potatoes

Susan Rizzo

Oven: 400°F. Prep time: Less than 30 minutes
Tme: 1–2 hours Yield: Serves 8

6 lb. leg of lamb
3 stems rosemary
3–4 garlic cloves, cut into slivers
6 large potatoes, peeled and sliced thinly
4 onions, sliced thinly
Sea salt and freshly ground black pepper
1 oz. butter, plus a little extra for the gravy
18 oz. chicken stock
1 bottle (750 ml /26 fl. oz.) good red wine
1¾ pints beef stock
3 oz. malt vinegar
1 pinch caster sugar
1 large bunch mint leaves, finely chopped
Salt
Olive oil

Preheat the oven to 400°F. Using a small sharp pointed knife, make a series of small deep slits about 1½" apart all over the leg of lamb. Into each cut insert a sliver of garlic and a small sprig of rosemary, pressing them right down inside. Drizzle with the olive oil and a good sprinkling of salt, then set aside while you build the potato dish.

Layer the potatoes and onions in a large ovenproof tray, seasoning each layer with salt and black pepper, and finishing with a layer of potatoes. Dot with butter, then pour over the stock and press down lightly. Put the roasting dish into the bottom of the oven, and place the lamb on a small wire rack on the oven rack directly above the potatoes. This is so that any juices from the lamb will *weep* onto the potatoes below. (Continue on next page).

Leave to roast for 1½ hours, or until the potatoes are cooked through, pressing the potatoes down into the cooking liquid every 30 minutes as it cooks. Remove the lamb from the oven when cooked to your liking and let it rest for 15 minutes before carving.

Pour the red wine and beef stock into a sauté pan or large frying pan and set over a medium heat, bring to the boil and cook for 30–45 minutes, or until reduced to a quarter of the original volume and is thickened to make a glossy gravy. Add a little knob of butter and check the seasoning.

Meanwhile, heat the malt vinegar, sugar and a pinch of salt in a clean pan until just simmering, then add the mint and stir until wilted.

To serve: Carve the lamb and serve with the potatoes, gravy and mint sauce.

Veggies

Apple Couscous Recipe
Susan Rizzo

1½ cups instant couscous
1 cup apple juice
½ cup frozen apple juice concentrate
1 large crisp apple, chopped
½ cup dried cranberries
1½ Tbsp. maple syrup
½ cup toasted almonds

Bring apple juice to a boil. Add apple juice concentrate. Bring to a boil.

Place couscous in a medium mixing bowl. Pour apple juice over couscous and allow to sit for 10 minutes. Fluff with a fork; add apples, cranberries, maple syrup, and toasted almonds. Serve immediately.

Easy Asparagus
Kathy Birkner
Oven: 350°F. Time: 20 minutes

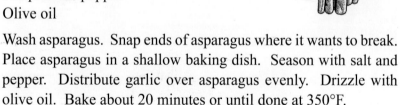

1 bunch asparagus
2–3 cloves garlic, minced finely
¼–½ tsp. salt
¼ tsp. black pepper
Olive oil

Wash asparagus. Snap ends of asparagus where it wants to break. Place asparagus in a shallow baking dish. Season with salt and pepper. Distribute garlic over asparagus evenly. Drizzle with olive oil. Bake about 20 minutes or until done at 350°F.

Asparagus with Mary Ann's Sauce
Mary Ann Karam

1 bunch asparagus
Water
Salt

Sauce

1 stick butter
2 egg yolks
Juice of 2 lemons
½ tsp. salt
¼ tsp. white pepper
2 tsp. prepared horseradish

Arrange stalks in a large pan. Pour in about ½" of boiling water. Salt to taste and cover pan. After water begins to boil, lower heat and cook approximately 10 to 12 minutes until asparagus is tender. Drain and serve with the following sauce.

Sauce: Melt butter on top of double boiler. Combine lemon and salt to slightly beaten egg yolks. Gradually add egg yolk mixture to melted butter, beating constantly. Cook until the sauce is slightly thickened and hot. Add prepared horseradish to sauce. Serve hot over asparagus.

Baked Blooming Onion
Kathy Birkner
Oven: 400°F. Time: 35 minutes Yield: 1 blooming onion

For the Onion:

1 large Vidalia onion
⅔ cup Panko bread crumbs with garlic
⅛ to ¼ tsp. cayenne pepper
¼ tsp. salt
2 eggs
Alternative sides: ketchup, spicy dipping sauce (see below), ranch dip, honey mustard

For The Spicy Dipping Sauce:

½ cup Greek yogurt (or mayo)
2 Tbsp. ketchup
2 tsp. horseradish sauce
¼ tsp. salt
¼ tsp. smoked paprika
⅛ tsp. garlic powder
½ tsp. ground cumin
⅛ tsp. oregano

Preheat oven to 400°F.

For the blooming onion: Place onion on a cutting board, and cut off the top (not the root end) one-quarter (¼)" of the onion until a few of the inside layers are exposed. Peel the outermost layer of the onion down to the root, but leave the root intact.

Lay the onion on the cutting board so that the flat side is down on the cutting board. Using a knife, divide the onion into 16ths, beginning with your knife one-eighth (⅛") away from the root and cutting straight down. After the entire onion is cut, turn the onion over and set on a piece of parchment paper on a baking sheet. Then separate the petals gently with your fingers. If any of your cuts did not go all the way through, use a paring knife to make sure the whole onion is cut into 16ths.

In a separate small bowl, whisk together the Panko, cayenne pepper, and salt until combined.

In another separate bowl, whisk the eggs until combined.

Start with the bottom layers of the onion, brush the top of each petal with the egg mixture until coated, and then immediately sprinkle with the panko mixture. Repeat until all petals are coated well. (*Hint:* The panko does not completely stick when the egg is wet, but press it on with your fingers. The process is slow and tedious, but well worth it!)

Form an aluminum tent over the baking sheet so the onion is totally covered. Place in the preheated 400°F. oven and bake for 5 minutes. After 5 minutes, remove the foil tent and bake for an additional 10–15 minutes until the onion is soft and the tips are lightly crisp. Remove and serve with different sauces.

To Make The Spicy Dipping Sauce: Combine all of the ingredients and whisk together until mixed. Serve immediately or refrigerate in a sealed container for up to 1 week.

Variation:

1) Use 1 Tbsp. Cajun or blackening seasoning
2) Use Italian seasonings in place of cayenne pepper. Taste a pinch of the dry seasoning before applying it to the onion to see if more seasoning (salt and pepper) is needed.

Baked Lima Beans
Frances Jerome
Oven: 300°F. Time: 2½ hours

1 lb. dried baby lima beans
6 cup water
1 cup chopped onion
½ lb. bacon, chopped
½ cup chili sauce
½ cup molasses
½ tsp. dry mustard
1 Tbsp. cider vinegar

Place beans in water in non-aluminum pan and soak overnight. Bring beans to a simmer and cook very gently for 30 minutes. Drain beans and measure cooking liquid. There should be 2 cups. If not, add water. Add liquid to beans in baking dish. Preheat oven to 300°F. Brown bacon; add onion and cook until soft and lightly browned. Add bacon, onions and rest of ingredients to beans. Bake covered, 2 hours until tender. Remove cover, bake 30 minutes longer to thicken sauce. Adjust seasonings before serving.

Basic Baked Stuffed Mushrooms

Martha Sweeney

Oven: 375°F. Time: 15 minutes

1 lb. large mushrooms
½ cup fine bread crumbs
½ cup finely shredded Gruyere or Swiss cheese
4 Tbsp. grated onion and the juice
½ tsp. tarragon (scant since as it is a very strong herb)
½ tsp. salt
½ tsp. pepper
2 Tbsp. Half & Half or cream or milk
Parmesan or Romano grated cheese
Butter

Carefully remove stems from mushrooms, but set mushroom caps aside. Chop stems fine or use grater.

Sauté onions and chopped mushrooms in butter; add crumbs, cheese, Half & Half, salt, pepper, and tarragon. Mixture should be sticky, add more crumbs and cream, if necessary.

Oil the mushroom caps. Stuff caps with mixture. Sprinkle Parmesan cheese on top of caps.

Oil baking dish and add a bit of water. More water should be added as baking progresses to keep mushrooms from drying out. Bake at 375°F. oven for 15 minutes.

Note: This is a basic recipe so you can add whatever you wish to it.

Mixed Vegetables
Broimi (Greek)

Gloria Marek-Kuranie (Corning, NY)

1 lb. eggplant
1 lb. zucchini
½ lb. fresh green beans
2 large potatoes
2 large carrots
2 medium green peppers
6–8 large mushrooms
2 lb. fresh tomatoes chopped
½ cup olive oil
2 medium onions sliced
Salt, pepper
2–3 garlic cloves sliced
½ cup parsley
½ cup kefalotyri* or Romano cheese grated
Oil for frying

Wash and trim eggplants and zucchini. Cut in large chunks, salt each generously, and put into separate colanders, allow to stand for 1–2 hours. Rinse in a lot of water and squeeze out. Fry in oil lightly, set aside. Clean potatoes, carrots, green beans, and green peppers. Cut in large pieces and fry each one lightly in hot oil. Fry mushrooms, set aside. Heat the onion and garlic, salt lightly. Add tomatoes and sauté about 10 minutes. Add parsley and seasoning. Remove from heat and add all the fried vegetables. Sprinkle cheese over dish.

Name in English	Name in Greek	Pronunciation
*kefalotyri	Κεφαλοτύρι	keh-fah-lo-TEE-ree

Blooming Onion
Katie Brown
Total Time: 1 hour Prep: 1 hour Cook: 6 minutes
Yield: 4 servings

Dip

2 Tbsp. mayonnaise
2 Tbsp. sour cream
1½ tsp. ketchup
½ tsp. Worcestershire sauce
1 Tbsp. drained horseradish
¼ tsp. paprika
Pinch of cayenne pepper
Kosher salt and freshly ground black pepper

For the Onion

1 large sweet onion, such as Vidalia (about 1 pound)
2½ cups all-purpose flour
½ tsp. cayenne pepper
2 Tbsp. paprika
½ tsp. dried thyme
½ tsp. dried oregano
½ tsp. ground cumin
Freshly ground black pepper
2 large eggs
1 cup whole milk
1 gallon oil
Kosher salt

For the Dip:
Combine all of the dip ingredients in a bowl, cover and refrigerate.

For the Onion: Slice off one-half (½") from the pointy stem end of the onion, then peel down to the root, but leave the root intact. Place the onion cut-side down. Starting one-half (½") from the root, cut downward all the way through to the board. Repeat to

(Continue on next page.)

make four evenly spaced cuts around the onion. Continue slicing between each section until you have 16 evenly spaced cuts. Turn the onion over and use your fingers to gently spread apart the petals.

Whisk the flour, cayenne, paprika, thyme, oregano, cumin and ½ teaspoon of black pepper in a bowl. In a small deep bowl, whisk the eggs, milk, and 1 cup water.

Place the onion in a separate bowl with cut-side up, then pour all of the flour mixture on top. Cover the bowl with a plate, then shake back and forth to distribute the flour. Check to make sure the onion is fully coated, especially between the petals. Lift the onion by the core, turn over and pat off the excess flour; reserve the bowl of flour.

Using a slotted spoon under the onion, and spoon on top, dunk the onion in the egg mixture. Let excess egg drip off, then repeat duplicating the flouring process again. Take out onion. Keep the onion refrigerated until ready to cook.

Heat the oil in a deep pot over medium to high heat (400 °F.). Gently pat off any extra flour from the onion. Using a wire skimmer, carefully submerge the onion into the oil with the cut-side down. If the oil temperature drops, increase the heat so the temperature of the oil remains fairly constant. Fry the onion about 3 minutes, then flip the onion over and continue cooking until golden brown about 3–4 minutes. Drain on paper towels. Season with salt. Serve with the dip.

Broccoli Puff
Theresa Birkner
Oven: 350°F. Time: 45 minutes Yield: 6 servings

10 oz. pkg. frozen cut broccoli
1 can cream of mushroom soup
½ cup sharp cheese, shredded
¼ cup milk
¼ cup mayonnaise
1 beaten egg
¼ cup fine bread crumbs
1 Tbsp. butter, melted

Cook broccoli without salt; drain. Spray 10" x 6" x 2" dish with cooking spray. Stir soup and cheese together. Add milk, mayonnaise, and egg gradually until well-blended. Pour over broccoli. Combine crumbs and butter. Sprinkle over top. Bake at 350°F. for 45 minutes until crumbs are brown.

Broccoli Salad
Elmosa Herrera

½ lb. bacon, chopped and cooked
1 large bunch broccoli, cut small
2 cups celery, chopped
6 small green onions, chopped
1 cup pecan or almonds, chopped
1 cup raisins
2 cups red seedless grapes

Dressing:

1 cup mayonnaise
¼ cup milk
1 Tbsp. vinegar
¼ cup sugar

Combine all but bacon and nuts. Chill. Add dressing, bacon, and nuts before serving.

Black-Eyed Peas

Kathy Birkner
Yield: 8 servings

1 lb. dried black-eyed peas
8 cups water

Wash dried beans with cold water. Pick out any bad, floating, or foreign materials. Cover the peas and allow to soak overnight. Use about 8 cups of water to cover the beans for soaking. Soaking reduces the cooking time. The next morning drain the water and discard. Reserve peas.

½ cup onion, diced
½ to 1 green pepper, diced finely
2 Tbsp. olive or canola oil
2 oz. ham, diced finely
1 lb. prepared black-eyed peas
4 cups water
½–1 tsp. salt (or to taste)
¼ tsp. black pepper

In a large sauce pan, sauté onion in oil, when about half translucent, add green pepper, and continue to sauté until onions are translucent. Add black-eyed peas, ham, and water. Add salt and pepper. Bring to a boil, reduce heat to simmer; cook peas until tender, about 1–1½ hours. As peas cook, add more hot or boiling water, if needed. Serve.

Broccoli Slaw
Susan Rizzo
Yield: 10 servings

3 packets chicken-flavored ramen noodles
2 bags (16 oz.) broccoli slaw
1 bunch green onion, cut into thin slices
1 cup sunflower seeds
1 cup sliced almonds

Dressing

1 cup. oil
½ cup sugar
¼ cup white vinegar
Seasoning packs from ramen noodles

Combine salad ingredients: Remove seasoning packets from ramen noodles and set aside. Pour noodles, slaw, onion, seeds, and almonds into a bowl. Do not mix.

Prepare the dressing: Combine oil, sugar, and vinegar with contents of ramen seasoning packets.

Assemble the salad: Pour dressing over top of salad. Do not mix. Let stand 20 minutes. Mix salad and serve immediately.

Broccoli, Cheese & Rice in Three Quarter Thyme
Melinda McMath
Oven: 350°F. Cook time: 45 minutes

3 cups cooked brown rice
4 beaten eggs
¼ cup vegetable oil
½ lb. (or more) chopped broccoli
½ cup chopped onion
1 Tbsp. soy sauce
½ to 1 tsp. thyme
1 lb. shredded cheddar cheese

Combine ingredients and bake in a greased casserole dish at 350°F. for 45 minutes.

Broccoli Slaw
Cathy Van Delden

1 bag broccoli slaw
4 green onion, chopped
⅛ cup olive oil
2 Tbsp. balsamic vinegar
½ tsp. pepper
2 Tbsp. sugar or Splenda
Seasoning package from top ramen roasted chicken or chicken ramen; reserve noodles
½ cup sliced almonds
½ cups sunflower or pine nuts
2 Tbsp. sesame seeds

Mix slaw and onions together and put in plastic bag. Whisk oil, vinegar, pepper, sugar, and seasoning; pour over slaw and marinate overnight or at least 8 hours.

Toast nuts and sesame seeds separately before serving. Mix together the nuts, top ramen noodles that have been broken up, then sprinkle over broccoli mixture. Serve immediately.

Brussels Sprouts
with Chestnuts, Bacon and Parsley

Susan Rizzo
Prep Time: 15 minutes Time: 10 minutes Serves: 8 servings

1¼ lb. Brussels sprouts
1 Tbsp. vegetable oil
9 oz. bacon, cut into small pieces
2 Tbsp. butter
About 8 to 9 oz. vacuum-packed chestnuts
2 fluid oz. Marsala wine
1 large handful fresh parsley, chopped, divided
Freshly ground black pepper

Slice the bottoms off each of the brussels sprouts, cutting a cross onto the base as you go. Place the brussels sprouts into a large saucepan of salted boiling water. Cook the brussels sprouts for 5 minutes, or until they are tender, but still retain a bit of bite.

Remove the pan from the heat and drain the excess water from the Brussels sprouts.

Heat the oil in a large clean saucepan. Add the bacon pieces to the pan and cook until they are crisp and golden-brown in color, but not cooked to the point of having dried out.

Add the butter and the chestnuts to the bacon saucepan and with a wooden spoon or spatula, press down on them to break them up into pieces. Once the chestnuts have been warmed through, turn the heat up, and add the Marsala to the pan. Cook until the mixture has reduced and thickened slightly. Add the sprouts and half the parsley to the saucepan and mix well. Season the Brussels sprouts with freshly ground black pepper.

To serve, place the Brussels sprouts onto a warmed serving plate and sprinkle the remaining chopped parsley over the top.

Cathy's Spinach Casserole
Cathy Van Delden
Oven: 350°F. Time 30 minutes Yield: 8" x 8" pan

4 small pkg. (10 oz.) chopped spinach
1 medium onion, chopped
4 cloves garlic, diced
5 oz. or 1 small can evaporated milk
1 small pkg. hot Velveeta cheese
Salt and pepper to taste
½ cup slivered almonds

Thaw spinach. Squeeze out water in spinach with hands until dry. Set aside.

In microwave bowl, add onion, garlic, and milk. Cook 1 minute. Chop cheese and add to milk mixture. Microwave 1 minute at a time, stirring until cheese melts. Add salt and pepper to taste. Flake apart spinach. Add to cheese mixture. Spray 8" x 8" pan with cooking spray and put in mix. Sprinkle with slivered almonds. Bake at 350°F. for 30 minutes or until casserole bubbles.

Note: Double recipe for a 9" x 13" pan.

Dirtiest 12 Fruits and Veggies
Most Pesticides

1. Peach
2. Apple
3. Bell pepper
4. Celery
5. Nectarines
6. Strawberries
7. Cherries
8. Kale
9. Lettuce
10. Grapes (Imported)
11. Carrot
12. Pear

Fresh Cauliflower Salad
Elsa Mery

Prep and make at least ½ day in advance.

1 head cauliflower
½ cup olive oil
½ cup vinegar
Seasoning salt (HEB Hill Country or McCormick)
½ tsp. salt or to taste
⅛ tsp. pepper or to taste
8 oz. mushroom pieces
1 small onion, thinly slice

Break cauliflower into bite sized flowerets. In a large bowl combine flowerets, mushrooms, and onions. Mix oil and vinegar; add salt and pepper, stir. Pour over cauliflower mixture and toss to mix well. Prepare at least ½ day ahead; then mix intermittently every 30 minutes to 1 hour. Serve.

Couscous with Raisins and Carrots
Susan Rizzo

2 cups couscous
32 oz. can vegetable broth
1 small onion, finely chopped
1 cup raisins
1 cup carrots thinly sliced

In a saucepan, combine vegetable broth, onion, and carrots and bring to a boil. Reduce heat to low and simmer for 5–8 minutes. Return to a boil and add couscous.

Remove from heat and add raisins. Cover and allow to sit for 10 minutes or until vegetable broth is absorbed.

Fluff couscous with a fork and serve immediately.

Note: Couscous with raisins and carrots is the perfect side dish to poultry dishes. I like to serve this as a side dish for Thanksgiving, but it is perfect for every day.

Chicken or Pork Fried Rice
Carrie Lyons
Yield: Serves 6-8

5–6 Tbsp canola oil
2 cups cooked white rice
2 cups cut-up cooked chicken or pork
4 eggs beaten with ¼ cup water
1 cup chopped celery
1 cup chopped onion
1 can sliced bamboo shoots
1 can sliced water chestnuts
Garlic salt to taste
Pepper to taste
Lite soy sauce

In large skillet heat 2 tablespoons of oil, pour in ¼ of the eggs spread real thin, cook, then turn onto cookie sheet. Repeat with the remainder of eggs in one-fourth (¼) increments, let cool, set aside.

Pour 2 tablespoon oil into a pan, add celery and onions, and sauté 3–4 minutes; then add meat and sauté until blended and hot. Add bamboo shoots, water chestnuts, and rice with more oil as needed up to 2–3 additional tablespoon. Add garlic salt and pepper to taste. Finally add soy sauce for color and flavor as desired. Add eggs sliced up at the end.

Note: Recipe was given to Carrie Lyons by a military friend while in the Philippines.

Confetti Corn Relish

2 (12 oz.) cans whole kernel corn
⅔ cup green pepper, diced
⅔ cup onion, diced
⅔ cup pimento, diced
½ cup. white vinegar
2 Tbsp. vegetable oil
¼ cup sugar
2 tsp. dry mustard
½ tsp. salt
½ tsp. pepper
½ tsp. celery seed (optional)

Drain liquid from corn. Reserve ½ cup. Combine the corn, onion, pepper and pimento in large bowl. Combine the reserved corn liquid, vinegar, oil, sugar, mustard, salt and pepper in small saucepan. Bring to boiling. Pour over vegetables. Cover with plastic wrap. Refrigerate overnight. Stir well before serving.

Hot German Potato Salad
Theresa Birkner
Servings: 6

6 oz. bacon, diced
5 potatoes, cooked in jackets (about 3½ cups cubed)
1 onion, chopped
½ tsp. salt
¼ tsp. pepper
1 tsp. sugar
½ cup vinegar
1 beaten egg

Cook bacon until crisp. Remove bacon; save drippings. Combine cooked and skinned *hot* potatoes, bacon, and onion.

Add remaining ingredients to bacon drippings; heat thoroughly, stirring constantly. Then pour over potato mixture, and combine well.

Creamy Spinach Bake
Kathy Birkner
Bake: 400°F. Yield: 4 large servings

3 Tbsp. butter
9 oz. spinach, cooked and drained
½ cup onion, diced
3 Tbsp. flour
1 Tbsp. tarragon, snipped finely
¼ tsp. salt
1 cup 1% milk
2 oz. Parmesan cheese
5 eggs, separated

Separate eggs; allow egg whites to warm to room temperature about 20 to 30 minutes. Grease 2-quart casserole or baking dish. Set aside.

In a Teflon coated pan, melt 3 tablespoons butter over medium heat. Add onion, sauté for 2 minutes, then add spinach and continue cooking for 4 more minutes. Stir in flour, tarragon, and salt. Then add milk. Cook until thickened. Remove from heat and allow cooling.

In a bowl, combine spinach mixture, parmesan cheese, and 5 eggs yokes. Beat egg whites until stiff peaks form, and then fold into spinach mixture adding one-half at time. Pour into prepared baking dish and bake at 400°F. uncovered for 15 to 20 minutes.

Note: Use parsley or dill in place of tarragon.

Eggplant Burgers
Kathy Birkner
Yield: 8 (8 oz.) burgers

2 large eggplant, shredded (about 8 cups)
1 cup Parmesan cheese
1 medium onion, finely chopped
1 tsp. salt or to taste
¼–½ tsp. black pepper
½ tsp. garlic powder
1 cup garlic panko crumbs (less or more as needed)
½ cup Italian bread crumbs
2 eggs, beaten well
½–1 cup flour
Olive oil

Combine all ingredients. Form into patties from 4 to 8 oz. depending on the size you want.

Pour enough olive oil to coat a non-stick pan; put on medium heat. Place burgers into pan and cook about 3 to 4 minutes per side. Serve with lettuce and condiments on pita bread.

Note: Make the burgers in advance if you like. Place formed burger on a saran coated cookie sheet; cover. Freeze. After burgers are frozen, individually wrap and place in a plastic or freezer bag for storage. When ready to cook, follow cooking instructions.

Eggplant Casserole
Elsa Mery

2 lb. chuck steak, cubed
1 large eggplant
2 medium potatoes, peeled and cubed
1 medium onion, chopped
1–2 tsp. salt
½ tsp. pepper
8 oz. can tomato sauce

Peel eggplant and slice crosswise into ¼" slices. If not cooking immediately, place in salted cold water so it does not turn dark and so the eggplant absorbs less oil when frying. In a frying pan brown eggplant in oil until nicely browned. Place in paper towels to hold and remove excess oil. Then cook potatoes in same oil, adding more oil as needed, until soft. Remove potatoes from pan and set aside. Using same pan, sauté the onion until soft, remove from pan, and set aside. Then brown meat, add salt and pepper. Add tomato sauce to meat and cook about 2 minutes until it bubbles. Then add other reserved ingredients along with 2 cans of water. Bring to a boil and simmer for about an hour. Add more water if it cooks down.

Fresh Tomatoes with Mozzarella
Helen Antonelli

Cluster of tomatoes on the vine
Fresh mozzarella cheese
Fresh basil
Extra virgin olive oil

With a snap of your fingers, detach tomato from vine. Rinse briefly. Slice tomato and cheese. On a serving dish alternate slice and garnish with fresh basil. Drizzle with olive oil or your favorite dressing. Serve and enjoy!

Good Luck Jambalaya
Cathy Van Delden

½ cup salt pork strip
2 cloves garlic, minced
1 large onion, chopped
2 cans black-eyed peas with jalapeños, undrained
1 medium bell pepper, chopped
⅔ cup of Bloody Mary mix or V8 with Tabasco
1¼ lb. raw shrimp
Celery leaves
⅓ cup uncooked long grain rice

Cook salt pork in a large skillet until golden brown. Add garlic, onion, and bell pepper and sauté until tender.

Add black-eyed peas, Bloody Mary mix and rice. Bring the mixture to a boil over medium heat. Cook and reduce the heat to low and simmer for 20 minutes. Add the shrimp and cook for 5 minutes.

Place on serving tray and garnish with celery leaves.

Parmesan Spinach
Kathy Birkner

1 lb. fresh spinach
3 tsp. olive oil
1 tsp. minced garlic
½ cup Parmesan cheese
Salt and pepper (to taste)

Sauté minced garlic in olive oil in non-stick frying pan until golden brown. Pour spinach into pan and sauté for a minute or two until wilted. Remove from burner; add Parmesan cheese, salt, and pepper to taste. Toss to mix. Serve.

Mary's Guacamole
Mary Karam

6 ripe avocados
2 ripe tomatoes
1 clove of garlic
1 lemon, juiced
1 tsp. salt (or to taste)
¼ tsp. ground black pepper
1 small onion, finely chopped
2 small hot peppers

Peel and seed the avocados. Put in food processor or smash with potato masher. Add lemon juice. Grind together onion, garlic, and hot pepper. Add to avocado mixture. Squeeze all the liquid out of the tomatoes, do not add peel. Mix all ingredients together. Great as a dip or with a lettuce salad.

Pea Salad

Arlene Coury

10 oz. pkg. frozen peas
½ cup + cheddar cheese, diced
2 hard-boiled eggs, sliced
¼ cup celery, chopped
2 Tbsp. onion, chopped
⅓ cup mayonnaise
½ tsp. salt
¼ tsp. Tabasco sauce
⅛ tsp. black pepper

Combine together the peas, sliced eggs, celery, cheese, and onions. Combine the mayo, salt, pepper, and Tabasco.

To serve: Mix the mayo mixture into the pea mix and serve. Keep refrigerated.

Potato Leek Soup
Karen Sacre
Yield: 4–6 servings

3 large leeks, chopped (white & pale green and yellow parts only)
2½ lb. potatoes, peeled and diced into ½" cubes
2 Tbsp. butter
2 cups water
2 cups broth (chicken or vegetable)
Salt and pepper to taste
Sage, thyme, or marjoram to taste
½ can evaporated milk

Sauté leeks in butter 10 minutes. Add other ingredients except the milk. Simmer 20 minutes. Purée in blender or food process. Add milk. Serve.

Oriental Rice and Vegetables
Karen Sacre

1 onion, sliced
6 garlic cloves, sliced
½ green cabbage, sliced
½ purple cabbage, sliced
2 green bell peppers, sliced
2 red bell peppers, sliced
1 bunch broccoli, chopped
8 oz. package mushrooms, sliced
1 cup rice, uncooked
Soy sauce (to taste)
Pepper (to taste)
Turmeric (to taste)
Cumin (to taste)
Coriander (to taste)

Sauté onion and garlic in olive oil; add the remaining vegetables and soy sauce to taste. Season with pepper, turmeric, cumin, and coriander. When vegetables are tender, add 3 cups of rice, and 3 cups of boiling water. Simmer until the water is absorbed.

Spinach Balls
Elmosa Herrera
Bake: 350°F. Cook: 20 minutes

2 pkgs. frozen chopped spinach, cooked and drained
4 eggs, beaten
1½ sticks oleo
½ cup Parmesan cheese
2 cups stuffing mix (herb)
1 onion, chopped
¼ tsp. thyme
½ tsp. salt
½ tsp. pepper

Mix all ingredients and form into 1" balls. Chill or freeze. Bake for 20 min. at 350°F. in regular oven.

Spanish Rice
Annie Molina

¼ cup Crisco or oil
1 cup uncooked rice (not instant)
½ cup onion, diced
8 oz. can tomato sauce
2 cups water
1 tsp. sugar
1 Tbsp. chili powder
¼ tsp. salt
½ green pepper, diced
1 stalk celery, diced

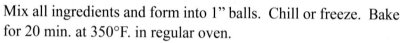

Heat oil in heavy 10" frying pan. Add rice, cook stirring over medium heat until golden in color; add onion, cook 1 minute. Add tomato sauce, water, seasonings, green pepper, and celery. Cover, cook over low heat 25 minutes or longer until rice is tender. Stir. Serve.

Roasted Cauliflower
with Cumin, Sumac and Lemon

Susan Rizzo
Oven: 375°F. Cook time: 45 mins. Yield: 6 servings

2 small or 1 large cauliflower
½ tsp. sumac
½ tsp. ground cumin
Lemon juice
2 Tbsp. parsley, chopped
Olive oil
Sea salt

Preheat the oven to 375°F. Separate cauliflower into florets. Drizzle the cauliflower liberally with oil, and sprinkle with salt, sumac and cumin.

Roast for 45 minutes to an hour. (Turn the temperature down if the cauliflowers start to get too dark.) Cook until lightly browned ,and an inserted fork meets with just a little resistance.

Before serving, drizzle again with good quality olive oil and a fair squeeze of lemon, then sprinkle with parsley, and a little more salt.

Spicy Roasted Cauliflower

Kathy Birkner

Oven: 400°F. Time 30-40 minutes Yield: 6 servings

1 Tbsp. vegetable oil
1 head cauliflower
1½ cups plain Greek yogurt
1 lime, zested and juiced
2 Tbsp. chili powder
1 Tbsp. cumin
1 Tbsp. garlic powder
1 tsp. curry powder
2 tsp. Kosher salt
1 tsp. black pepper

Preheat the oven to 400° F. Lightly grease a small baking sheet with vegetable oil. Set aside.

Remove the green leaves and the stem of the cauliflower.

In a medium bowl, combine the yogurt, lime zest and juice, chili powder, cumin, garlic powder, curry powder, salt, and pepper.

Dunk the cauliflower into the bowl and apply with a brush or your hands to spread the marinade evenly over the cauliflower. If you have any extra marinade, store it in an airtight jar in the refrigerator for up to three days. Use it on veggies, meat, or fish.

Place the cauliflower on the prepared baking sheet and roast until the surface is dry and lightly browned, about 30 to 40 minutes. The marinade makes a crust on the surface of the cauliflower.

Let the cauliflower cool for 10 minutes before cutting it into wedges, and serve with a big green salad.

Split Red Lentils (Keftah)
Thelma O'Shannessy

1 cup split red lentils
3 cups water
1 tsp. salt
1 tsp. red pepper flakes
1 cup medium bulghur
½ cup butter or margarine, melted
1 medium onion, chopped
2 scallions, chopped (green onion)
½ sweet green pepper, chopped
2 cups parsley, chopped

Rinse lentils. Boil lentils 30 minutes in water. Add salt and red pepper flakes and additional water, if needed, boiling 2 minutes longer. Put bulghur in large bowl and pour lentils over it. Mix, cover, and let cool 1 hour.

Sauté the onions in melted butter and add to the bulghur-lentil mixture. When cool enough to handle, knead 5 minutes until well blended. Mix in the chopped vegetables (scallions, green pepper, and parsley). Add more salt and red pepper flakes to taste.

Sweet Potato Casserole

Thelma O'Shannessy
Oven: 350°F. Cook time: 35 minutes

Filling

3 cups fresh sweet potatoes, cooked and mashed
1 cup sugar
½ cup margarine, melted
2 eggs beaten
1 tsp. vanilla
½ cup milk

Topping

1 cup brown sugar
½ cup flour
½ cup margarine
1 cup pecans, chopped

Filling: Mix together with electric mixer and put in a 9" x 13" baking dish.

Topping: Mix together, sprinkle on top of sweet potatoes and bake at 350°F. for 35 minutes.

Vegetable Casserole

Thelma O'Shannessy

Oven: 350°F. Cook time: 20–30 minutes Yield: 6 servings

1 eggplant, diced
1 yellow squash, diced
1 zucchini squash, diced
1 jar artichokes
1 Tbsp. oregano (optional)
1 large onion, chopped
2 cloves garlic, shredded fine
½ cup parsley, chopped
1 can tomatoes, diced
½ cup oil (corn)
Salt to taste

Wash and dice eggplant, squash, parsley, onion, and garlic. Spray baking dish. Put in eggplant and squash, then artichokes. Season with salt as desired. Pour tomatoes and oil over eggplant-squash mixture; sprinkle parsley and oregano. Bake uncovered at 350°F. for 45 minutes or until vegetables are tender. Dish may be served hot or cold.

Variation: Add mushrooms, if desired.

Zucchini Boats
Kathy Birkner
Oven: 350°F. Time: 20–30 minutes Yield: 6 boats

6 medium zucchini or Tatume (light green) squash
2 cup Italian dry bread crumbs
2 eggs, lightly beaten
1 large tomato, diced
½ cup grated Parmesan cheese
¼ cup minced fresh parsley
2 garlic cloves, minced
½ cup chicken broth
½ tsp. salt
⅛ tsp. pepper
Olive oil spray

Cut zucchini in half lengthwise. Scoop out pulp, leaving a ¼" shell; save pulp. Cook shells in salted water for 2 minutes. Remove; drain. Set aside.

Coarsely chop zucchini pulp in food processor. Transfer to a large bowl. Add the Italian bread crumbs, eggs, tomato, Parmesan cheese, parsley, and garlic; mix. Stir in broth, salt, and pepper. Fill zucchini shells, and place in a greased 9" x 13" baking pan. Spray with olive oil. Bake uncovered at 350° for 20 to 30 minutes or until golden brown.

Variation: Add pinch of crushed red pepper flakes (will make them slightly spicy) or a pinch cayenne pepper.

If you would like crispier boats, place on wire rack and bake. Prepare as above.

Zucchini Casserole

Annie Molina
Oven 350°F. Time: 30 minutes

4 cups zucchini, chopped, steamed until tender, then drain
1 cup onion, chopped
1 cup (8 oz.) sour cream
1 can cream of chicken soup
1 pkg. corn bread such as Stove Top Dressing
1 cube butter (2 Tbsp.)
2 carrots, grated

Steam zucchini until tender, then drain, and put in a mixing bowl. Add sour cream, carrots, onions, and soup; mix.

In a 2-quart casserole, spoon half of the stuffing mix with butter in bottom of casserole. Spoon squash filling on top of mix. Put rest of stuffing mix on top of squash. Bake in a preheated 350°F. oven for 30 minutes.

Note: Do NOT salt as there is enough seasoning in the Stove top dressing.

Zucchini Casserole

Minnie Mery

Oven: 350°F. Cook time: 20–30 minutes Yield: 6 servings

1 lb. zucchini
2 large cloves garlic
1 Tbsp. fresh mint or 2 Tbsp. dry mint
salt and fresh black pepper to taste
⅓ cup oil

Wash zucchini; cut into quarters. Pulverize or use mortar and pestle to combine the garlic, dried mint, and salt together. Place some of the zucchini in a baking dish, then sprinkle with garlic mixture. Continue layering until all is used ending with the garlic mixture. Season with some black pepper. Drizzle the oil over the zucchini and bake in 350°F. oven for 20 to 30 minutes or until zucchini is tender and done.

Zucchini Sticks
Kathy Birkner
Oven: 375°F. Time: 30–35 minutes Yield: 8 slices per zucchini

3–4 zucchini
2 eggs
½ cup water
1 cup Panko crumbs
½ cup Parmesan cheese
¼ tsp. salt
⅛ tsp. pepper

Cut zucchini in half and then in half again, lengthwise; if thinner sticks are desired, cut in half again. If zucchini are large, you can cut in half to shorten.

Have a cookie sheet pan with a wire rack ready. In a shallow wide pan, combine panko crumbs, salt and pepper. In another shallow wide pan, beat eggs slightly, then add water; mix well. Dip zucchini in egg mixture, then panko crumbs. Place on wire rack. After completing all of the zucchini, spray each with olive oil spray. Bake 350°F. for 30–35 minutes. Cook less time if you want crispy, crunchy sticks.

Variation: Add some cayenne or red pepper flakes to Panko crumbs.

Vegetables and Fruits Lowest in Pesticides

1. Onion	7. Sweet Peas
2. Avocado	8. Kiwi
3. Sweet Corn	9. Cabbage
4. Pineapple	10. Eggplant
5. Mango	11. Papaya
6. Asparagus	12. Watermelon

Desserts and More

Cakes
Cookies
Bars
Pies
Candy

Apple Cake Supreme
Regina Aune
Oven: 325°F. Cook Time: 1¾ hours Serves: 16

1½ cups oil
1½ cups granulated sugar
½ cup brown sugar
3 cups flour
3 eggs
1½ tsp. cinnamon
1 tsp. nutmeg
½ tsp. salt
1 tsp. baking soda
3½ cups tart apples, peeled
1 cup walnuts, coarsely chopped
2 tsp. vanilla

Glaze:

3 Tbsp. butter
3 Tbsp. granulated sugar
3 Tbsp. light brown sugar
3 Tbsp. heavy cream
¼ tsp. vanilla

Dice apples into large pieces and place in bowl of lightly salted water until ready to use. (Do not drain, but lift apple pieces out with hands into mixture.) Generously grease and flour 10" tube pan, shaking out excess flour.

Combine oil and sugars in large bowl, blending well. Add eggs, 1 at a time, beating thoroughly with each addition. Sift dry ingredients together and add to first mixture, blending well. Fold in apples, nuts, and vanilla. Spread evenly in prepared pan and bake until cake tests done, about 1¾ hours. Let cool in pan about 30 minutes before turning out onto wire rack.

Combine glaze ingredients in saucepan and bring to a boil for 1 minute. Spoon over warm cake.

Apple Pie Cake

Kathy Birkner

Oven: 350°F. Time: 40–45 minutes
Yield: 9" x 13" pan or bundt pan

½ cup shortening
2 cups flour
2 cups sugar
2 eggs
2 tsp. vanilla
2 tsp. baking soda
2 tsp. cinnamon
1 tsp. salt
4 Tbsp. hot water
1 cup chopped nuts
5 cups apples, diced (I use 4 cups so it doesn't get soggy.)

Cream shortening and sugar. Stir in eggs and vanilla. Add dry ingredients, and mix. Add apples, combine. Fold in nuts. Turn into a greased 9" x 13" or greased Bundt pan. Bake 350°F. for 35–45 minutes or until toothpick inserted comes out clean.

Note: I have substituted ⅜ cup (6 Tbsp.) canola oil for the shortening.

Bacardi Rum Cake

Louise Malouff
Oven: 325°F. Time: 1 hour Yield: bundt or tube pan

Cake:

1 cup chopped pecans or walnuts
18½ oz. pkg. yellow cake mix (regular or pudding cake mix)
3¾ oz. pkg. vanilla instant pudding and pie filling
4 eggs
½ cup cold water
½ cup oil
½ cup Bacardi dark rum (80 proof)

Glaze:

¼ lb. butter
¼ cup water
1 cup sugar
½ tsp. Bacardi dark rum (80 proof)

Preheat oven to 325 degrees. Grease and flour 10" tube *or* 12 cup Bundt pan. Sprinkle nuts over bottom of pan.

Mix all cake ingredients together. Pour batter over nuts. Bake 1 hour. Cool. Invert on serving plate. Prick top.

Glaze: Melt butter in saucepan. Stir in water and sugar.

Boil 5 minutes, stirring constantly. Remove from heat. Stir in rum. Spoon and brush glaze evenly over top and sides. Allow cake to absorb glaze. Repeat until glaze is all used up.

Note: If using yellow cake mix with pudding *already* in the mix, omit instant pudding, use 3 eggs instead of 4, and ⅓ cup of oil instead of ½.

Optional: Decorate with border of sugar frosting or whipped cream.

Blueberry Cheesecake
Kathy Birkner

Oven: 325°F. Time: 40 minutes Yield: 10" pie cheesecake

Graham cracker crust

1⅓ cups Graham cracker crumbs
¼ cup sugar OR Splenda
⅓ cup butter

Pulse in food processor until combined. Pour into pie tin and push to cover pan evenly. Bake at 325°F. for about 10 minutes.

Cheesecake

2 pkg. cream cheese (I use 1 low fat and 1 fat free at room temp)
1 cup Splenda OR sugar
2 Tbsp. lemon juice
Dash salt
1 tsp. vanilla
2 eggs

Beat cream cheese until smooth. Then add Splenda (or sugar), salt, lemon juice, and vanilla; combine. Then add 1 egg at a time and mix thoroughly, but do not over mix. Pour into pie crust and cook for about 40 minutes at 325°F. To check that cake is done, make small slit with butter knife. If knife comes out clean, cheesecake is done. Remove from oven, and allow cooling.

Blueberry Topping

2 cups blueberries
½ cup Splenda OR sugar
½ cup water
1 Tbsp. cornstarch and 1 Tbsp. cool water

Place blueberries, Splenda, and water in heavy saucepan and cook over medium heat until blueberries soften and begin to expel some juice. Remove from heat. Combine tablespoon of water and cornstarch mixing until smooth, then add to blueberry mix; stir to combine. Place back over medium heat and bring to a boil. Cook for 30 seconds, then remove from heat. Allow to cool for 15 minutes; then pour over cheesecake. Cover and refrigerate for 30 minutes to 1 hour before serving.

Carrot Cupcakes

Oven: 350°F. Time: 20–23 minutes Yield: 16 cupcakes

1 cup whole wheat flour
1¾ cup flour
2 tsp. baking soda
½ tsp. salt
½ tsp. cinnamon powder
½ tsp. ginger powder
¾ cup coconut oil, melted
1 cup brown sugar
½ cup unsweetened applesauce
2 oz. Greek yogurt
3 eggs
1 tsp. vanilla extract
2 cups carrots, grated
½ cup raisins
½ cup walnuts (lightly toasted and roughly chopped)

Preheat the oven to 350°F. Line cupcake tins with 16 liners. Sift the flours, baking soda, cinnamon powder, ginger, and salt together.

Mix sugar and oil together. Then add yogurt and applesauce mixing only until combined. Add the eggs one by one and then the vanilla. Sprinkle the flour mixture over the wet ingredients, then mix, taking care not to over mix the batter. Fold in the carrots, raisins and walnuts. Drop spoonful of the batter into the cupcake liners and bake 20–23 minutes until a toothpick is inserted comes out clean. Leave to cool. While the cupcakes are baking, make the frosting.

Icing recipe follows next page.

Icing

1 cup confectioners' sugar
¾ cup butter, softened
6–7 oz. cream cheese
1 lemon (zest grated off and juiced)

Cream the butter and cream cheese together along with the lemon zest and juice until smooth. Sift the confectioners' sugar and add to butter mixture, beating until smooth. Set aside.

When the cupcakes have cooled, spoon the frosting into a piping bag fitted with a big star nozzle and pipe the icing onto the cupcakes. If you don't have star nozzle, place frosting in a plastic bag, then snip the corner and drizzle over cupcakes. Serve.

Cream Cheese Coffee Cake
Frances Jerome
Oven: 350°F. Time: 1½ hours   Yield: 16 Servings

1 cup soft butter
8 oz. pkg. cream cheese
1½ cup sugar
1½ tsp. vanilla
4 eggs
2¼ cups unsifted flour
1½ tsp. baking powder
¾ cup raisins
Chopped nuts

Grease a 10" tube pan. Sprinkle with nuts. Beat butter until fluffy; add sugar beating until light and fluffy. Add eggs one at a time, scraping bowl, then add vanilla. Add flour and cream cheese alternately beating after each addition until combined. Pour into pan. Bake in 350°F. oven about 1½ hours, cool on wire rack 15 minutes. Remove from pan cool. Sift with powdered sugar if desired.

Choco-Caramel Cheesecake Bites

Oven: 350°F. Bake: 35–40 minutes Yield: 36 bites

Crust

1¼ cups finely crushed chocolate cookie crumbs*
¼ cup butter, melted

Filling

20 caramels, unwrapped
2 Tbsp. fat-free Half & Half
8 oz. package cream cheese, softened
⅓ cup sugar
1 egg
½ tsp. vanilla
¼ cup sour cream, fat free

Coating

12 oz. package (about 2 cups) real semi-sweet chocolate chips
¼ cup shortening

Preheat oven to 350°F. Line 8" square baking pan with parchment paper bring paper up over sides. Lightly spray paper with cooking spray. Spray foil with cooking spray. Combine cookie crumbs and melted butter. Press into the bottom of the 8" pan.

Combine caramels and Half & Half in medium sized glass bowl. Microwave on HIGH (100% power) for 1 minute; stir. Then continue microwaving at 30 second intervals until the mixture is smooth; pour over crust in pan. Sprinkle with pecans. Place in refrigerator while you are preparing cream cheese filing.

Combine cream cheese and sugar in large mixing bowl. Beat at medium speed, scraping bowl often, until creamy. Add egg and vanilla, only beating until the mixture combines. Stir in sour cream, and pour over caramel mixture.

Bake 350°F. for 35 to 40 minutes or until just set 2 inches from edge of pan. Cool on wire rack for 2 hours. *Cover loosely and refrigerate for at least 4–5 hours.* Lift cheesecake from pan using parchment paper. Cut into 36 squares.

Place cooling rack over large piece of waxed paper on counter (to catch drips). Combine chocolate chips and shortening in 1-quart saucepan. Cook over low heat, stirring constantly, until smooth (4 to 5 minutes). Pierce each cheesecake square with fork. Spoon chocolate over top and sides of each cheesecake square, letting excess chocolate drip back into pan. Place onto cooling rack. Let stand about 20 minutes or until chocolate is firm. Store refrigerated.

Note: Substitute finely crushed chocolate sandwich cookie crumbs for cookies.

Hint: Don't over beat the cheesecake batter. Just beat until the ingredients combine. Over beating produces too much air causing cheesecakes to rise during baking, then fall, and crack while it cools.

Dump Cake
Alice Casillas
Oven: 350°F. Time: 30-45 minutes or until golden brown.

1 can crushed pineapple or 1 can cherry pie filling
1 cup shredded coconut
1 box yellow cake mix
1½ sticks butter
1 cup chopped pecans

Do not mix ingredients. Pour entire contents of can into PAM sprayed oblong pan. Sprinkle entire can of coconut over bottom layer. Sprinkle cake mix over coconut. Slice butter into patties and arranges over cake mix. Cover and press chopped pecans into butter.

Note: Any fruit pie filling can be used.

Delicious Norwegian Fruit Cake

Alice Casillas

Oven: 350°F. Time: 2½ hours Yield: 1 cake

2 cups sugar
3 cups butter, softened
6 eggs, separated
3 cups sifted cake flour
2 Tbsp. lemon extract
1 lb. candied cherries, cut
4 oz. candied pineapple, cut
1 lb. golden raisins
1 lb. pecan or walnuts (optional)

Preheat 350°F. Grease and flour tube pan.

In a very large mixing bowl, cream the softened butter. Add sugar, beat well. Beat egg yolks. Add beaten egg yolks to the creamed butter and sugar. Continue creaming and beating. Add lemon extract. Gradually add 2 cups flour.

Dredge cut fruit and nuts with remaining cup of sifted cake flour. Add to butter. When mixed well, fold in stiffly beaten egg whites.

Bake 2½ hours or until done. Fruit cake is done when an inserted toothpick comes out clean.

Easy Chocolate Almond Cake
Regina Aune
Oven: 350°F. Time: 30 minutes Yield: 9" x 13" pan

Cake

½ cup butter or margarine, softened
1 cup sugar
4 eggs
1 cup all-purpose flour
1 tsp. almond extract
1 tsp. baking powder
¼ tsp. salt
16 oz. can chocolate syrup

Icing

1 cup sugar
½ cup butter or margarine
⅓ cup evaporated milk
6 oz. semi-sweet chocolate chips

Preheat oven to 350°F.

To make cake: Mix together butter, sugar, eggs, flour, almond extract, baking powder, and salt. Add chocolate syrup and mix well. Pour into a greased 9"x 13" pan and bake for 30 minutes.

For icing: Heat sugar, butter, and evaporated milk over medium heat, stirring constantly until it come to a rapid boil. Boil for 1 minute. Remove from heat. Add chocolate chips, stirring until well mixed. Then pour over warm cake.

Fruit Cocktail Cake

Louise Malouff

Oven: 350°F. Time 35–40 minutes Yield: 9" x 13" pan

Cake:

2 cups flour
1½ cups sugar
2 eggs
16 oz. can fruit cocktail
2 tsp. baking soda
½ tsp. salt
1 tsp. vanilla

Topping

½ cup evaporated milk
1 cup sugar
1 stick butter
½ lb. coconut (optional)
½ lb. nuts (optional)

For cake: Mix the ingredients very well. Butter only the bottom of baking pan, then pour ingredients into pan. Bake at 350°F. for 35 minutes.

For topping: Put milk, sugar, and butter in bowl, and place in oven until butter dissolves with sugar. Remove and add coconut and nuts, if desired. Pour over cake.

German Butter Pound Cake

Kathy Birkner

Oven: 350°F. Bake 50 minutes
Yield: 1 bundt cake (16 servings)

6 eggs, separated
1 cup butter, softened
2 cups sugar
1 Tbsp. grated lemon peel
1 tsp. vanilla extract
½ tsp. almond extract
1½ cups spelt or King Arthur flour
2 tsp. baking powder
½ tsp. salt
½ tsp. ground cardamom
½ tsp. cinammon
6 Tbsp. 2% milk
2 Tbsp. confectioners' sugar

Separate eggs and put egg whites in large bowl. Allow eggs to come to room temperature (about 30 minutes). Generously, grease with solid shortening and flour a Bundt or 10" tube pan.

In a large mixing bowl, cream sugar and butter until light and fluffy. Then add egg yolks, one at a time, beating well after each yolk. Beat in vanilla and almond extracts and lemon peel. In another bowl, combine dry ingredients of flour, baking powder, salt, cardamom, cinnamon; then add to creamy ingredients alternating with milk, mixing thoroughly with each addition. Remove beaters and clean or use clean whip to beat egg whites until soft peaks form. Fold into cake batter.

Transfer to the prepared cake pan. Bake 350°F. for 50–60 minutes or until toothpick inserted comes out clean. Allow cake to cool 10 minutes before removing to a wire rack to cool. Sprinkle with confectioners' sugar after cooling. Serve.

Harvey Wallbanger Cake

Kathy Birkner

Oven: 350°F. Time: 45–50 minutes Yield: 12–16 servings

1 pkg. yellow cake mix
1 pkg. instant pudding
⅓ cup canola oil
½ cup unsweetened applesauce
⅛ cup vodka
¼ cup Galliano liquor
¾ cup orange juice

Preheat oven to 350°F.

Mix and beat with electric mixer for 4 minutes. Pour into a greased and floured Bundt pan. Bake for 45 to 50 minutes at 350°F. or until toothpick inserted in center comes out clean. Allow to cool 10 to 15 minutes before turning cake onto a serving dish. Frost. Serve.

Note: Galliano can be expensive. See below for a recipe, if you want to make your own.

Substitutions for Galliano are Neopolitan and Sambuca. I have also used cuarenta y tres liqueur.

Homemade Galliano

2 cups distilled water
½ cup sugar
2–3 drops yellow food coloring
1½ cups 188 Proof grain alcohol
6 drops anise extract
2 tsp. vanilla extract

Boil water, corn syrup and sugar for 5 minutes. Add the remaining ingredients and stir. Cover and let stand 1 month in a tightly closed glass container.

Hot Sherry Glaze Cake

Cathy Van Delden

Oven: 350°F. Time: 1 hour Yield: 1 bundt pan

1 butter recipe yellow cake mix
½ cup water
⅓ cup cream sherry
½ cup cooking oil
4 eggs
1 cup pecans, finely chopped

Glaze

1 cup sugar
1 stick butter
½ cup cream sherry

Combine all cake ingredients except pecan in a mixing bowl, and beat for 2 minutes. Fold in chopped pecans. Pour into greased and floured Bundt tube or floured tube pan. Bake 350°F. for 1 hour. Immediately pour hot glaze over the cake and edge after removing from oven. Wait 30 minutes before turning cake out of pan. Enjoy!

Glaze: Mix all ingredients and boil for 2 to 3 minutes. Pour hot glaze immediately after removing cake from oven.

Million Dollar Pound Cake

Frances Jerome

Oven: 350°F. Time: 1 hour 20 minutes Yield: 10" tube pan

2 cups butter
3 cups sugar
6 eggs
4 cups unsifted flour
¾ cup milk
1 tsp. almond extract
1 tsp. vanilla extract

Grease a 10" tube pan. Have ingredients at room temperature. Cream butter; add sugar and beat until light and fluffy. Add eggs one at a time, beating well after each addition. Mix flavorings in milk. Alternately, add one-fourth of the flour with one-third of the milk, ending with the flour. Place in prepared pan. Bake at 350°F. for 1 hour and 20 minutes or until cake tester comes out clean. Cool 15 minutes. Remove from pan.

Mini Cheese Cupcakes

Heidi Van Delden

Oven: 300°F. Time: 20 minutes

¼ cup margarine
3 (8 oz.) pkg. cream cheese
1 Eagle brand condensed milk
¼ cup sugar
1½ cup graham cracker crumbs
2 tsp. vanilla
3 eggs

Preheat oven to 300°F. Combine crumbs, sugar, and margarine. Press equal portions into cups. Beat cheese until fluffy in large mixing bowl, gradually beat in milk until smooth. Add eggs and vanilla. Mix. Pour into cups. Bake at 300°F. 20 minutes.

Mississippi Mud Cake
Elva
Oven: 350°F. Cook time: 45 min. Yield: 1 cake

1 cup margarine
4 eggs
1 cup flaked coconut
1½ cups flour
½ cup cocoa
1 tsp. vanilla
1 cup coarse nuts
13 oz. jar of marshmallow crème

Frosting

½ cups margarine
6 Tbsp. milk
½ cup cocoa
1 box (lb.) powdered sugar
1½ cups nuts

In a large bowl with an electric mixer, cream butter at high speed. Add eggs one at a time, beating well after each addition. Add coconuts, sugar, flour, cocoa, vanilla, and nuts. Stir with a large spoon until well mixed. This is a heavy batter; do not beat. Spread batter in greased 9" x 13" x 2" pan. Bake in 350°F. oven for 45 minutes. As soon as the cake is taken from the oven, spread marshmallow crème over hot cake. Let cool for 20 minutes.

Frosting: Make frosting in a large bowl. Mix together all of the ingredients except nuts. Blend at low speed of electric mixer. Gradually increase speed and blend together until smooth. Stir in half of the nuts. With a large spoon spread frosting on top of the cake. Swirl through marshmallow crème. Sprinkle with remaining nuts.

Pineapple Orange Cake

Cookie (Catherine Hammer)

Oven: 350°F. Time: 25 minutes Yield: 9" X 12" pan 12 servings

1 box yellow cake mix
4 eggs
¾ cup oil or 1 stick butter
1 small can mandarin oranges with juice

Topping

8 oz. Cool Whip
6 oz. instant vanilla pudding
1 small can crushed pineapple with juice

Preheat oven to 350°F.

Mix together the cake mix, eggs, oil and oranges with juice.

Pour batter into a 9"x 13" cake pan. Cook for about 25 minutes or until done. Cool and frost with topping.

For topping: Mix whipped topping, pudding and pineapple with juice. Frost cake. Refrigerate.

Pistachio Marble Cake
Louise Malouff
Oven: 350°F. Time: 50–55 minutes Yield: 1 tube pan

1 pkg. (2 layer size) yellow or white cake mix
3 oz. pkg. pistachio flavor instant pudding and pie filling
4 eggs
1 cup water *
¼ cup oil
½ tsp. almond extract
¼ cup chocolate syrup
*or use: pudding included cake mix and ¾ cup water

Combine cake mix, pudding mix, eggs, water, oil and extract in large mixer bowl. Blend, then beat at medium speed of electric beater for 2 minutes. Measure 1 cup of the batter into a separate bowl and blend in chocolate syrup to that. Spoon batters alternately into greased and floured tube pan. Zigzag spatula through batter to marble.

Bake at 350° F. for 50–55 minutes. Do not *under-bake*.

Rosebud's Frosting for Chocolate Cake
Louise Malouff

1 pkg. powdered sugar
1 stick oleo (½ cup)
2 scant tsp. powdered instant coffee
8 drops maple flavoring
6 drops vanilla flavoring

Sift powdered sugar then add instant coffee. Set aside.

Whip oleo margarine with mixer.

Then add alternately the powdered sugar mixture and margarine. Add flavorings, then add just enough milk for creamy consistency .

Note: *Do not put too much milk in at first. Go very slowly as it is very easy to make too runny!!*

Polish Papal Cream Cake

Kremowka Papieska

Regina Aune

Oven: 400°F. Time: 15 minutes dough Yield: 9" x 13" pan

2 sheets (1.1 lb.) frozen puff pastry dough, thawed
1 tsp. vanilla
Pinch of salt
5 Tbsp. cornstarch
6 large egg yolks
Confectioners' sugar
2 cups milk
¾ cup sugar

Roll out each piece of puff pastry slightly to blend the seam lines. Lightly score each pastry sheet into 9 sections.

Sandwich each puff pastry between two pieces of parchment paper and two cooling racks.

Bake 15 minutes, then remove top rack and top sheet of parchment paper. Cool completely.

Place one layer of the cooked pastry into a 13" x 9" inch pan.

Pour hot pastry cream over it and place the second puff pastry layer on top (see below for making pastry cream). Refrigerate until set.

When ready to serve, dust with confectioners' sugar and cut according to the pre-scored markings.

Pastry Cream: In a medium saucepan, bring milk, sugar, vanilla, salt, cornstarch, and egg yolks to a boil, stirring constantly with a wire whisk.

Reduce heat slightly and continue to boil for 1 minute stirring constantly with a wooden spoon to get in the corners of the pan.

Remove pan from heat and plunge into an ice water bath. Pour cream over cooled puff pastry (as above). Serve.

Revised Red Velvet Cake
Dora Cuellar
Oven: 350°F. Time: 14–16 minutes for 9" pan; 30–40 minutes for Bundt pan Yield: 2 (9" rounds) or 1 Bundt pan

¼ cup butter, softened
1¼ cup sugar or Splenda
2 eggs
½ cup unsweetened applesauce
1 bottle (1 oz.) red food coloring, if desired
1 tsp. white vinegar
1 tsp. vanilla extract
2 cups flour
¼ cup cornstarch
2 tsp. baking cocoa
1 tsp. baking soda
1 tsp. salt
1 tsp. cinnamon
1 cup buttermilk

Frosting:

4½ tsp. all-purpose flour
½ cup fat-free milk
½ cup butter, softened
½ cup sugar
½ tsp. vanilla extract

Line two 9" round baking pans with parchment paper; coat paper with cooking spray and sprinkle with flour. OR use greased and floured Bundt pan. Set aside.

In a large mixing bowl, beat butter and sugar until well blended. Add eggs, one at a time, beating well after each. Add applesauce, food coloring, vinegar and vanilla, beat well. In a small bowl, combine the flour, cocoa, baking soda, cornstarch, cinnamon, and salt. Add to butter mixture alternately with buttermilk. Pour into prepared pans. Bake at 350° for 14–18 minutes for 9" pan or 30–40 minutes for Bundt pan or until a toothpick inserted near the center comes out clean. Cool for 10 minutes before removing from pans. Allow cake to cool completely.

Frosting: In a small saucepan, add milk slowly to flour, whisk flour and milk until smooth. Bring to a boil, then cook and stir for about 2 minutes. Allow milk mixture to cool to room temperature. In a small bowl, cream butter and sugar until light and fluffy. Beat in flour mixture and vanilla. Spread between layers and over top of cake.

Roman Apple Cake

Cathy Van Delden

Oven: 350°F. Time: 40 minutes Yield: 9" x 13" pan

1 cup sugar
½ cup Crisco shortening
1 egg
½ cup milk
1½ cups flour
Dash salt
1 tsp. baking soda
¼ tsp. baking powder
1 tsp. vanilla
2 cups chopped apples

Topping

2 Tbsp. butter, melted
½ cup brown sugar
2 Tbsp. flour
3 tsp. cinnamon
½ cup nuts, chopped

Mix all ingredients except the apples with a mixer. Fold in apples. Pour into a greased 9" x 13" pan.

Prepare topping by combining all of the ingredients and sprinkle over top of cake before baking. Bake at 350°F. about 40 minutes.

Sour Cream Coffee Cake
Oven: 350°F. Time 45 minutes Yield: 9" x 13" pan

Topping

8 oz. walnuts, chopped
3 Tbsp. cinnamon
1 cup sugar

Cake

½ lb. butter (2 sticks)
2 cups sugar
4 eggs
2 tsp. baking powder
½ tsp. salt
2 tsp. baking soda
2 cups flour
2 cups sour cream
2 tsp. vanilla

Cream butter and sugar until fluffy. Beat in eggs one at a time, mixing well after each addition. Stir in vanilla.

Sift dry ingredients together and add to creamed mixture, alternately with sour cream.

Turn half of the batter into a well-floured 9" x 13" pan and sprinkle with half of the topping. Cover with remaining batter and sprinkle the rest of the topping. Bake 350°F. for 45 minutes or until cake tests done.

Salad Oil Chocolate Cake

Louise Malouff

Oven: 350°F. Time: 20-25 minutes Yield: 8" x 8" pan

Sift and mix into bowl:

1 cup sugar
¼ cup cocoa
1½ cup flour

Make hole in middle of flour mixture.

Mix in:

1 cup water
½ cup salad oil
2 tsp. vinegar
1 tsp. baking soda
Dash salt
2 tsp. vanilla

Mix well. Bake until a toothpick inserted near the center comes out clean.

Note: Double recipe for 9" x 13" x 2" pan.

Apple Yogurt Cake
with Cinnamon-Sugar Streak

Oven: 350°F. Bake: 45 to 55 minutes Serves: 8 or more

1½ cups whole-milk yogurt, well-stirred
⅔ cup olive oil
1 lemon, juiced (about ¼ cup)
1 cup sugar
3 large eggs
1½ tsp. vanilla
4 small tart apples (Granny Smith~1½ pounds), peeled, cored
2½ cups all-purpose flour
2½ tsp. baking powder
¾ tsp. baking soda
½ tsp. salt
Pinch of freshly ground nutmeg
2½ tsp. cinnamon, divided
½ cup brown sugar
2 Tbsp. unsalted butter, softened

Heat the oven to 350°F. Lightly grease a 9" x13" baking pan with baking spray or olive oil. Whisk together the yogurt, olive oil, lemon juice, sugar, eggs, and vanilla in a large bowl. Prepare the apples, and chop into chunks about ½" across. You need 3½–4 cups of apples. Stir the chopped apple into the liquid ingredients. Add the flour, baking powder, baking soda, salt, nutmeg, and ½ teaspoon right into the liquids and stir just until no lumps remain. In a small separate bowl, mix the remaining 2 teaspoons cinnamon with the brown sugar and butter. Pour half of the batter into the cake pan. Sprinkle the batter with half of the cinnamon-brown sugar mixture, dropping it on the batter in small lumps. Spread the rest of the batter over top, and sprinkle with the remaining cinnamon-brown sugar.

Bake for 45–55 minutes, cover with foil at the end if the top browns. When a tester comes out clean, transfer the cake to a cooling rack; let cool for at least 15 minutes before cutting. Serve the cake warm or at room temperature. This keeps very well for several days, and it gets even moister as it sits, due to the apples.

Spiced Yogurt Pound Cake

Oven: 350°F. Time: 30–35 minutes Yield: 9" x 13" pan

2 cups sugar
1 cup butter, softened
2¼ cups all-purpose flour
1 cup plain yogurt
1 tsp. vanilla extract
1 tsp. cinnamon
1 tsp. allspice
½ tsp. nutmeg
¼ tsp. cloves
½ tsp. salt
½ tsp. baking soda

Preheat oven to 350°F. Grease and flour a 9" x 13" baking pan.

In a large bowl, cream the butter with sugar until light and fluffy. Beat in flour, yogurt, eggs, vanilla, cinnamon, allspice, nutmeg, cloves, salt, and baking soda. Mix until combined, then beat at high speed for 2 minutes.

Pour batter into prepared pan. Bake at 350°F. for 30 to 35 minutes or until a toothpick inserted near the center comes out clean. Cool cake in pan on wire rack for 15 minutes. Remove and continue to cool.

Note: This is a rich, moist, and delicious spiced pound cake usually made during the fall and winter months. The cake does not need any frosting, except maybe a dusting of confectioners' sugar.

Strawberry Glazed Cream Cheese Cake
Oven: 350° F. Time: 9" 40 to 45 minutes; 10" 50 to 55 minutes

Crust

¾ cup coarsely ground walnuts (3 ounces)
¾ cup finely crushed graham crackers
3 Tbsp. melted unsalted butter

Filling

4–8 ounce packages cream cheese, room temperature
4 eggs
1¼ cups sugar
1 Tbsp. fresh lemon juice
2 tsp. vanilla

Topping

2 cups sour cream
¼ cup sugar
1 tsp. vanilla

Strawberry Glaze

1 quart medium strawberries
12 oz. jar red raspberry jelly
1 Tbsp cornstarch
¼ cup Cointreau
¼ cup water

Position rack in center of oven, preheat to 350°F. Lightly butter 9" to 10" spring form pan.

Crust: Combine walnuts, graham cracker crumbs, and butter. Press compactly into pan.

Filling: Beat cream cheese in large bowl with an electric mixer until smooth. Add eggs, sugar, lemon juice, and vanilla, then beat thoroughly. Spoon over crust.

Set pan on baking sheet to catch any butter that may drip out. Bake 10 inch cake 40 to 45 minutes or 9 inch 50 to 55 minutes.

(Cake may rise slightly and crack in several areas; it will set-
tle again, crack will minimize, and topping will cover cracks.)
Remove from oven and let stand at room temperature 15 minutes.
Retain oven temp at 350°F.

Topping: Combine sour cream, sugar, vanilla; blend well. Cover
and refrigerate. When cake is finished baking, spoon topping
over, starting at the center and extending to ½" of edge. Return
to oven and bake 5 minutes longer. Let cool, then refrigerate
cheesecake for at least 24 hours, preferably 2 to 3 days.

Glaze: Several hours before serving, wash and hull berries, let
dry completely on paper towels. Combine a little jelly with cornstarch in saucepan and mix well. Add remaining jelly, Cointreau
and water, and cook over medium heat stirring frequently until
thickened and clear, about 5 minutes. Cool to lukewarm, stirring
occasionally.

Using knife, loosen cake from pan; remove spring form. Arrange
berries pointed in up over top of cake. Spoon glaze over berries,
allowing some to drip down the sides of cake. Return to refrigerator until glaze is set.

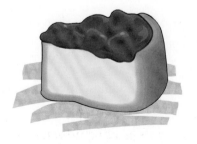

Wacky Cake
Louise Malouff
Oven: 300°F. Time: 40–45 minutes Yield: 1 cake

1½ cups flour
1 cup sugar
½ tsp. salt
1 tsp. baking soda
3 Tbsp. cocoa

1 Tbsp. vinegar
1 tsp. vanilla
5 Tbsp. melted butter
1 cup cold water

Make, mix and bake in ungreased pan.

Sift together flour, sugar, salt, baking soda and cocoa into a cake pan.

Make 3 holes evenly opposite each other.

In first hole, put 1 tablespoon vinegar.

In second hole, put 1 teaspoon vanilla.

In third hole, put 5 tablespoons melted butter.

Pour 1 cup cold water over mixture and stir well.

Bake at 300°F. for 40–45 minutes.

Gingerbread Cake

Oven: 350°F. Time: 50–55 minutes Yield: 8" x 8" pan

½ cup brown sugar
⅓ cup canola
1 large egg
⅓ cup applesauce
½ cup molasses
½ cup agave
2½ cups whole wheat flour
1½ tsp. soda
2 tsp. cinnamon
1 tsp. cloves
2 tsp. ginger
½ tsp. salt

Cream sugar and oil together. Add egg, applesauce, molasses, and agave then beat in. Sift together the dry ingredients and add to creamed mixture slowly beating until smooth. Pour into a 8" x 8" prepared pan. Bake at 350°F. for 50–55 minutes or until a toothpick comes out clean.

Buttermilk Cake

Oven: 375°F. Time: 40–45 minutes Yield: 11" x 7" pan

2 cups flour
½ tsp. soda
½ tsp. baking powder
Pinch of salt
2 sticks butter
2 cups + 2½ Tbsp. sugar divided
4 eggs
1 tsp. vanilla
1 cup buttermilk
1 cup half & half

Sift dry ingredients together. Cream butter with sugar, add eggs one at a time. Add flour mixture alternating with buttermilk mixture. Spray a 11" x 7" baking pan with cooking spray. Pour into pan and bake. After removing cake from oven, combine half and half with sugar in a saucepan and heat, *but do not boil.* Pour over warm cake. Serve from baking dish.

Orange Cake

Oven: 350°F. Time: 40–45 minutes Yield: 11" x 7" pan

1 box butter cake mix
3 eggs
1 can mandarin oranges, cut up, do not drain
¾ cup oil

Mix above ingredients. Grease and flour 9" x 13" x 2" cake pan. Bake at 350° for 25–30 minutes (watch carefully).

Icing

8 oz. pkg. cream cheese, softened
1 small can crushed pineapple, drained
Powdered sugar

Beat cream cheese until fluffy. Add pineapple and enough powdered sugar for proper spreading consistency. (Beat well after adding pineapple and powdered sugar.) Spread on top of cake (I leave mine in pan).

Easy Italian Cream Cake

1 butter pecan cake mix
½ cup pecans
½ cup sour cream

Prepare cake according to box directions. Mix in sour cream and pecans. Bake according to cake box instructions.

Icing

8 oz. pkg. cream cheese at room temperature
1 box powdered sugar
½ cup butter (1 stick)

Chocolate Frosting

Louise Malouff

¼ cup Crisco
½ cup cocoa
¼ salt
⅓ cup milk
1½ tsp. vanilla
3½ cups confectioners' sugar (sift if lumpy)

In a saucepan, melt Crisco. Remove from heat after melting and add cocoa and salt. Stir in milk and vanilla. Put sugar into a bowl. Add chocolate mixture to sugar. Mix at medium speed until smooth and creamy. Add 1 Tbsp. more milk, if needed for good spreading consistency.

Cream Cheese Frosting

Louise Malouff

Soften 3 oz. cream cheese with 1 Tbsp. milk. Gradually blend in 2½ cups sifted confectioners' sugar, ½ tsp. vanilla. Mix well and spread.

Chocolate 'Philly' Frosting

Louise Malouff

3 oz. pkg. cream cheese
1 Tbsp. milk
2½ cups sifted confectioners' sugar
1 oz. square unsweetened chocolate, melted
1 tsp. vanilla
Dash of salt

Combine cream cheese and milk. Add sugar gradually, blending thoroughly. Add chocolate, vanilla and salt. Mix well.

Note: Enough to frost a 2 layer, 8" cake.

Cookies, Bars, & Candy

Anise Biscotti
Pasquale A. Perillo
Oven: 350°F.; 300°F. Bake: 20–22 minutes

6 whole eggs
1 cup sugar
1 cup canola oil or other healthy oil
4 tsp. anise extract
2½ tsp. anise seeds, crushed
4 cups flour
5 tsp. baking powder

Beat eggs, sugar and oil in sequence with an electric mixer until fluffy and well blended. Add anise extract and seeds and beat one minute. Mix flour and baking powder together and add one cup at a time into the wet mixture until the dough can be formed into a thoroughly blended and smooth ball.

Divide dough into four equal balls and form into slightly raised loaves approximately 3 inches wide, 12 inches long and 1 inch high. Place loaves on greased baking sheet and bake in 350°F. oven for 20 to 22 minutes until a toothpick inserted in center of loaf comes out dry. Loaves should be lightly browned. Reduce oven temperature to 300°F. to prepare for the second baking.

When loaves are cool, slice each loaf diagonally with a serrated knife to form small rectangular slices. Place sliced biscotti on a baking sheet ½" apart. The biscotti may be baked standing on the flat edge for 30 minutes in a 300°F. oven; or they may be laid on the flat side and baked for 15 minutes, then turned to the opposite side and bake for an additional 15 minutes.

Remove from oven and allow to cool thoroughly before storing in an air tight container. Biscotti may be consumed immediately or wrapped and frozen for later use for up to two months.

Note: Biscotti are a traditional cookie served with coffee. Biscotti refers to cooking twice. The loaf is baked, sliced and *cooked again* to crisp the cookie to a texture that can be dipped in coffee. These little treasures are low in sugar and fat and versatile when made with seasonal or holiday flavors.

Anise Crescents
Louise Malouff
Oven: 350°F. Time: 15–20 minutes until lightly browned
Yield: 2½ dozen

1 cup butter
½ cup sugar
¼ tsp. salt
¾ tsp. crushed anise seeds
2½ cups sifted flour

Work butter with a *wooden* spoon until creamy. Blend in sugar, salt, and anise seeds; beat until fluffy. Gradually add flour and blend thoroughly. Chill dough one to 2 hours or until stiff enough to handle. Shape into crescents.* While still warm, roll in confectioners' sugar.

*Note: Cookies can also be made into small balls.

Italian Anisette Cookies
Phillip LaMonica
Oven 375°F. Bake: 8 Minutes Yield: 3 dozen

4 cups flour
1 cup sugar
½ cup milk
2 eggs
1 Tbsp. baking powder
¾ cup canola oil
1 Tbsp. anise extract

Icing

1 tsp. anise extract
1 cup confectioners' sugar
2 Tbsp. hot water

Preheat oven to 375° degrees F.

In large bowl, mix flour, baking powder and white sugar. Make a well in the center, then add oil, milk, 1 tablespoon anise extract, and eggs. Mix together until dough is sticky.

Oil fingers and pinch off dough in 1 inch pieces. Roll into a ball and place on sheet of parchment paper, 1 inch apart, flatten top slightly. Bake for 8 minutes. Dip cookies in Icing while warm.

To Make Icing: Blend in 1 teaspoon anise extract and start with 1 tablespoon hot water to 1 cup confectioners' sugar. Add another tablespoon of hot water, if needed to make smooth icing.

Apricot Bars
Regina Aune
Oven: 375°F. Time: 10; then 30 minutes Yield: 75 bars

2 cups Mariani apricots
½ cup firm margarine or butter
½ cup sugar
2½ cups all-purpose baking mix
2 cups packed brown sugar
4 eggs
⅔ cup all purpose baking mix
1 tsp. vanilla
1 cup nuts, chopped
Powdered sugar

Preheat oven to 375°F.

Place apricots in a 2 quart sauce pan, add enough water to cover. Heat to boiling, reduce heat and simmer uncovered for 10 minutes. Cool, chop, and set aside. Cut butter into sugar and 2½ cups all-purpose baking mix until crumbly. Pat into an ungreased jelly roll pan, 15" x 10½" x 1." Bake 10 minutes. Beat brown sugar and eggs. Stir in apricots, ⅔ cup all-purpose baking mix, vanilla, and nuts. Spread over baked layer. Bake 30 minutes longer. Cool completely. Cut into 1" x 2" bars. Roll in powdered sugar.

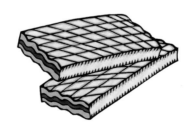

Boiled Chocolate Cookies
Louise Malouff

2 cups sugar
½ cup + 2 Tbsp. milk
½ cup butter or margarine
3 Tbsp. cocoa
½ cup peanut butter
3 cups oatmeal
1 tsp. vanilla
½ cup nuts or coconut (optional)

Boil the sugar, milk, butter and cocoa for 2 minutes.

Remove from heat. Add peanut butter, vanilla and oatmeal plus optionals. Drop by teaspoonful on waxed paper and let cool.

Bourbon Balls
Louise Malouff
No-Bake Yield: 4½ dozen

6 oz. pkg. (1 cup) semi-sweet chocolate morsels
½ cup sugar
3 Tbsp. light corn syrup
⅓ cup bourbon
2½ cups finely crushed vanilla wafers
1 cup walnuts, finely chopped

Melt semi-sweet chocolate morsels over hot (not boiling) water (possibly use a double-boiler pan). Remove from heat.

Stir in sugar and corn syrup. Blend in bourbon. Combine crushed vanilla wafers and walnuts. Add semi-sweet chocolate mixture. Mix well.

Form into 1" balls, then roll in granulated sugar. Let *ripen* in covered container at least several days.

Butterscotch Brownies
Suzanne Karam
Oven: 350°F. Time: 25 minutes
Yield: 8" x 8"; Double for 9" x 13" pan

¼ cup shortening
1 cup packed light brown sugar
1 egg
¾ cup flour
1 tsp. baking powder
½ tsp. salt
½ tsp. vanilla
½ cup chopped nuts

Grease 8" square pan.

Melt ¼ cup shortening, stir in 1 cup packed light brown sugar. Cool completely. Add 1 egg.

Mix remaining ingredients together, *do NOT beat.* Mix with the back of your spoon until combined, pour into greased pan and bake for 25 min.

I always double this recipe and spread in a 9" by 13" pan. Been making these since I was in grade school!

Variation: My mother adds dates and we sprinkle with powdered sugar before cutting.

Cashew Sugar Cookies

Oven: 375°F. Bake Time: 8–10 minutes Makes: 40–42 cookies

1¼ cups all-purpose flour
½ cup ground lightly salted cashews or ground almonds
¼ cup granulated sugar
¼ cup packed brown sugar
½ cup butter
Granulated or coarse sugar
Whole cashews or blanched whole almonds, toasted

In a medium bowl combine flour, ground nuts, granulated and brown sugars. Using a pastry blender, cut in butter until mixture resembles fine crumbs. Form mixture into a ball and knead gently until smooth.

On a lightly floured surface, roll dough until ¼" thick. Using a 1½" cookie cutter, cut into desired shapes. Place 1 inch apart on an ungreased cookie sheet. Lightly sprinkle with additional granulated sugar. Lightly press a whole nut in the center of each cookie.

Bake in a 375°F. oven for 8 to 10 minutes or until lightly browned. Transfer cookies to a wire rack and let cool.

Charles' Peanut Butter Cookies
Charles Malouff
Oven: 350°F. Time: 8–10 minutes

2 cups peanut butter
1 cup sugar
2 eggs
1 cup chocolate chips

Combine ingredients. Stir well. Drop by teaspoons onto cookie sheet.

Chickpea Flour Chocolate Chip Cookies
Gluten-Free
Susan Rizzo
Oven to 350°F. Prep Time: 10 min. Cook Time: 10 min.
Yield: 28 cookies

½ cup butter
2 cups brown sugar
2 eggs
¼ tsp. vanilla
2 cups chickpea flour
½ tsp. salt
½ tsp. baking soda
½ tsp. baking powder
⅔ cup chocolate chips (optional)
chopped nuts (optional)

Mix butter, sugar, eggs, and vanilla.

Mix chickpea flour, salt, soda, and baking powder in a separate bowl. Add dry ingredients to wet ingredients and mix thoroughly. Stir in chips and nuts.

Drop by the tablespoon onto a baking sheet. I use parchment paper, but if you don't, grease the baking sheet. (If your dough is very thick, push it down and spread it out a little. My dough was soft and sticky, and it melted and spread out in the oven.).

Bake at 350°F. for 10-15 minutes. These cookies will have to be a little darker than golden brown so that they will set and hold together

Let cool on the baking sheet for a few minutes before removing. Cool completely on a wire rack.

Brownie Surprises
Oven: 375°F. Cook Time: 7 min. Yield: 4 servings

4 brownies (about 2" x 3") homemade or store bought
¼ cup nutella
¼ cup chopped toasted hazelnuts
¼ cup mini chocolate chips (try a mix of white, semisweet, and milk chocolate)

Spread each of the brownies with 1 tablespoon of nutella. Sprinkle each of the brownies with 1 tablespoon chopped hazelnuts. Top the nuts with 1 tablespoon mini chocolate chips. Place the brownies on a baking sheet and bake for 5 to 7 minutes until the chocolate is starting to melt. Transfer the brownies to the refrigerator and let cool until the chocolate hardens, about one hour.

Bizcochitos - New Mexico Style
Annie Molina
Oven: 400°F. Time: 10 minutes

5–6 cups flour
3 tsp. baking powder
1 ¼ tsp. salt
3 Tbsp. anise seed
2 cups lard (1 lb) (be sure and use lard)
2 large eggs
1 cup sugar
6–7 Tbsp. whiskey or wine
1 tsp. vanilla

Cream together really well the first six ingredients. Add remaining 3 items. Roll to ¼ " thickness, cut with cookie cutter, traditional cutter is fleur-de-lis design. Dip cookie in mixture of ½ cup sugar to 1 Tbsp. ground cinnamon. Place cookies onto baking sheets. Bake.

Chewy Chocolate Chip Cookies
Kathy Birkner
Bake: 350°F. Time: 10–12 minutes Yield: 3 dozen

1 cup sugar
1 Tbsp. molasses
½ cup unsalted butter, room temperature (can use ghee)
½ cup unsweetened applesauce
¼ cup milk (or soy milk)
1 egg
½ tsp. vanilla extract
½ tsp. cinnamon
2 cups rolled oats
1 cup whole-wheat flour or spelt flour
½ cup cocoa powder
½ cup puffy rice cereal
½ tsp. salt
½ tsp. baking soda

Heat oven to 350°F.

Beat sugar, butter, applesauce, milk, egg, cinnamon, and vanilla extract in a large bowl with an electric mixer on medium speed until smooth. Stir in remaining ingredients.

Drop dough by rounded tablespoonfuls about 2 inches apart onto a cookie sheet lined with parchment paper. Bake 10–12 minutes, until cookies are just barely set in the center. Cool 1–2 minutes; remove from cookie sheet to wire rack.

Coconut-Peanut Cookies
(Galletas Maria)

Susan Rizzo
**Oven: 400°F. Prep Time: 20 minutes Inactive: 30 minutes
Yield: Makes about 3½ dozen Cook Time: 12 minutes**

1½ cups all-purpose flour
1 tsp. baking powder
¼ tsp. baking soda
1 tsp. fine salt
¾ cup (1½ sticks) unsalted butter, slightly softened
¾ cup packed light brown sugar
1 large egg
1 cup flaked or shredded sweetened coconut
1 cup old fashioned oats
¾ cup chopped unsalted roasted, skinless peanuts

Preheat to 400°F., place racks in the middle of the oven. Line baking sheets with parchment paper or silicone baking mats. (If you only have 1 baking sheet, let it cool completely between batches.)

Whisk the flour, baking powder, baking soda and salt together in a medium bowl.

Melt the butter in medium saucepan over low heat. Remove the pan from the heat, and stir in the brown sugar with a wooden spoon. The sugar will get soft and saucy, but there may still be a layer of butter on top; don't worry, the mixture comes together as you add the rest of the ingredients.

Stir in the egg, then the flour mixture, taking care not to over mix. Stir in the coconut, oats and nuts dough will look rough and textured. Let dough set until it gets to room temperature, about 30 minutes.

Using a tablespoon-sized ice cream scoop (#60), scoop balls of the dough onto the prepared pans, arranging them about 2½" apart.

Bake until the cookies are golden brown with toasted edges, about 12 minutes. Cool cookies on the pan for a couple minutes. Then transfer to racks to cool.

Store unshaped dough for up to 3 days in the refrigerator.

Store cookies in airtight containers for up to a week. Freeze for 1 month for longer storage.

Cowboy Cookie
Kathy Birkner
Oven: 350°F. Prep Time: 25 minutes Bake Time: 10 minutes

1 cup shortening
1 cup granulated sugar
1 cup brown sugar
2 eggs
1 tsp. vanilla extract
2 cups all-purpose flour
1 tsp. baking soda
½ tsp. salt
½ tsp. baking powder
2 cups rolled oats
½ cup chopped pecans
6 oz. package chocolate chips
½ cup shredded coconut

In a large bowl, using an electric mixer, cream the shortening, granulated sugar, and brown sugar. Add eggs and the vanilla and beat until well blended. Stir in the flour, baking soda, salt and baking powder. Add oats, nuts, chocolate chips, and coconut; mix until combined. Spoon cookie mixture onto greased foil lined cookie sheet. Bake for 8–10 minutes. Transfer cookies to a wire rack to cool.

Chocolate Potato Candy
Susan Rizzo

1 medium potato, peeled
½ cup melted semisweet chocolate
4 cups confectioners' sugar
1 cup peanut butter

Boil potato until very tender. In small bowl, mash potato with fork or masher. Add 3½ cups of confectioners' sugar slowly until thick dough like consistency. Spread remaining sugar on flat surface and roll out dough evenly. Spread on peanut butter and chocolate. Roll into log and cut into 1 inch pieces!

Crisp Date Balls
Theresa Birkner
No-Bake Yield: 24 balls

4 Tbsp. butter
½ cup sugar
1 egg, lightly beaten
1 cup dates, finely chopped
Dash cinnamon
2 cups crisp rice cereal, such as Rice Krispies
½ cup toasted walnuts, chopped (optional)
1 cup flaked unsweetened coconut

Melt butter in a small heavy pan over low heat, and then add sugar. Then add egg stirring until warmed through to combine. Add dates and increase heat to medium. Cook stirring continuously until the mixture thickens, usually about 6–7 minutes. Remove from heat, then add crisp rice cereal and nuts, mix and stir until the rice cereal is coated. As soon as the mixture is cool enough to handle (but usually still very warm), shape heaping teaspoonful of mixture into a tight ball. Roll in coconut to lightly coat the balls. Allow to cool, then store in airtight container.

Date and Nut Pinwheels

Theresa Birkner

Oven: 400°F. Time: 10–12 minutes Yield: 5 dozen cookies

2¼ cups pitted dates, cut up
1 cup sugar
1 cup water
1 cup chopped walnuts
1 cup shortening
2 cups brown sugar, firmly packed
3 eggs, well beaten
4 cups flour
½ tsp. salt
½ tsp. baking soda

Combine dates, white sugar, and water in a pan. Cook over low heat until thick. Add nuts. Set aside to cool.

Cream shortening, add brown sugar gradually, working until light. Add eggs and mix well. Add remaining ingredients. Cover and chill thoroughly. Divide mixture into two parts. Roll each into a rectangle a little less than ¼ inch thick. Spread each with date filling. Roll from long side as you would a jelly roll. Wrap in wax or plastic wrap. Chill in refrigerator overnight.

Cut into one-fourth (¼") slices. Arrange on a greased cookie sheet or parchment paper. Bake 400°F. for 10 to 12 minutes.

Date Apple Bars

Kathy Birkner

Oven: 350°F. Time: 20–25 minutes Yield: 18 bars

5 Tbsp. butter (room temperature)
⅔ cup packed brown sugar
1 large egg
3 Tbsp. milk
½ cup peeled and diced apple
1⅓ cups flour, preferably whole wheat
¾ tsp. baking soda
1 tsp. cinnamon
½ tsp. allspice
¼ tsp. ground nutmeg
½ cup walnut pieces, chopped
½ cup dried dates, pitted and chopped

Preheat the oven to 350°F. Grease a 9" x 13" inch pan.

Cream the butter and brown sugar in a large mixing bowl. Add eggs and milk, mix. Stir in the apple. Add the dry ingredients (flour, baking soda, cinnamon, allspice, and nutmeg) and mix thoroughly. Fold in nuts and dates.

Pour batter into a greased pan and spread. Bake for 20 to 25 minutes, until firm to the touch. Remove from the oven and cool for 10 minutes before cutting in 2" x 3" pieces.

Note:
1) An easy way to chop the dates in a food processor is to take 1 to 2 tablespoons of the flour and sprinkle over dates in a processor; process by pulsing until chopped.
2) These bars can be baked ahead, cut and frozen in plastic bags and kept up to 2 months in the freezer.

Easy Cream Cheese Brownies
Helen Antonelli
Oven: 350°F. Bake Time: 40 minutes Yield: 24 squares

4 squares Unsweetened Baking Chocolate
¾ cup (1½ sticks) of salted butter
2½ cups sugar, divided
5 eggs
1¼ cups flour, divided
1 pkg. (8 oz.) Cream Cheese, softened

Line 13" x 9" inch baking pan with foil extending over edges to form handles. Grease foil.

Microwave chocolate and butter in large microwaveable bowl on HIGH 2 minutes until melted. Stir until chocolate is completely melted.

Stir 2 cups of the sugar into chocolate until well blended. Mix in 4 of the eggs. Stir the flour until well blended.

Spread batter into prepared pan.

Beat cream cheese remaining ½ cup sugar, remaining egg and remaining ¼ cup flour in same bowl with wire whisk until well blended. Spoon mixture over brownie batter.

Swivel knife over the top to marbelize.

Bake at 350°F. for 40 minutes or until toothpick inserted in center comes out clean. (If baking in glass dish, reduce oven temperature to 325°F.) *DO NOT OVERBAKE.* Cool in pan. Lift out of pan onto cutting board. Remove foil. Cut into 24 squares.

Eskimo Snowballs
Susan Rizzo
No-bake recipe

1 cup butter or margarine (softened)
4 Tbsp. water
1 tsp. vanilla extract
6 Tbsp. cocoa powder
1½ cup granulated sugar
4 cups quick-cooking oats
Powdered sugar
Flaked coconut
Chopped nuts

Cream butter with water and vanilla. Add sugar, cocoa, and oatmeal; mix well. Roll into 1" balls. Add more water if necessary to make the dough stick together. Divide the balls in half. Roll half the balls in confectioners' sugar and coconut, then roll the other half in the chopped nuts. Refrigerate until serving.

Tipsy Balls
Louise Malouff

9 oz. pkg. vanilla wafers, crushed fine with a rolling pin
1 cup powdered sugar, sifted
2 Tbsp. cocoa
1½ cup nuts, chopped fine
4 jiggers of whiskey
2 Tbsp. white corn syrup

Combine powdered sugar, cocoa, and nuts; mix well. Then add whisky and corn syrup mixing again. Make into small balls. Roll in more powdered sugar.

Ghiradelli White Blondies

Kathy Birkner

Yield: 10–12 servings

Oven: 350°F. Bake Time: 25 minutes Serving: 24 squares

2 bars (8 oz.) Ghirardelli white chocolate baking bars, broken into 1" pieces

½ cup unsalted butter, cut into small pieces

2 eggs

⅓ cup sugar

1 Tbsp. vanilla extract

1¼ cups flour

¾ tsp. salt

1 cup Ghirardelli semi-sweet chocolate or milk chocolate chips

Preheat oven to 350°F. Line a 9" square baking pan with waxed paper, then grease the paper. Melt white chocolate and butter in a double boiler over hot, but not boiling water. Stir mixture occasionally until smooth. Set aside.

In a large mixing bowl, beat eggs until foamy. Add sugar, vanilla extract, melted chocolate and butter slowly. Fold in flour, salt, and chocolate chips until well mixed. Spoon mixture into the prepared pan. Bake 25 minutes. Cut; serve warm or at room temperature.

Ginger Pecan Oatmeal Crisps

Oven Temp: 350°F. Times: Cook 15 minutes
Prep 15 minutes   Inactive Prep: 2 hours Yield: 4 dozen

¾ cup pecan halves
1 cup whole-wheat flour
¼ cup cornstarch
1 tsp. ground ginger
½ tsp. fine salt
¼ tsp. baking soda

¾ cup (1½ sticks, 6 ounces) unsalted butter, softened
¾ cup granulated sugar
⅓ cup light brown sugar
1 tsp. pure vanilla extract
1 large egg

Grind the oatmeal and pecan pieces in a food processor until they resemble cornmeal that is reasonably fine but with some texture. Whisk the whole wheat flour, cornstarch, ginger, salt and baking soda together in a medium bowl. Whisk in the oat/nut mixture.

In another medium bowl, beat the butter with an electric mixer until smooth and light, about 1 minute. Gradually add the granulated and light brown sugar; continue beating until evenly combined, about 3 minutes more. Add the vanilla and the egg.

Mix in the dry ingredients to make a textured dough. Line a 1½ quart loaf pan or 3 mini loaf pans with plastic wrap and pack dough into the bottom half of the pan. Press to level off the dough. Lay a piece of plastic wrap on top and refrigerate until completely firm, about 2 hours.

Preheat the oven to 350°F. Line 2 baking sheets with parchment paper or silicone mats. Remove dough from the pan and unwrap. Slice dough in half lengthwise if using a large pan. Slice each log crosswise into ¼" thick cookies. Place the cookies about a 1" apart on the prepared pans. Bake until golden brown, 15 to 18 minutes. Transfer cookies to a rack to cool and crisp. Serve.

Store cookies in a tightly sealed container for up to 1 week.

Ghiradelli Mississippi Mud Bars
Kathy Birkner

Oven: 350°F. Bake: 12–15 minutes Yield: 10–12 servings

½ cup butter or margarine, softened
¾ cup brown sugar, firmly packed
1 tsp. vanilla extract
1 large egg
1 cup all-purpose flour
½ tsp. baking soda
¼ tsp. salt
1 bar (4 oz.) Ghirardelli semi-sweet chocolate baking bar, chopped and divided
1 bar (4 oz.) Ghirardelli white chocolate baking bar, chopped and divided
1 cup walnuts, chopped and divided

Preheat oven to 350°F.

In a large bowl, beat butter, sugar, egg and vanilla at medium speed until light and fluffy. Mix in flour, baking soda and salt. Stir in half of the semi-sweet and white chocolate and ½ cup of the walnuts. Spread in greased foil-lined 9" square baking pan.

Bake 12–15 minutes or until toothpick inserted in center comes out almost clean. Sprinkle with remaining semi-sweet and white chocolates. Cover with foil. Let stand 5 minutes or until chocolates are melted.

Swirl chocolates with small knife to marbelize. Sprinkle with remaining ½ cup walnuts.

Cool in pan until firm, then cut into bars.

Gingersnaps

Oven: 325°F. Cook time: 8 to 12 minutes Yield: 2 to 3 dozen

¾ cup butter
1 cup sugar
1 egg
¼ cup molasses
2 cups flour
1 Tbsp. ginger, ground
1 tsp. cinnamon
½ tsp. salt
½ tsp. baking soda
1 cup sugar

Cream butter and sugar until light. Add egg, and molasses; beat well. Combine flour, spices, salt, and soda; add to creamed mixture, blending well. Shape into small balls and roll in sugar. Bake at 325°F. for 8 to 12 minutes.

Jean's Brownies
Jean Steigerwald

Oven: 375°F. Time: 20–25 minutes. Yield: 9" x 13" pan

Melt in pan on stove: Then set aside.

2 sticks oleo
8 Tbsp. cocoa

Mix in mixing bowl:

1¼ cups flour
2 cups sugar
4 eggs
2 tsp. vanilla

Add chocolate mixture and flour mixture. Add nuts, if desired.

Butter 9" x 13" pan, then pour in batter. Bake.

Kuluri (Cookies)
Thelma O'Shaughnessy
Oven: 350°F. Time: 15–20 minutes
Yield: About 100 cookies depending on size

6 large eggs
1 cup butter, room temperature
½ cup oil
1 tsp. vanilla extract
1 jigger whiskey or cognac
4 tsp. baking powder
½ tsp. baking soda
2 cups sugar
6–7 cups flour

Heat the oven to 350°F. Cream butter in mixer, then add sugar, mix. Add oil, mix. Then add eggs, vanilla, and whiskey. Add baking powder and baking soda. Then add flour slowly by the cup, mixing constantly until the mixture pulls away from sides, but is still soft and pliable. Using cookie press or other pressing device, make into desired shapes. Place on parchment covered baking sheet. Bake about 15 to 20 minutes until lightly browned.

Variation: Add peel of 1 grated orange

Note: Dough can be rolled and put into a loop ring, or rolled and twisted into a rope-like cookie, or a "S" shaped cookie. Your imagination is your guide.

Marshmallow Treats
Louise Malouff

¼ cup butter or margarine
7–10 oz. regular marshmallows (about 32) OR 3 cups miniature marshmallows.
5–6 cups Rice Krispies

Melt butter in 3 qt. saucepan. Add marshmallows and cook over low heat, stirring constantly until marshmallows are melted and mixture is well-blended. Remove from heat. Add Rice Krispies and stir until well coated. Press warm mixture into buttered 13 x 9" pan. Cut into squares when cool.

Variation: About 2 cups marshmallow crème may be substituted for marshmallows. Add to melted butter and cook over low heat about 5 minutes, stirring constantly.

Proceed as directed above.

Chocolate No-Bake Cookies
Louise Malouff

3 cups oatmeal
2 Tbsp. peanut butter
½ cup coconut (optional)
½ cup milk
4 Tbsp. cocoa
2 cups sugar
1 tsp. vanilla
¼ lb. margarine

In a bowl combine oatmeal, peanut butter and coconut.

In a pan boil milk, cocoa and sugar for 1 minute. Then add margarine and vanilla. Pour fudge mixture over dry mixture. Mix well then drop by teaspoons on waxed paper.

No-Bake Cookies
Louise Malouff

1 stick butter
1 cup sugar
⅓ cup cocoa
⅓ cup milk
3 cups oatmeal
½ cup peanut butter

Bring above ingredients to a boil, remove from heat.

Stir in 3 cups oatmeal and ½ cup peanut butter

Drop onto waxed paper.

Miniature Shoo Fly Pies
Louise Malouff
from 1976 Bicentennial Cookbook

Oven: 400°F. Time: 20 minutes Yields: 16 servings

1½ cup margarine or oleo
6 oz. cream cheese
3½ cups flour
2 eggs
1½ cup (packed) brown sugar
2 Tbsp. melted butter
¼ tsp. vanilla
1 cup sugar

Soften 1 cup margarine and cream cheese. Combine 2 cups flour, softened margarine and cream cheese to form dough. Line muffin tins with dough, pressing evenly around sides and bottom of tins.

Combine eggs, brown sugar, melted butter and vanilla. Pour into pastry-lined tins. Cut remaining margarine and sugar into remaining flour, sprinkle over filling in muffin tins.

Bake in 400°F. oven for 20 minutes or until golden brown.

Orange Zest Biscotti
Pasquale A. Perillo
Oven: 350°F., then later 300°F. Bake: 20–22 minutes 1st time; 30 minutes total 2nd time Yield: 4 loaves, sliced

6 whole eggs
1 cup sugar
1 cup canola oil or other healthy oil
1 tsp. orange extract
1 Tbsp. orange zest
4 cups flour
6 tsp. baking powder
1 cup dried cranberries or golden raisins
1 cup toasted pistachio nuts or slivered almonds (optional)

Beat eggs, sugar & oil in sequence with an electric mixer until fluffy and well blended. Mix flour and baking powder together and add one cup at a time into the wet mixture until the dough can be formed into a thoroughly blended and smooth ball. If cranberries and/or nuts are used, they should be added after the last cup of flour is added to the wet mixture.

Divide dough into four equal balls and form into slightly raised loaves approximately 3" wide x 12" long x 1." Place loaves on greased baking sheet and bake in 350°F. oven for 20 to 22 minutes until a toothpick inserted in center of loaf comes out dry. Loaves should be lightly browned. Reduce oven temperature to 300 degrees to prepare for the second baking.

When loaves are cool, slice each loaf diagonally with a serrated knife to form small rectangular slices. Place sliced biscotti on a baking sheet ½ inch apart. The biscotti may be baked standing on the flat edge for 30 minutes in a 300°F. oven; or they may be laid on the flat side and baked for 15 minutes, then turned to the opposite side and bake for an additional 15 minutes. Remove from oven and allow to cool thoroughly before storing in an airtight container. Consume immediately or wrap and freeze for later use for up to two months.

NOTE: Biscotti may be made in many sizes, textures and flavors. They may be rustic with large pieces of nuts and fruit, or "biscotti" may be made smaller and iced with chocolate glaze. Our recipe features a process that was used in home baking and ideal for morning or afternoon coffee with family, or stored in an attractive tin to serve guests. Experiment and discover how well this treat adapts to many flavors and additions to create your signature specialty!

Peanut Butter Bars
Kathy Birkner
Oven: 350°F. Time: 45–45 minutes Yield: 24 bars

⅔ cup butter, softened
⅔ cup creamy peanut butter
1 cup sugar
1 cup packed brown sugar
4 eggs
2 tsp. vanilla
2 cups flour
2 tsp. baking powder
½ tsp. salt
1 pkg. milk chocolate chips

Preheat oven to 350°F. Grease a 13" x 9" pan.

In a large bowl, cream the butter, peanut butter, and two sugars. Add eggs, one at a time, beating after each egg. Beat in vanilla. Mix dry ingredients of flour, baking powder, and salt. Slowly add the dry ingredients to the creamed mixture. Stir in chips.

Spread into the prepared pan. Bake in 350°F. for 45–50 minutes or until a toothpick comes out clean. Cut into bars while hot. Cool on a wire rack.

Peanut Butter Cookies

with Turbinado Sugar

Oven: 350°F. Bake: 16 min.

¼ cup (½ stick) unsalted butter
1 cup turbinado sugar
1 cup salted chunky natural peanut butter
1 large egg
½ tsp. vanilla extract
½ tsp. baking soda
¼ tsp. salt
¾ cup whole-wheat flour
Additional turbinado sugar

Position racks in center of oven and preheat to 350°F. Using electric stand mixer, beat butter and 1 cup turbinado sugar with paddle attachment until well blended. Add peanut butter and mix well. Beat in egg and vanilla. Mix in baking soda and salt. Thoroughly mix in flour.

Using hands, form dough into 1¼" balls. Dip half of each dough ball into additional turbinado sugar. Place dough balls sugar side up on ungreased cookie sheet, spacing about 3" apart. Using flat-bottomed glass and applying even pressure, flatten each ball to ¼" thickness.

Bake until golden brown, about 16 minutes. Cool 2 minutes. Using spatula, transfer cookies to wire rack to cool. Store cookies in airtight container.

Do Ahead Tip: Cookies can be made 1 day ahead. Store airtight at room temperature.

Pumpkin Whoopie Pie

Oven: 375°F. Time: 11 minutes Yield: 24 pies

2 cups spelt or whole grain flour
1 cup oatmeal, ground in food processor
½ tsp. salt
1 tsp. baking powder
1 tsp. baking soda
2 tsp. cinnamon
½ tsp. ginger
½ tsp. nutmeg
¼ tsp. cloves
½ cup sugar
2 eggs
¾ cup brown sugar, packed
15 oz. can canned pumpkin
½ cup applesauce
1 tsp. vanilla

Filling

4 oz. reduced fat or fat-free cream cheese
2 cups powdered sugar

Pies: Heat oven. Line a cookie sheet with parchment paper. Set to the side. Combine flour, oatmeal, baking powder, baking soda, salt, cinnamon, ginger, nutmeg, and cloves in a bowl.

In a large bowl, beat together sugar and eggs about a minute so it is fluffy and light. Add brown sugar, pumpkin, applesauce, and vanilla. Then add flour mixture and mix thoroughly. Drop by heaping tablespoon onto prepared cookie sheet. Bake 11–12 minutes. Allow to cool slightly before taking off cookie sheet. Place on wire rack to cool completely.

Filling: Combine cream cheese with powdered sugar in a small bowl. Mix until well combined, creamy and smooth. Spread filling on the flat side of a cookie and place a second cookie, flat side onto filling, making a sandwich.

Variation: Substitute equal amount of Splenda for white sugar. For brown sugar, substitute 2¼ cups Splenda + 2 tsp. molasses. Use Splenda in place of powdered sugar in filling.

Rum Balls
Nancy Karam
Yield: 3–4 dozen balls

3 cups ground vanilla wafers (one 12 oz. pkg.)
¾ cup finely chopped pecans
2 tablespoons cocoa
3 tablespoons dark corn syrup
½ cup rum (dark rum is better)
Confectioners' sugar

Chop vanilla wafers in food processor until consistency of coarse corn meal. You can also crush them between waxed paper sheets with a rolling pin. Mix ground wafers, nuts, and cocoa. Add corn syrup and rum and mix thoroughly by hand. Roll into balls about ¾ to 1" in diameter. Roll balls in confectioners' sugar then store in cookie tin for a day or so for best flavor.

Toffee Peanut Clusters
Prep/Total Time: 30 min. Yield: 60

1½ lb. milk chocolate candy coating, coarsely chopped
16 oz. jar dry roasted peanuts
8 oz. pkg. milk chocolate English toffee bits

In a microwave, melt candy coating; stir until smooth. Stir in peanuts and toffee bits. Drop by rounded tablespoonfuls onto waxed paper-lined baking sheets. Let stand until set. Store in an airtight container.

Symon Joy (candy)
Kathy Birkner

6 oz. sweetened condensed milk
1 tsp. vanilla
⅛ tsp. salt
2 cups powdered sugar
14 oz sweetened shredded coconut
¾ cup whole unsalted almonds (toasted; if desired)
16 oz. bittersweet chocolate or chocolate chips (1 bag)
2 Tbsp. canola oil
Cooking Spray

Line an 8" x 8" pan with foil, overlapping the edges, and lightly spray with cooking spray.

In a mixing bowl, combine the condensed milk, vanilla, and salt. Add and mix in the confectioners' sugar (1 cup at a time) until you have a smooth mixture. Then add the coconut mixing until combined and coated. Pour mixture into the prepared pan and press in to an even layer using your hands or rubber spatula lightly coated with cooking spray. If almonds are desired, place the almonds in single rows, about 8, leaving room in between, and press them slightly in to the Coconut mixture so they stick. Refrigerate for at least an hour, until firm enough to cut in to bars. When the Coconut mixture has set, lift out of the pan by the foil. Peel the foil off and place on a cutting board. Cut in to strips in between the rows of almonds; then cut in to bars, every 2 almonds. Keep refrigerated until ready to coat.

Set a medium mixing bowl over a small pot of simmering water and add chocolate chips to the bowl. Stir every so often until they have melted, and then add the oil. Stir until the oil and chocolate are completely blended and the chocolate is thinned and shiny. Using a fork, dip each bar in to the chocolate, letting any excess drip off. Place the dipped bars on a wax paper lined baking sheet. Dip all of the bars and then let them sit until the chocolate firms and sets up. Store at room temperature or refrigerate.

Three-Ingredient Peanut Butter Cookies

Charles Malouff, Jr.

Oven: 350°F. Time: 6–8 minutes Yield: 1 dozen

1 cup peanut butter
1 cup white sugar
1 egg

Preheat oven to 350°F. Line baking sheets with parchment paper.

Combine the peanut butter, white sugar and egg. Mix until smooth. Drop by teaspoonful of dough onto the prepared baking sheet.

Bake at 350°F. for 6 to 8 minutes. Do not over bake! These cookies are best when they are still soft and just barely brown on the bottoms.

Rugalach

Frances Jerome

Oven: 375°F. Chill 4 hrs. Bake: 15 minutes Yield: 40

2 cups sifted flour
½ tsp salt
1 cup softened butter
8 oz. pkg. cream cheese (room temperature)
⅓ cup sugar
1 Tbsp. cinnamon
½ cup finely-chopped nuts
¼–½ cup raisins

Cream butter and cheese until fluffy. Blend in flour and salt. Chill several hours in wax paper. Divide dough into four parts. Roll each part out to 10" to 12," with ¼" thickness. In a small bowl, mix sugar, cinnamon, raisins, and nuts. Sprinkle ¼ of filling on round and cut into 10 wedges. Starting a wide end, roll each wedge into crescent. Repeat with remaining 3 parts of dough. Bake at 375°F. for 15 minutes, until golden brown.

White Chocolate Macadamia Cookie
Oven: 300°F. Time 16–18 minutes Yield: 40–44 cookies

1½ cups brown sugar
¾ cup sugar
1¾ sticks unsalted butter (at room temperature)
1½ tsp. baking soda
1½ tsp. salt
2 large eggs + 1 yolk
6 Tbsp. agave
1 tsp. vanilla
3 cups flour
8 oz. white chocolate chips
4 oz. macadamia nuts, chopped

Line 2 baking sheets with parchment paper. In mixer bowl, cream together sugars, butter, baking soda, and salt beating at medium speed until mixture is soft and fluffy (about 3 minutes). Reduce mixer speed to low and gradually add eggs and egg yolk, agave, and vanilla, mixing well. Add flour, chocolate chips, and macadamia nuts and blend just to combine.

Spoon batter by round teaspoonful onto prepared baking sheets about 2" apart. Bake one sheet at a time rotating the pan half way through baking time for total of 16–18 minutes or cookies take on a lightly golden brown. After removing from oven, transfer the cookies using a spatula to a wire rack to cool. Repeat but allow baking sheet to cool between batches until all the cookie dough is used. Store in a sealed container or wrap air-tight and freeze for 2 months.

Pies & More

Apple Berry Pie
Theresa Rizzo
Oven: 425°F. Bake Time: 40–50 minutes Yield: 6–8 servings

3 cups chopped peeled apples
½ cup sugar
¼ cup chopped pecans or walnuts
¼ cup raisins
3 Tbsp. flour
½ tsp. cinnamon
¼ tsp. nutmeg
2 Tbsp. margarine melted
16 oz. can whole berry cranberry sauce
15 oz. pkg. pie crusts
1 tsp. flour

Prepare pie crusts according to package directions for two-crust pie using a 9" pie pan and a teaspoon of flour to smooth out pie crust.

Cut second crust into 6 or 8 wedges, set aside. Preheat oven to 425°F.

In a large bowl combine all filling ingredients; mix lightly. Spoon into pie crust lined pan. Arrange pie crust wedges over berry mixture points of wedges meeting in the center. (Do not overlap). Peel back the points of the pie crust to form petals, gently press the points into the crust. Fold outer edge of each wedge under bottom crust, flute.

Bake at 425°F. for 40–50 minutes or until crust is golden brown and apples are tender.

Note: Cover edge of pie crust with strip of foil during last 10–15 minutes of baking, if necessary, to prevent excessive browning.

Grandma's Apple Crisp
Louise Malouff
Oven: 375°F. Time: 30 minutes Serves: 6

Filling

6 tart apples, peeled and sliced
⅓ cup sugar
½ tsp. cinnamon
Butter

Crust

1 cup flour
1 cup sugar
1 tsp. baking powder
Dash of salt
1 stick cold butter
1 beaten egg

Dust apples with sugar and cinnamon and dab with butter. Place on bottom of 9" square cake pan.

To make crust, blend flour, sugar, baking powder and salt. Cut butter in small pieces and blend into flour mixture with pastry blender. Beat egg and drizzle into flour mixture. It will be crumbly. Pour over the apples. Bake at 375°F. for 30 minutes or until browned.

Louise's Pumpkin Pie
Louise Malouff
Oven: 425°F. / 350°F. Time: 15/45 minutes Yield: 9" pie

2 eggs, slightly beaten
1¾ cups pumpkin
¾ cup sugar
1 tsp. salt
2 tsp. cinnamon
1 tsp. ginger
½ tsp. cloves
1⅔ cups evaporated milk
9" unbaked pie shell

Mix ingredients in order given. Pour into pastry shell. Bake in hot oven 425°F. for 15 minutes. Reduce temperature to moderate 350°F. and continue baking 45 minutes longer or until knife inserted in center comes out clean.

Mango Mousse
Alice Casillas

1 can mangoes (liquid included)
8 oz. pkg. cream cheese (softened)
6 oz. pkg. orange gelatin
3 oz. pkg. lemon gelatin
2 cups boiling water
Fresh or frozen strawberries (optional)

In a blender, place mangoes and softened cream cheese; blend until smooth. Dissolve gelatins in boiling water. Add blended mango-cheese mixture to dissolved gelatins. Pour into greased mold. Chill until set. Garnish with fresh or frozen strawberries.

Note: Sugar-free gelatin may be substituted. Reduced fat or fat-free cream cheese may be substituted.

Siti's Apple Pie
Louise Malouff
Oven: 375°F. Time: 45 minutes Yield: 1 pie

Crust

2 cups flour
¼ tsp. salt
1 cup + 1 Tbsp. shortening
¾ cup cold water

Filling

4 large apples or 7 small apples per pie (Jonathan Apples or
    Winesap Apples work well), peeled and thin
¼ tsp. nutmeg
2 Tbsp. lemon juice
2 tsp. flour
1¼ tsp. cinnamon
¾ cup sugar (1 cup for larger pies)
Milk for sprinkling

Crust: Mix crust ingredients well and roll out (crust will make 2 pies). Put bottom layer of pie crust into pie pan.

Filling: Mix apples, spices, lemon juice, flour, and sugar; mix well. Pour apple mixture into pie shell and dot with 2 tablespoons of butter. Put top crust on and cut slits into top. Sprinkle with little milk and sugar.

Note: If frozen, take aluminum wrap off, and warm at 350°F. for ½ hour.

Walnut Pumpkin Pie
Rosemary Karam
Oven: 425°F. then 350° F. Yield: 8 servings

1 graham cracker pie crust
1 can pumpkin
14 oz. sweetened condensed
Milk (NOT evaporated milk)
1 egg
1¼ tsp. cinnamon
½ tsp. each of ground ginger, nutmeg and salt
½ cup packed brown sugar
2 Tbsp. all-purpose flour
2 Tbsp. cold margarine or butter
¾ cup walnuts, chopped

Heat oven to 425°F. In a mixing bowl, combine pumpkin, sweetened condensed milk, egg, ¾ teaspoon of cinnamon, ginger, nutmeg and salt; mix well. Turn into pie crust.

Bake 15 minutes; remove pie. Reduce oven temperature to 350°F.

In a small bowl, combine sugar, flour and remaining ½ teaspoon cinnamon; cut in margarine until crumbly. Stir in walnuts. Sprinkle walnut mixture evenly over pie.

Bake 40 minutes or until knife inserted 1" from edge comes out clean. Cool. Garnish as desired.

Never Fail Pie Crust
Kathy Birkner
Yield: 3 (9"–10") pie crusts

3 cups whole wheat or spelt flour
1 cup shortening
1 Tbsp. sugar
2 tsp. salt
1 Tbsp. vinegar
1 egg, beaten
½ cup water

Mix flour and shortening in food processor, pulsing into a crumbly mixture. If you do not have a food processor, use a fork to incorporate the shortening in the flour. Add sugar, egg, vinegar, and water; pulse to mix well and form into a ball. Roll into pie crust.

Note: roll crust between 2 pieces of plastic wrap for easy placement into pie dish. Any leftover portion can be frozen for use later.

Banana Split Dessert
No Bake Yield: 9"X 13"

Deborah Day

1 large pkg. No Bake Cheesecake (Mix according to pkg. directions.)
3–4 bananas, sliced
16 oz. can crushed pineapple, drained
16 oz. Cool Whip
1 jar strawberry topping
Chocolate and/or caramel syrup
Maraschino cherries with stems (optional)
Nuts (walnuts or pecans, if desired)

Make cheesecake according to directions on box; pour into pan and spread. Refrigerate for 1 hour. Then layer in order: bananas, pineapple, Cool Whip, strawberry topping. Drizzle chocolate and/or caramel over top. Top with Maraschino cherries. Refrigerate until ready to serve. Place cut nuts on top or serve in a bowl as desired.

Cheri's Apple Pie

Cheri Cole

Cream Filling

Large graham cracker crust
8 oz. cream cheese at room temperature
16 oz. sour cream
1 Tbsp. sugar or to taste

Apple Filling

20 oz. can apple pie filling
1 tsp. cinnamon
¼ tsp. nutmeg
¼ cup brown sugar
Cinnamon for garnish

Chop apple slices into smaller pieces; then add cinnamon, nutmeg, and brown sugar.

Whip cream cheese and sour cream together; add a tablespoon of sugar. Combine cream cheese mixture with apple mixture, then pour and spread into pie crust.

Sprinkle with cinnamon. Chill for at least 1 hour, Serve.

Pistachio Pie

Oven: 350°F. Serving: 6-8

2 pkg. instant pistachio pudding
12 oz. container Cool Whp
16 oz. can crushed pineapple
1 large graham cracker crust

Bake graham cracker crust for 6-7 minutes in a 350°F. oven. Allow to cool.

While crust is cooling, combine pudding, Cool Whip, and pineapple with juice using a mixer. Then pour mixture into cooled crust. Place in refrigerator for about an hour to allow time to set. Serve.

Miscellaneous

Drinks & Beverages

Spices

Make Your Own

Dog Treats and Food

Saline

Laundry Detergent

Different Flours

Green Living

Blessing for a Happy Home

Drinks & Beverages

Dad's Eggnog (Modified version)
Louise Malouff

6 eggs, whipped
1 cup sugar
3 Tbsp. vanilla
1 tsp. cinnamon
¼ tsp. nutmeg
Pinch of salt
6 cups light cream
¾ cup bourbon
⅓ cup dark Jamaican rum
Whipped cream
Nutmeg

Whip together eggs. Add sugar. Whip in the remainder of the ingredients, one ingredient at a time in order given. Top with whipping cream and nutmeg.

Lemonade
Yield: 10 (8 Oz.) Servings

1½ cups lemon juice (about 6 lemons)
1¾ cups sugar
8 cups water

Combine sugar and 1 cup water. Bring to a boil stirring to dissolve sugar. Remove from heat and allow to cool to room temperature. After syrup cools, refrigerate until it is chilled.

Put lemons in microwave for 15 seconds. Then squeeze removing the seeds, but leaving the pulp. Chill until syrup is ready. In a large pitcher combine syrup with the lemons and remaining water. Serve over ice.

Orange Julius

Louise Malouff
Yield: 6 cups

6 oz. can frozen orange juice
1 cup milk
1 cup water
½ cup sugar
1 tsp. vanilla
10–12 ice cubes

Combine all ingredients in blender. Cover and blend until smooth, about 30 seconds. Serve immediately.

Red Champagne Punch

Susan Rizzo

1 cup sugar
1 (750 milliliter) bottle Burgundy wine
2 (750 milliliter) bottles champagne, chilled
8 fluid ounces brandy
1 quart club soda

In a punch bowl, dissolve the sugar in the Burgundy wine. Stir in the champagne, brandy, and club soda just before serving.

White Vodka Punch

Susan Rizzo

1 (750 milliliter) bottle vodka
1 (46 fl. oz.) can grapefruit juice
1 (46 fl. oz.) can pineapple juice
2 liter bottle lemon-lime flavored carbonated beverage
2 trays ice cubes, or an ice ring

In a *swanky* punch bowl (a MUST), combine the vodka, grapefruit juice, pineapple juice, lemon-lime soda and ice, or ice ring. This punch is too good for the little punch glasses that come with the punch bowl so use your highball glasses, stand around the punch bowl and have a good time!

Arnold Palmer Tea

½ cup lemonade
½ cup basic tea
Sugar or sweetener, if desired

Combine the lemonade and tea. Add sugar or sweetener, if desired. Serve over ice.

Spices & Mixtures

Arabic 7 Seven Spice
(Bokharat)

Susan Rizzo

2 Tbsp. ground black pepper
2 Tbsp. paprika
2 Tbsp. ground cumin
1 Tbsp. ground coriander
1 Tbsp. ground cloves
1 tsp. ground nutmeg
1 tsp. ground cinnamon
½ tsp. ground cardamom

Mix all ingredients well. Store in an airtight container or in freezer. You can also roast and grind these spices yourself first before mixing.

Note: A great idea gift idea—make, decorate and wrap in a beautiful bottle glass. Not everyone is aware of this spice, it's great in many dishes such as beef and chicken, and gives a nice exotic flavor.

Poultry Rub
Kathy Birkner
Yield: about 3 Tbsp.

2 tsp. brown sugar
½ tsp. salt
1 tsp. black pepper
2 tsp. smoked paprika
1 tsp. garlic powder
1 tsp. dried basil
½ tsp. dried parsley
⅛ tsp. cayenne pepper (optional)

Combine all of the ingredients. Makes enough rub to season 8 chicken breasts with bone or without bone or a 4 pound chicken.

Salt & Spice

Susan Rizzo
Yield: ⅓ cup

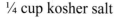

¼ cup kosher salt
2 Tbsp. McCormick® Perfect Pinch® Salt Free Garlic Pepper
Seasoning, McCormick® seasoned pepper Blend or Lawry's®
Seasoned Pepper
1 Tbsp. McCormick® garlic salt
1 Tbsp. McCormick® onion powder
1½ tsp. McCormick® celery seed, crushed

Mix all ingredients in blender/food processor until well blended.
Store in tightly covered jar in cool, dry place.

Note: This spice blend is similar to the discontinued Salt 'n Spice
product. It contains salt, pepper, onion, garlic and celery seed.

Usage Tips: Use this all-purpose seasoning as you would salt
and pepper. It tastes great on scrambled eggs, potatoes, hamburg-
ers, potato salad and vegetables.

Jalapeno Spice

Kathy Birkner
Yield: 2 tsp. ground spice

12 jalapeno peppers (or other spicy hot peppers)

Rinse peppers in cold water and remove stem. Slice into small
rounds. Place on a tray and let dry in the sun for 5-7 days (with
at least 5 hours of direct sunlight). Bring inside at night to avoid
moisture OR place peppers on a foil-lined pan in the oven and
bake at 250°F. for 15–30 minutes until dry (don't overheat) so
you can grind them. When dry, grind in a food processor taking
care not to inhale the spice or get it in your eyes. Then place in an
airtight shaker container and store in a cool place.

Baking Powder

Kathy Birkner

Yield: 1⅔ cup

⅓ cup potassium bicarbonate
⅔ cup cream of tartar
⅔ cup arrowroot

Combine and store in a glass jar. Use instead of commercially prepared baking powder.

Note: Most store baking powders have high sodium content as well as aluminum. Rumford brand is the only baking powder available that does not contain aluminum.

Sweetened Condensed Milk Substitute

Kathy Birkner

1 cup instant nonfat dry milk
⅔ cup granulated sugar
½ cup boiling water
3 Tbsp. butter, melted

Combine, then let cool. Use instead of commercial condensed milk.

Note: Substitute ⅔ cup Splenda or Xylitol for sugar if you are cooking for a diabetic. Do not let your dog taste as it causes low blood sugar that can kill him.

Orange Flower Water

Azizi Karam

1 tsp. orange blossom extract
½ cup cup water

Combine to make orange blossom water.

Pet Foods and Treats

Home Cooked Dog-Cat Diet

Kathy Birkner

Yield: Basic recipe feeds 50 pound dog for 1 day. Increase or decrease amount prepared according to your dog's size. For a 15–20 pound dog, give about 4½ to 5 oz. per day.

10 oz. cooked meat (beef, turkey, pork, or chicken)
7 oz. steamed vegetables, grated or chopped
1 to 1¼ tsp. salt
750 mg of bone meal (not plant kind) or calcium citrate (available at health food stores)
Missing Link (Omega 3 and other vitamins and nutrients) Use according to dog's weight.
Taurine (500 mg capsule), opened and sprinkled and mixed well into mixture Taurine is an amino acid for heart and eyes.

Vary the type of meat and vegetable used to guard against food sensitivities or nutritional deficiencies arising from always using the same ingredients. Lightly cooked meats have higher nutrient content. Do not drain fat off meat.

Avoid carbohydrates (unless your pet has trouble gaining weight.) High carbs include: peas, wheat, corn, rice, oats, grains, potatoes, and carrots.

Vegetables supply the right amount of carbohydrates. Any vegetable is okay. Suggested vegetables: broccoli, squash, yams (sweet potatoes), parsnips, spinach, kale, parsley, garlic, bok choy, lettuce, apples, kelp, or Swiss chard. Grate, chop, or puree and steam or sauté vegetables to make them more digestible.

Pre-prepared frozen meat and vegetable diets sold to be fed raw, can be instead lightly stir-fried and fed as home cooked diet. Do not feed raw food diets that contain bone fragments.

A raw quartered knuckle bone or other rounded bone can be given daily to help maintain dental health. Never feed poultry or pork bones and never feed cooked bones.

Modify for Cats

Use organ meats. Add taurine.
Less veggies (5–10% less)
Use Salmon oil instead of *Missing Link*

Apple Carrot Dog Treats
Kathy Birkner
Oven: 350°F. Cook Time: 30–40 minutes
Yield: About 2 dozen small treats

1 cup of whole wheat flour, brown rice flour, or gluten free flour
1 cup of grated carrots
1 tsp. baking powder
1 egg
½ cup unsweetened apple sauce

Preheat oven 350°F.
Mix ingredients together until dough forms. Roll dough into small balls and place on a cookie sheet lined with parchment paper. Press dough down slightly so the biscuits are about one-fourth (¼") thick. Bake until golden brown and let cool on a wire rack.

Note: ½ teaspoon of salt can be added to these treats to help extend the shelf life, but it is optional.

Laundry

Homemade Laundry Detergent
Kathy Birkner

1 cup Borax
1 cup Washing Soda
¾ cup Castile soap
4½ gallons water
5 gallon bucket

Put liquid Castile Soap in saucepan and cover with water; heat on low until heated and thinner. Fill bucket with hot water and add soap. Stir to combine. Add 1 cup Washing Soda and 1 cup Borax and mix well. As it cools, it will thicken. If mixture becomes too thick, add hot water to thin it to a desired consistency. This detergent can be used without more ado. Mix well before each use. Use ½ cup for a normal load and 1 cup for a heavy load.

Note: Safe for babies and allergy–free.
Tip: Turn simple baking soda into washing soda by baking in a shallow pan at 400°F. for 30 minutes, stirring occasionally.

Nasal Rinse

Nasal Saline Solution
Kathy Birkner

1 qt. distilled or bottled water that does NOT contain chlorine
2–3 heaping tsp. pickling salt (Kosher)
1 tsp. baking soda
Boil water for 2 minutes. Then add salt and soda while hot. Allow to cool then carefully, pour into a clean glass jar to store.

After solution has cooled, use a bulb syringe or Nettie pot to put saline in the nose to rinse.

Note: 1.) *Do not cut the recipe down.*

2.) *Do not use regular salt as it has additives that dry the nose.*

3.) Solution is good for *one* week.

Variation: Hypertonic saline helps fight allergies and helps wash out bacteria that cause sinus infections. *To make hypertonic saline,* increase salt to 4½ tsp.

Adding a tablespoon of Xylitol helps keep bacteria in your nose from adhering that can lead to a sinus infection. Be extremely careful not to let your dog or cat taste it as Xylitol causes extreme hypoglycemia (low blood sugar) and can kill them.

Different Flours

Almond Flour

Naturally grain-free, this Paleo-friendly flour contains protein, healthy fats, and 35 percent of your RDA for vitamin E. One caveat: You must refrigerate or freeze it after opening to prevent spoiling.

Best For: Coating chicken or fish; in meatballs, crab cakes, or anywhere else you'd use bread crumbs; or for replacing up to one-fourth of the white flour in cakes, muffins, pancakes, and cookies.

Nutrition: Per 4 oz. 160 calories: 108, 14 g. fat, 6 g. carbs, 3 g. dietary fiber, 6 g. protein, iron 6%.

Soy Flour

Ground soybeans provides calcium, fiber, and three time the protein of white flour.

Best For: Thickening sauces, gravies, or soups. Swap up to a third of white flour with soy in recipes not using yeast.

Nutrition: Per 1 oz. (28 g.) calories: 92, 0 g. fat, 11 g. carbs, 5 g. dietary fiber, 13 g. protein, iron 14%, calcium 7%

Quinoa Flour

Quinoa is a whole grain grown in the Andes region of South America. This nutrient-packed flour contains a complete protein and provides all eight essential amino acids. Quinoa is about 60% protein. Quinoa is easily digested and gluten-free. Quinoa has a delicate nutty flavor and is versatile for baking. To get rid of quinoa's natural bitterness, grind your own flour, baking the quinoa first on a parchment-lined sheet at 215°F. for 10 minutes. Be sure to wash the seeds.

Best For: Upping the healthiness of cookies and cakes. Cut it with an equal amount of white flour—the texture will be a bit more grainy than usual, but the result will be so much better for you.

Nutrition: Per 1 oz. (28 g.) calories: 34, 1 g. fat, 6 g. carbs, 1 g. dietary fiber, 1 g. protein, iron 2%.

Spelt Flour

Spelt is an old grain (ancient) wheat that has been around since the birth of Christ. Since it is an old grain, people that are intolerant of the current day whole wheat, easily tolerate spelt flour. Spelt four has a slightly sweet and nutty flavor. Spelt flour is available in whole grain and also white spelt. Spelt flour bakes up lighter and softer than whole-wheat flour, but it's still fiber-rich. (Be sure the label says whole-grain—not all varieties are.)

Best For: Baked goods, pizza crusts, and breads. Unlike some other flours (soy, quinoa), spelt can be subbed for white flour cup for cup without changing the consistency of the end product. Use cup for cup instead of regular flour.

Nutrition: Per ¼ cup: 120 calories, 1 g. fat (0 g sat), 22 g. carbs (0 g. sugar), 1 mg sodium, 4 g. fiber, 4 g. protein

Brown Rice Flour

Brown rice is a staple food in Asia where it is grown on small paddies and harvested by hand. Brown rice is the world's second largest crop. Brown rice is higher in fiber, vitamins, and minerals than white rice, is gluten-free, and nutty tasting.

Uses: Baking for gluten free recipes, sauces, shortbread, and for coating foods.

Nutrition: Per ¼ cup, calorie 130; 1 g. fat, 27 g. carbs, 3 g. protein, 75 mg potassium, 4% iron

Coconut Flour

Coconut flour is an excellent source of gluten-free protein, low glycemic index (low carb), 40% dietary fiber, promotes lipid oxidation (helps burn fat), and helps balance blood sugar levels.

Uses: Baking, thickening gravies, or to increase fiber in smoothies or any recipe. Coconut readily absorbs moisture so use a ratio of ¼ cup coconut flour and ¾ cup of flour. If using only coconut, it is necessary to add eggs at a ratio of 4 eggs to 1 cup flour. Additionally, increase the liquid. Refrigerate after opening.

Nutrition: Per 2 Tbsp., calories: 62, 1.5 g. fat, 9 g. carbs, 6 g. dietary fiber 6 g., 3.5 g. protein.

Kamut Flour (Khorasan wheat)

Kamut was rediscovered in the 1940, but has been around since the Roman empire. Kamut is higher in protein and has many minerals especially zinc, selenium, and magnesium compared to modern wheat. Kamut contains an unusually high content of selenium, a mineral known for its high antioxidant capacity. Kamut is considered a high energy wheat since it has a higher percentage of lipids. An alternate name for kamut is Balady durum. Legends say that Khorasan wheat is also called Camel's Tooth or the Prophet's Wheat was the grain Noah brought with him on the ark. Kamut is well tolerated by people can do not do well with modern wheat. Use cup for cup instead of regular flour.

Uses: Baking, thickening gravies, and use for white flour cup for cup without changing the consistency of the end product.

Nutrition: Per 1 cup calories: 627 (186 g.), 4 g. fat, 131 g. carbs, 17 g. dietary fiber, 27 g. protein, iron 46%, 249 mg magnesium.

Barley Flour

High in fiber, barley can help lower blood cholesterol and sugar levels. Just make sure to look for a whole-grain variety.

Best for: Fluffy biscuits, breads, and pancakes that are less dense than made with wheat flour.

Nutrition: Per 1 oz. 97 calories, 0 g fat, 21 g carbs (0 g sugar), 3 g. fiber, 3 g. protein, iron 4%

Chickpea Flour

A healthful gluten free flour, popular in Indian cuisine. Also known as Besan or garbanzo bean flour, and is high in protein.

Nutrition: Per 1 oz. (28 g) calories: 108, 2 g. fat, 16 g carbs, 3 g. dietary fiber, 6 g. protein, iron 8%.

Greener Living

What to use after you have been creative in your kitchen, and save in your pocketbook. Make your cleaning supplies!

All Purpose Cleaner

For a 16 ounce spray bottle, add ingredients in order:

1 tsp borax
2 Tbsp. vinegar

Fill bottle with hot water to dissolve borax. Then add:

1 Tbsp. castile soap or natural dish washing soap

Shake. Label. You are ready to clean! Use on shower stall, kitchen sink, mirrors, shine chrome. *Test before using on granite.*

Alternative for Soft Scrub

16 oz. squirt bottle
1⅔ cup baking soda
½ cup liquid soap
½ cup water
2 Tbsp. vinegar

Mix baking soda with liquid soap in a bowl. Add water. Then add vinegar last. Stir until lumps are gone. If mixture is too thick, add more water. Shake before using. Label.

Shower Cleaner

Spray bottle
5% vinegar
Fresh herbs or your favorite essential oil

Use portion of 1 part herb to 4 part vinegar. Shake every few days and after two weeks strain using coffee filter or cheese cloth. Do not leave herbs in the vinegar for more than 14 days or it will spoil the batch. Use your favorite essential oil if you do not have fresh herbs. Label. *Do not use on wood or granite without trying first* to make sure it won't harm surface.

Air Freshener

8 oz. spray bottle
20–30 drops of your favorite essential oil
5% white vinegar

Mix essential oil in vinegar. Label. Shake before using. Spray.

Furniture Polish and Cleaner

Spray bottle

¼ cup olive oil OR baby oil OR mineral oil
4 Tbsp. vinegar
20–30 drops lemon oil

Pour into a spray bottle. Shake before using. Label. Use a soft cloth or old kitchen towel to clean and polish your furniture.

Fabric Softener

Yield: about a gallon

Large gallon plastic jug
6 cups vinegar
8 cups water
1 cup baking soda
25 drops orange essential oil or your favorite essential oil (such as lavender, lemon grass, peppermint, cinnamon, sandalwood, or wintergreen).

Combine all of the ingredients in a plastic jug. Shake well to mix, and shake before adding ½ cup to your rinse cycle. Label.

Note: Vinegar softens hard water while decreasing static cling. The essential oil gives your laundry a fresh, clean smell.

Fabric Softener 2

Borax

Add ½ to 1 cup of borax to your washer in the wash cycle. The borax will soften, disinfect, and boost your laundry detergent cleaning ability. Borax works great as a fabric softener.

Sink and Shower Scrubber

8 oz. empty cheese shaker
Baking soda
1 Tbsp. dried herbs (such as mint) or 5–10 drops essential oil
1 tsp. borax

Pour about 4 oz. of baking soda into cheese shaker. Add dried herbs or essential oil and borax. Close and shake to mix. Then fill with another 4 oz. baking soda. Shake to mix again. Label.

Sprinkle onto a wet sponge or cloth and scrub sink or shower. Rinse.

Scented Baking Soda

Mix dried herb or ground cinnamon with baking soda for a fresh-smelling cleanser. Label.

Garbage Pail Odor

Scented baking soda

Sprinkle a quarter cup (¼ cup) of scented baking soda into your trash pail to reduce odor.

Phone Rescue

If you accidently drop your cell phone into water, rescue it by putting in a bag of rice to dry it out.

Bed Bugs

When traveling, put a few fabric softener sheets in your suit case to deter bed bugs from coming home with you.

Ant Killers

1) 5% Vinegar Spray with squirt bottle.

2) Mix ½ tsp. borax with cup of sugar. Moisten with a table-spoon hot water. Stir to dissolve. Place it in a shallow dish in an area where you have ants. ***Caution:*** *Be careful where you place where children or pets can get ahold of it.*

3) Aspartame: Mix small packet of the blue stuff with 1 cup sugar. Stir to dissolve. Place it in a shallow dish in an area where you have ants. *Caution: Be careful where you place where children or pets can get a hold of it.*

4) Hot water: Pour into the center of a mound. It kills the ants instantly and is environmentally safe.

For Greener Plants

Epson Salt

Add tablespoon to a gallon of water. Water your plants. They will green up immediately. Use sparingly on cactus.

Odor Eater

Save used dryer sheets, and put a few drops of essential mint oil on them. Place in shoes or boots to refreshen and remove odor.

Soothing Bath

Add 25 to 30 drops of essential oil such as lavender or chamomile to 2 lb. (32 oz.) of Epsom salt. Add cup to your bath for a soothing soak.

Glass and Mirror Cleaner

Spray bottle
2 oz. vinegar
1 oz. alcohol
2 drops of essential lemon oil (if desired)
Water
Newspaper

Put vinegar, alcohol and essential oil in spray bottle. Fill with water. Spray. Wipe glass or mirror with newspaper to clean. Newspaper has no lint, and does a marvelous job.

Blessing for a Happy Home

*Lovingly Dedicated to the Memory of Hannah (Annie) Akkary Allen
By her Loving Grandchildren and Great-Grandchildren*

Who remember and seek to imitate her *"Special Recipe"* for Life

Ingredients

Begin with several "green fig" cuttings whose roots flourish in Barhalioun, Lebanon.

Transport them over the Atlantic Ocean carefully wrapped in a suitcase through Ellis Island.

Tenderly plant and nurture the twigs everywhere you live in San Antonio America.

Pick the fruit as a delicious treat in the summer and preserve it to savor through the winter.

Prune the tree on the Feast of St. Joseph, March 19th, and take more cuttings for the future.

If you move, bring the cuttings for the new house.

Share the cuttings with all your neighbors and friends at St. George Maronite Church.

Always prune, keep the strongest cuttings and plant them for the future, for others!

Teach your daughters to make the preserves, give them cuttings to share.

There are fig trees from Bartholin bearing fruit today because "Tita" treasured her homeland, her family, her figs and gave them away. All her trees grew with loving care, and the birds came and ate of the fruit, and like the Biblical message would *bear good fruit.*

By their fruits you will know them . . .

Do people pick grapes from thorn bushes, or figs from this-tles?

Just so, every good tree bears good fruit, and a rotten tree bears bad fruit.

A good tree cannot bear bad fruit, nor can a rotten tree bear good fruit.

Every tree that does not bear good fruit will be cut down and thrown into the fire.

So by their fruits you will know them.

Matthew 7: 17-20

Measures

1 teaspoon	1/6th fluid oz.		5 ml
1 table-spoon	½ fluid ounce	3 teaspoons	15 ml
¼ cup	2 fluid ounces	4 tablespoons	50 ml
1/3 cup	2 ⅔ fluid ounces	5 tablespoons + 1 teaspoon	75 ml
½ cup	4 fluid ounces	8 tablespoons	125 ml
2/3 cup	5⅓ fluid ounces	10 tablespoons + 2 teaspoon	150 ml
¾ cup	6 fluid ounces	12 tablespoons	175 ml
1 cup	8 ounces	16 tablespoons	240 or 250 ml
2 cups	16 fluid ounces	1 pint	500 ml
4 cups	32 fluid ounces; 2 pints	1 quart	1000 ml (little < 1 liter)
4 quarts	128 fluid ounces	1 gallon	Little < 1 liter

Dry Measures

1 ounce (oz.)		25 or 30 g
4 ounces (oz.)	¼ pound (lb.)	115 or 125 g
8 ounces	½ pound (lb.)	225 or 250 g
12 ounces	¾ pound (lb.)	340 or 375 g
16 ounces	1 pound (lb.)	450 or 500 g.
32 ounces	2 pounds (2¼ lb.)	1000 g or 1 kg.

Abbreviations

Teaspoon = tsp.
Tablespoon = Tbsp.
Pound = 1b.
Gram = g.

Dozen = 1 doz.
Package = pkg.
Ounce = oz.
Liter = L.

Substitutions

Baking powder	¼ tsp. soda + ½ tsp. cream of tarter
Buttermilk	1 Tbsp. lemon juice or vinegar plus enough milk to make 1 cup (let stand 5 minutes before using) or 1 cup plain yogurt
Buttermilk	⅔ cup Greek yogurt + ¼ cup buttermilk
Butter, 1 cup	1 cup shortening plus ¼ tsp. salt (optional)
Cake flour, 1 cup	1 cup all-purpose flour less 2 tablespoons
Chocolate, semisweet (1 oz.)	3 Tbsp. semisweet chocolate pieces or 1 Tbsp. cocoa powder + 2 tsp. sugar and 2 tsp. shortening
Chocolate, sweet baking (4 oz.)	¼ cup cocoa powder + ⅓ cup sugar and 3 Tbsp. shortening
Chocolate, unsweetened (1 square)	3 Tbsp. cocoa + 1 Tbsp. oil or shortening
Cornstarch. 1 Tbsp.	2 Tbsp. flour
Corn syrup	1 cup sugar plus ¼ cup water
Cream cheese	1 cup plain Greek yogurt
Egg	2 egg whites or 2 egg yolks
Garlic	½ tsp. bottled minced garlic or ⅛ tsp. garlic powder
Ginger, 1 tsp. grated fresh	¼ tsp. ground ginger
Half & half	1 Tbsp. melted butter + enough whole milk to make 1 cup
Mayonnaise	1 cup plain yogurt or use ½ mayo and ½ yogurt
Molasses	Honey, equal amounts
Onion, chopped, ½ cup	2 Tbsp. dried minced onion or ⅛ tsp. onion powder
Oil, 1 cup	¾ cup Greek yogurt OR ½ cup oil + ½ cup applesause
Sour cream	1 cup plain yogurt
Sugar	1 cup packed brown sugar or 2 cups confectioner's sugar
Sugar, brown	1 cup sugar + 2 Tbsp. molasses
	1 cup Splenda + 2 Tbsp. molasses
Vanilla bean	2 tsp. vanilla extract
Yeast, 1 pkg.	2¼ tsp. active dry yeast

Equivalents and Other Measures

	Volume	*Weight*
Sugar	2¼ cups	1 lb.
Confectioners' Sugar	3½ cups	1 lb.
Brown sugar	2¼ cups	1 lb.
Dried Beans	1 cup	2½ cups cooked
Rice	2⅓ cups	1 lb.
Rice, uncooked	1 cup	3 cups cooked
Lentils	2⅓ cups	1 lb.
Meat, diced	2 cups	1 lb.
Butter	2 cups	1 lb.
Butter, rendered	3½ cups	2 lb.
Burghur	3 cups	1 lb.
Cream, heavy	1 cup	2 cups whipped
Dates	2½ cups	1 lb.
Dried fruit	2 cups	1 lb.
Flour	4 cups (500 g)	1 lb.
Onions	½ cup, chopped	1 medium
Potatoes	3 medium	1 lb.
Salt	2 Tbsp.	1 oz.
Lemon	3–4 Tbsp.	1 medium
Orange	⅓ cup juice	1 medium
Almonds	2⅔ cups whole	1 lb.
Almonds	4 cups ground	1 lb.
Walnuts	4 cups chopped	1 lb.
Walnuts	5⅓ cups ground	1 lb.

Oven Equivalents

Fahrenheit Setting	*Celsius Setting*	*Gas Mark Setting*
300°F.	150°C.	2
325°F.	160°C.	3 (Slow)
350°F.	180°C.	4 (Moderate)
375°F.	190°C.	5
400°F.	200°C.	6 (Hot)
425°F.	220°C.	7
450°F.	230°C.	8 (Very Hot)
475°F.	240°C.	9
500°F.	260°C.	10
Broil	Broil	Grill

Lebanese To English Translations

Aboona	Priest (Father)
Adas	Lentils
Assal	Honey
Ah-seer il li-moon	Lemon juice
Ahweh	Coffee
Ajeen	Dough
Ameh	Whole wheat
Araq	Anise liqueur
Arnabeet (Zahra)	Cauliflower
Ater	Syrup
Baqdunis	Parsley
Batinjan	Eggplant
Baklawa	Layered pastry
Banadoora	Tomatoes
Bassal	Onions
Batata	Potatoes
Bayd	Eggs
Bamyeh	Okra
Bhaar heloo	Allspice
Burghul (Bulgur)	Cracked wheat
Djaj (Djaaj)	Chicken
Bhaar Aswad	Pepper
Fatayer	Triangle pies
Fool, Ful	Fava beans
Habaq	Basil
Habash	Turkey
Haleeb	Milk
Haliyun (Halyun)	Asparagus
Hummus	Chickpeas
Hashweh	Filling
Jibneh	Cheese
Jazar	Carrot
Khebez	Bread
Kafta	Ground meat, seasoned

Khass	Lettuce
Khyar	Cucumbers
Kibbeh (Kibbi)	Ground meat with burghul
Koossa	Squash
Laban	Yogurt
Labneh (Labnee)	Yogurt cheese (cream cheese)
Lahem	Meat
Lifit	Turnip
Lowz	Almonds
Loobyeh	Green beans
Mahlab	Seasoning for pastries
Malfoof	Cabbage
Maward	Rose water
Mehsheh	Orange blossom water
Mihshi	Stuffed meat or vegetables
Naanaa	Mint
Nbeed	Wine
Rakweh	Arabic coffee pot
Rizz	Rice
Salsa	Sauce
Samak	Fish
Sbanekh	Spinach
Sikkar	Sugar
Smid	Grain, like farina
Snoobar	Pine nuts
Tahini	Ground sesame seed
Teen	Figs
Toom	Garlic
Waraq (Malfoof Areesh)	Leaves such as grape, cabbage
Waraq ghar	Bay Leaf
Yansoon	Anise seed
Zaatar	Thyme
Zayt	Oil
Zaytoon	Olives
Zbeeb	Raisins
Zebdeh	Butter

English to Lebanese Translations

English	Lebanese
Allspice	Bhar heloo
Almonds	Lowz
Anise liqueur	Araq
Anise Seed	Yansoon
Arabic coffee pot	Rakweh
Asparagus	Haliyun (Halyun)
Basil	Habaq (Habaa)
Bay Leaf	Waraq ghar
Beans, fava	Fool (Ful)
Bread	Khebez
Butter	Zebdeh
Cabbage	Malfoof
Cabbage leaves	Waraq (Malfoof)
Carrot	Jazar
Cauliflower	Aranabeet (Zahra)
Cheese	Jibneh
Chicken	Djaj (Djaaj)
Chickpeas	Hummus (Hommos)
Coffee	Ahweh
Cracked wheat	Burghul (Bulgur)
Cucumbers	Khyar
Dough	Ajeen
Eggplant	Batinjan
Eggs	Bayd (Beyd)
Figs	Teen
Fish	Samak
Farina	Smid
Filling	Hashweh
Garlic	Toom
Grape leaves	Waraq Areesh
Green beans	Loobyeh
Ground meat, burghul, spices	Kibbeh (Kibbi)
Ground meat, seasoned	Kafta
Ground sesame seed	Tahini
Honey	Assal

Layered pastry	Baklawa
Lemon juice	Ah-scer il li-moon
Lentils	Adas
Lettuce	Khass
Meat	Lahem
Milk	Haleeb
Mint	Naanaa
Oil	Zayt
Okra	Bamyeh
Olives	Zaytoon
Onions	Bassal
Orange blossom water	Mehsheh
Parsley	Baqdunis
Pepper	Bhaar Aswad
Pine nuts	Snoobar
Potatoes	Batata
Priest (Father)	Aboona
Raisins	Zbeeb
Rice	Rizz
Rose water	Maward
Sauce	Salsa
Seasoning for pastries	Mahlab
Spinach	Sbanekh
Stuffed meat or vegetables	Mihshi
Sugar	Sikkar
Squash	Koossa
Syrup	Ater
Thyme	Zaatar
Tomatoes	Banadoora
Triangle pies	Fatayer
Turkey	Habash
Turnip	Lifit
Whole wheat	Ameh
Wine	Nbeed
Yogurt	Laban
Yogurt cheese (cream cheese)	Labneh

Index